WOMEN PLAYWRIGHTS
The Best Plays of 2003

SMITH AND KRAUS, INC.
Contemporary Playwrights / Full-Length Play Anthologies

Humana Festival 1993: The Complete Plays
Humana Festival 1994: The Complete Plays
Humana Festival 1995: The Complete Plays
Humana Festival 1996: The Complete Plays
Humana Festival 1997: The Complete Plays
Humana Festival 1998: The Complete Plays
Humana Festival 1999: The Complete Plays
Humana Festival 2000: The Complete Plays
Humana Festival 2001: The Complete Plays
Humana Festival 2002: The Complete Plays
Humana Festival: 20 One-Acts Plays 1976–1996

New Dramatists 2000: The Best Plays by the Graduating Class
New Dramatists 2001: The Best Plays by the Graduating Class

New Playwrights: The Best Plays of 1998
New Playwrights: The Best Plays of 1999
New Playwrights: The Best Plays of 2000
New Playwrights: The Best Plays of 2001
New Playwrights: The Best Plays of 2002

Women Playwrights: The Best Plays of 1992
Women Playwrights: The Best Plays of 1993
Women Playwrights: The Best Plays of 1994
Women Playwrights: The Best Plays of 1995
Women Playwrights: The Best Plays of 1996
Women Playwrights: The Best Plays of 1997
Women Playwrights: The Best Plays of 1998
Women Playwrights: The Best Plays of 1999
Women Playwrights: The Best Plays of 2000
Women Playwrights: The Best Plays of 2001
Women Playwrights: The Best Plays of 2002

If you require prepublication information about forthcoming Smith and Kraus books, you may receive our semiannual catalogue, free of charge, by sending your name and address to *Smith and Kraus Catalogue, PO Box 127, Lyme, NH 03768*. Or call us at (800) 895-4331, fax (603) 643-1831. www.SmithKraus.com.

WOMEN PLAYWRIGHTS

The Best Plays of 2003

Edited by D. L. Lepidus

CONTEMPORARY PLAYWRIGHTS
SERIES

SK
A Smith and Kraus Book

Published by Smith and Kraus, Inc.
177 Lyme Road, Hanover, NH 03755
www.SmithKraus.com

First Edition: March 2004
10 9 8 7 6 5 4 3 2 1
Manufactured in the United States of America

Cover and text design by Julia Hill Gignoux, Freedom Hill Design

The Library of Congress Cataloging-in-Publication Data
Women playwrights : the best plays of 2003 / edited by D. L. Lepidus
p. cm. — (Contemporary playwrights series)
ISBN 1-57525378-X-
1. American drama—women authors. 2. American drama—20th century.
3. Women—drama.
I. Smith, Marisa. II. Series: Contemporary playwrights series.
PS628.W6W668   1994
812'.540809287—dc20
94-10071
CIP

CONTENTS

Foreword vii

Introduction ix

The Psychic Life of Savages by Amy Freed 1

The Dianalogues by Laurel Haines 59

Daisy in the Dreamtime by Lynne Kaufman 89

The Last Schwartz by Deborah Zoe Laufer 123

String Fever by Jacquelyn Reingold 175

Waiting by Lisa Soland 221

Permissions 261

FOREWORD

As any sentient being knows, "best" lists are entirely subjective. In this book you will find six fine new plays by women playwrights. These are the "best" plays produced during the 2002–2003 theatrical season. The ones that I liked the best.

In choosing plays for this annual series, I try to include as eclectic a mix as I possibly can, both in style and in subject matter. Also, although I live and attend the theater in New York City (approximately two hundred times a year) and know more about what's done on the stages there, I make a concerted effort to find plays that have not seen the light of night in New York, obsessed as I am with the belief that New York should not be the ultimate arbiter of what constitutes Our American Drama.

To date, neither Laurel Haines's *The Dianalogues*, Lisa Soland's *Waiting*, Amy Freed's *The Psychic Life of Savages*, nor Deborah Zoe Laufer's *The Last Schwartz* have been produced in New York City. *The Dianalogues*, a witty and original collection of monologues for women about Princess Diana as an object of obsession, was originally developed at Arizona State University and has had several productions around the country — one done by men in drag. *The Psychic Life of Savages* has had a few regional productions. The one I saw was at Yale Rep. It's a witty and inventive satire on confessional poetry not unlike that of Sylvia Plath, Robert Lowell, and Ted Hughes. *The Last Schwartz* is a realistic Jewish family drama, which received sensational reviews when it was produced by a small professional theater in Florida. Ditto good reviews for *Waiting*, done in a small theater in Los Angeles.

As regards the New York plays, *String Fever*, a comedy about romance and physics, was wonderfully done by Ensemble Studio Theatre, starring Cynthia Nixon. *Daisy in the Dreamtime* was also beautifully produced by Abingdon Theatre, whose artistic director, Jan Buttram, has kindly written the introduction to this book. It's based on the true story of a woman who spent most of her adult life living in Australia among the aborigines and whose published diaries contain invaluable material about their fast-disappearing culture, even though she was not a trained anthropologist.

My very great thanks to the authors of these fine plays for allowing me to put them in this book, thereby calling them to your attention.

D. L. Lepidus

INTRODUCTION

I believe that all playwrights have a responsibility to carry a torch. They must deliver this message, over and over again, that theater is alive, vibrant, and is a truthful reflection of our times. Playwrights observe society, and the best of us are combing this human terrain, gleaning lessons for the future. Women playwrights have an unparalleled responsibility. Our strong and proud heritage has been passed down from generations of amazing storytellers; all were subject to the critical scrutiny that we experience today. As a fellow torchbearer and playwright, I beseech you, every time a producer says those well-worn words, "This is not right for me," grow another layer of tough skin. Grow it! Nurture that tough hide! Because one person's opinion of your work must never change your steadfast belief that you have worthy stories to tell with fascinating characters peopling them.

As artistic director of Abingdon Theatre Company, a not-for-profit company dedicated to the development and production of new plays by American playwrights, I am proud of Abingdon's open-submission policy. *Daisy in the Dreamtime* by Lynne Kaufman was an unsolicited submission in fall 2000. Lynne continued to develop it through Abingdon's process, and her play was produced on our main stage at the Abingdon Theatre Arts Complex in spring 2003. She was patient and persistent. Find theater companies like Abingdon that celebrate the playwright.

Follow Ms. Kaufman's example by being patient and persistent. We are living in a world gone mad, and our earth time is finite. It's our amazing good fortune to be living in a nation that allows women to speak loud and freely, that enables women to change lives. Congratulations to all the talented women playwrights included in this volume of plays. Read them. Study them. Learn from them. And take hold of your own playwriting torch and light up the world!

Jan Buttram
Artistic Director, Abingdon Theatre Company

The Psychic Life
of Savages

By Amy Freed

*For Will Marchetti, a great actor and a great friend
who created the role of Robert Stoner.
With gratitude.*

PLAYWRIGHT'S BIOGRAPHY

Amy Freed's most recent play, *The Beard of Avon,* premiered at the South Coast Rep and has been produced by the Goodman Theatre, American Conservatory Theater (ACT), and Seattle Rep among others. Her play *Freedomland* was a Pulitzer finalist in 1998, with productions at South Coast Rep, Woolly Mammoth, and Playwrights Horizons. *The Psychic Life of Savages* was the 1995 recipient of the Joseph Kesselring Award, a national award presented each year by the New York Arts Club to an outstanding new play. *Psychic Life* was also named the winner of the prestigious Charles McArthur Award for Outstanding New Play at the annual Helen Hayes awards in Washington, D.C. The play had an extended run after a successful premiere at the Woolly Mammoth Theatre. An earlier version of the play was first developed and performed in San Francisco under the title *Poetomachia,* where it was recognized by the Bay Area Critic's Circle and awarded an Outstanding Achievement Award for an Original Script. In its earlier version, it was also a finalist for the Susan Smith Blackburn Prize in 1994.

A native New Yorker and former actress, Freed lives in San Francisco. She has worked as an acting teacher and director for the various training programs of ACT, VITA Shakespeare Festival, and California Shakespeare Festival, as well as conducting playwriting workshops for ACT and San Francisco State University. She has a BFA from Southern Methodist University and an MFA from ACT.

ORIGINAL PRODUCTION

The Psychic Life of Savages premiered at the Woolly Mammoth Theatre, Washington, D.C.; artistic director, Howard Schwalwitz.

The Psychic Life of Savages was presented by Yale Repertory Theatre in February and March of 2003. James Bundy, artistic director; Victoria Nolan, managing director, and Mark Bly, associate artistic director. It was directed by James Bundy. Cast and crew included:

Scenic Design	Young Ju Baik
Costume Design	Corrine Larson
Lighting Design	Torkel Skjaerven
Sound Design	Sten Severson
Dramaturg	Emily V. Shooltz
Vocal Coach	Pamela Prather
Fight Director	Rick Sordelet
Stage Manager	Laura MacNeil

Casting . . . . Johnson-Liff Associates, Ltd.
Interviewer, Tito, Student, Party Guest . . . . Bill Kux
Ted Magus . . . . John Hines
Dr. Robert Stoner . . . . Will Marchetti
Anne Bittenhand . . . . Meg Gibson
Rebecca, Kit-Kat, Student, Party Guest . . . . Robyn Ganeles
Sylvia Fluellen . . . . Fiona Gallagher
Emily Dickinson, Vera . . . . Phyllis Somerville

PLAYWRIGHT'S NOTE

This play is a work of dramatic fiction inspired in the loosest sense by the lives and writings of several major poets. The persons, events, and relationships described are imaginary and are not intended to be in any way factual or biographical. All poems are my invention.

My own advice to the players: This play best succeeds when the actors don't shrink from the scale of its emotional stakes or the precision of its verbal attack. The circumstances must be invested in. All the characters are strong and gifted. One should find their occasional grandiosity by inhabiting them, not mocking them. The success of the play's comedy depends on realizing this distinction.

Once the turns of the scenes are really located, they can play fast. Every scene has a crescendo and a point of maximum tension. Every scene has a step that relates to the internal journey of each character and to Sylvia. The protagonist, Sylvia, moves inexorably from the perimeter to the center, from manic-depressive schoolgirl to nightmare wife to great scary poet, in three acts. That which she feeds on, as she and we discover, is trauma and conflict. Whether she (and the others) orchestrate their sexual and private lives to create necessary and cathartic frictions is a question without an easy answer, but it's a right question for this play, for all the characters.

Generally, I think it helps to remember that there was a time (late fifties to early sixties) when it seemed like artists and writers could change the direction of the world. At least so it seemed to the artists and writers. The century saw two atrocious wars waged with "perverted science" — and the grotesquely sanitized repressions of the mid-fifties played out absurdly against the nightmare vision of a gigantic mushroom cloud. No wonder psychological repression — everyday lies and concealment — seemed to some to be implicated deeply in the core of human destructive behavior.

To reveal the hidden devils of the human mind became a goal of psychotherapy. Some poets followed suit. Violence, sex, mental illness, grief, failure, and despair, formerly taboo topics, were violently wrested into mainstream discussion and into art and writing. A cultural revolution began to gather force that struck a death blow at an old society of frozen lies and toxic manners. My poets hoped that their poems could heal by violent exhortation or shocking confession in a way the church no longer could. Ridiculous? Sure. Maybe. But, as Ted Magus might say, Good.

Good. It's a start.

CHARACTERS

SYLVIA FLUELLEN: A young American poet.

TED MAGUS: A young English poet.

ANNE BITTENHAND: An American poet in her forties.

DR. ROBERT STONER: A man in his sixties, the American Poet Laureate.

Ensemble: Two Women and One Man

EMILY: The ghost of Emily Dickinson.

VERA: Dr. Stoner's wife, played by the actor playing Emily.

TITO: Anne's husband.

RADIO INTERVIEWER: Played by the actor playing Anne's husband.

KIT-KAT: Anne's daughter.

REBECCA: A young mental patient, played by the actor playing Kit-Kat.

FEMALE COLLEGE STUDENTS/PARTY GUESTS: Played by the actors playing
    Tito and Kit-Kat.

TIME

Not that long ago. And sometime later.

PLACE

New England

The Psychic Life of Savages

Act I

Scene One

A radio station. Ted Magus, Dr. Robert Stoner, and Interviewer are on the air.

INTERVIEWER: Welcome to Potshots. I'm interviewing Britain's Ted Magus and our own American Poet Laureate Dr. Robert Stoner here at Wardwell College. Mr. Magus, you say, in your introduction to *Songs of the Fen*, "Bark and bleat. Reach into your own darkness and remember how to howl. Ask the beasts. Ask the birds." What does that mean?

TED: Call to a hawk in a foul black wind and have him scream his answer to you. I have.

INTERVIEWER: What are you suggesting — ?

TED: I'm sure Dr. Stoner would share my belief that the poet is the shaman, chosen to heal our soul-sick society —

STONER: I couldn't agree less.

TED: Oh, really?

INTERVIEWER: Would you like to say more about that, Dr. Stoner?

STONER: No.

INTERVIEWER: Mr. Magus. You consistently use nature as metaphor — the hawk, a symbol of freedom and release, the cow for domestic stagnation . . .

TED: A trout don't think when he leap for the sky.

(Pause.)

INTERVIEWER: Let's talk about some of your poetic techniques. Your unique use of rhythm, for example.

TED: Rhythm. It's both awakening and sleep inducing. Trance. The fall-through to the spirit world. I'm very interested in that. Paradox. We are surrounded by paradox. In sleep, we wake. In waking, we sleep. We starve in the midst of plenty. And in fasting, we become full.

STONER: If my aunt had a dick, she'd be my uncle.

TED: Oh, but exactly. Dr. Stoner, you're joking, but the joke is, you've actually touched something far truer —

STONER: Oh, please.

INTERVIEWER: You've said a lot, here, Mr. Magus, let me pick up on what you said about rhythm. Do you actually attempt to induce a trancelike state in the reader?

TED: Well, there's an instance, in the title poem, for example, where I say:
Skirts of the wind sweep
dry rustle grasses
shuka shucka shucka
There go me glasses
The green bog trembles, a night hunter screeches
I thrust into the darkness —
And think about the leeches.
Deeper and deeper the green muck sucks
And still am I reaching down. Down Down.
Good night little peepers, little sleepers, God's sticky creatures . . .

INTERVIEWER: It seems that there's almost a tribal intensity at the beginning and then it slides imperceptibly towards what's a really hypnotic lullaby near the end.

TED: Exactly.

INTERVIEWER: Extraordinary.

TED: Well, do you know what's even more extraordinary, I came to find out later what I heard in the bog that day was known in ancient Bali as the monkey chant. Identical! It goes —
shak shaka shak
shak shaka shaka shaka shak,
shak shak shak
shak shaka shaka shaka shak . . .

INTERVIEWER: Fantastic.

TED: Chanted by hags. Women are more connected with the occult.

INTERVIEWER: Which brings us to you, Dr. Stoner.

STONER: Why?

INTERVIEWER: You said in a recent interview, Dr. Stoner, that you are not convinced of the innocence of the Salem witches.

STONER: There's a lot of room for doubt in my book.

INTERVIEWER: And quite a "book" it's going to be. I doubt any book of poems has been awaited with as much eagerness as your free-verse cycle on the life of Cotton Mather. Will you give us a little teaser?

STONER: Well, there is this one little piece I've begun about the witch-girls. Now, I have the image, the spear is in my hand, as it were, but I'm having trouble with the target. Frankly, I think that what with the damned insulin therapy that maybe my focus is a little off, but well, here goes. Mather knew —
And for this they hated him, all the dark daughters,

Old Cotton, he was blessed with eyes that see 'round corners
Eyes that through God's hard grace could render even
Termites translucent.

With those pale and potent eyes
Mather could see the Witch Girls —

And then it goes something — something — something —
I don't know. And that's where I've been stuck with it for years, now.
(Pause.)

INTERVIEWER: Interesting. The whole process, I mean —

STONER: I can hear the shrill of a high wind, and a chill, like a damp petti-
coat. Oh, they're around, all right, and they're probably out to fuck me up.

INTERVIEWER: Who, Dr. Stoner?

STONER: The witch-girls, of course.

INTERVIEWER: What?

TED: *(Slowly, as if feeling his way in a trance.)* One. Mather sees in a dream. A
young witch screams astride the bucking buck from Zanzibar. Her ice-
cold teat reminds him of his wife.

STONER: Hah Hah! Not bad, Son.

TED: Wait! Wait! I'm getting . . .

Two. Seen in residue of
Lumpy morning porridge —
Bowl uncleared by slattern daughter,
Does she dance now with the broom — ?

STONER: An old witch and a young one
An old witch and a young one
With their mobcaps cast aside
Stand in skanky petticoats
Bare toes sunk in stable muck —
Hold a jar,
It's full of winter wheat —
And something fat and white.
Floating closer, Father Mather sees
His member, long and hungry — !
Too large to be a maggot, with that freckle on the tip!

TED: *(Angry and excited.)* Mather, in a lather, now
Knows the way is stony

But that fire will be the answer,
If he wants his penis back!

STONER: My boy! My boy! My boy!

INTERVIEWER: We've just witnessed an astonishing improvisation between two remarkable poets, it seems to have surprised them as much as it did me, they're embracing now, on the stage floor, much moved, much emotion, and Ted Magus is now drumming in what seems to be a tribute to the senior poet, who has his eyes closed and is covered in sweat. Our time is up and — astonishing program — good night, this was Pot Shots, live from Wardwell College.

TED AND STONER: Shak shak shak shak shaka shaka shaka shak!
Shak shak shak shak shaka shaka shaka shak!

Scene Two

A mental institution. Anne is on phone. Rebecca, a young mental patient, is sitting on the floor drawing on a large pad.

ANNE: I'm OK, I'm not OK. I'm OK. Stop yelling at me! Would I be back in the nuthouse again if I knew why I did it! Use your head, Tito! I'm sorry, lover. I can't really make sense of it to you. Because you won't — no, you don't — do you remember that thing I was describing? What happened last week at the hairdresser's, where the tops of the trees started forming into a hostile pattern? I can just tell! For God's sake!

(Pause.)

Don't you think I'd rather be home taking the lamb chops out of the oven? Or whatever you cook them in. If I could cook, I mean. It's not a matter of making an effort! I have a time bomb in my brain, and it just — WENT OFF! That's all.

(Pause.)

Did my agent call? Well, why didn't you say so? They're taking *Thoughts on My First Bleeding Time!* That's wonderful! Did you tell her where I was?

(Pause.)

Listen! My readers do not *care* that I'm a *nut!* My readers *love* that I'm a nut. So tell her. No, Baby, not this weekend!

Because. I can't handle it, that's why. Don't you understand that it's a little hard for me to be playing wife and mother for you and our daughter right now? I just feel like the whole world is one big stinking gas chamber! Don't come up yet!

(She hangs up. Pause. She crosses to Rebecca, who is muttering to herself as she draws. Anne looks at Rebecca's drawing.)

ANNE: What's that?

REBECCA: My dog.

ANNE: Why does he have so many legs, Baby?

REBECCA: *(Upset.)* Because his name is Spider!

ANNE: That's just what I thought. Isn't he beautiful!

REBECCA: Hey, Anne. I'm going home for the weekend. *(Stabbing her drawing pad.)* I hate it there! *(Hopefully.)* Want to come?

ANNE: Oh, Baby. I've got a home of my own not to go to.

REBECCA: *(Resuming her savage drawing.)* Last time I was home, my mother made a pot roast. And the funniest thing — right as we sat down? It started to bleed. Then it started moving and she really knew she had done something wrong. She was screaming at it and waving her feelers. Wow.

ANNE: *(Intensely.)* Oh, yes. That is very interesting. Yes.

(She lights a cigarette, groping with her words to capture the images of her most recent breakdown.)

Breakfast is crawling all over the house —

The toast is coming out of the drain —

(Rebecca begins to draw her.)

The cereal is gossiping.

The fried eggs are swimming like devilfish.

I look into the garbage disposal —

That dark stinky navel

And it is saying Mmmm.

It is saying Mmmm. Mmmm. Mmmm.

ANNE: Mmmm. Mmmm. Mmmm.   REBECCA: Mmmm. Mmmm. Mmmm.

(Orderly enters with Sylvia in a wheelchair. She is radiant with malice and rigid with self-loathing. Her arms are covered with bandages. She does not move or speak.)

ANNE: Who's this?

ORDERLY: New roommate. C'mon Rebecca, time's up.

(Rebecca backs out, frightened by Sylvia's appearance. Orderly exits. Anne sizes up Sylvia. Sylvia stares at something invisible. A pause.)

SYLVIA: *(Her enunciation is savagely perfect and perfectly savage.)*

What odd Godmother, what withered Aunt?

Did you invite —

Mother, oh Mother — to my first birthday party?
Where everyone danced the Hanukkah dance, but me —

Standing alone, all foolish and Unitarian, my tea set filled
With scummy water.
You wept, but could not help me.
I have still not the ear for jigging.
(A pause.)

ANNE: *(Shocked.)* That's — very good.

SYLVIA: *(Looking at Anne for the first time.)* Thank you.

ANNE: *(Appalled, but fascinated.)* What a strange, gritty . . . somethingness . . . it has. You're very talented. *(Lighting a cigarette.)* So what happened to you, Miss Golden Girl?

SYLVIA: *(Rarely looking at Anne and speaking with the same frightening enunciation.)* I live in a house on campus with some of the other girls. Everyone gathers in the common room at night, to dry their hair and paint their nails. Much laughter, and vicious, cozy gossip. But whenever I spoke, there was a potent silence. As if a foreigner had just — farted.

ANNE: I see.

SYLVIA: I tried to blend in. Mother told me to let down my hair. No one likes a grind. So I wore a mud-pack to dinner in an attempt at henhouse sisterhood. Mistake! I was the only one. My world flickers around me, soundless. Faces look like soap bubbles. When I close my eyes, the faces disappear. I want to keep them closed.

ANNE: *(Pulling her chair closer.)* Oh, Baby. Death is a big commitment . . .

SYLVIA: For a while, I thought of leaving school. But that would have killed Mother. She would have loved that. No. There is no dropping out for a Golden Goose. So I just said "No Thank You."

ANNE: Oh, yes! The lovely "no thank you" moment! Haa!

SYLVIA: Some time back I'd discovered a trick of cutting myself with a penknife to get me in the mood for composition. It's how I came to write "Rose Red at the Big Game" for *Seventeen* last year. Second prize, maybe you saw it . . . ?

ANNE: I'm sorry, I . . .

SYLVIA: So it didn't take much, just a little extra pressure, and —

ANNE: There you were . . .

SYLVIA: My heart started to beat faster. I was real! An excursion into the fabled third dimension!

ANNE: Oh really? For me it's more like —

SYLVIA: At first it was like flying . . . you really do start seeing —

ANNE: Seeing your *life!* Like pictures in a scrapbook! Oh, I *know!* Mummy and Grandma dressed me in a bunny suit!

SYLVIA: Me, standing in a soggy gym suit, when I'd wet myself in fear before the teams were chosen . . .

ANNE: Padding my first bra!

SYLVIA: *(Increasingly excited.)* Mother walking me to school on the first day of college . . .

ANNE: *(Trumps her.)* Making love in the backseat of the family Ford . . . with — Daddy!

(Anne is shocked at this memory — the women turn to stare at each other.)

SYLVIA: *(Turns away again, suddenly composed.)* Then something changed. Suddenly I couldn't see. A ringing in my ears. Terrifying, but at the same time so *important* . . . like I was going —

ANNE: Where?

SYLVIA: I never found out. But I felt I was expected. Then, of course, my *mother* broke down the door. And here I am.

(Pause.)

ANNE: Got a fella?

SYLVIA: Flesh disgusts me. My own face sickens me! Encrusted, swollen, greasy in the cracked yellow mirror over the dormitory sink. Well, hello, Truth! There you are! No wonder it was darkness that seemed more . . . forgiving.

(Pause.)

ANNE: No one special, huh. I'm beginning to get the picture.

SYLVIA: *(Crumpling a bit.)* Nobody wants to go out with me. *(She looks away.)*

ANNE: Yes, they do. Oh, sure they do. Why not? Why ever not, Baby-girl?

SYLVIA: My hair is rat-colored and my lips are smeary and — *(Savagely.)* I've never got below an A MINUS!

ANNE: Lip liner! Peroxide! Blow an exam! C'mon, Baby! Live a little!

SYLVIA: I don't want it. I just want to stay here forever and watch the hair grow on my legs. *(Discovering.)* —I love it here.

ANNE: Me too.

(Orderly enters begins to wheel Sylvia away.)

SYLVIA: Where are we going?

(Orderly wheels Sylvia to shock treatment station.)

Scene Three

A dark wing in the psychiatric hospital. Lit by the lightning flashes of the ECT unit. Sylvia is receiving electro-convulsive therapy.

SYLVIA: *(Ecstatic with electricity.)* Yes! Yes! Yes!
  (She catapults to a sitting position. Sound of an astral wind. Emily is blown forcefully in. She's a small, terrible ghost dressed in an elaborate white Civil War dress. Her words are unimaginably fraught — an escapee from the terrors of Eternity, desperate for company before she's recaptured.)
EMILY: *(Trembling, hungry, lit up.)* "Convulsion — pleases — for it does not counterfeit."
SYLVIA: Who are you? A hallucination? I did not expect this.
EMILY: Oh, phoo. Let me try again.
  (She clears her throat modestly. Braces herself for the coming image — it lands like fire on her brain.)
  The pink and tender earthworm
  Waits the rending of the beak —
  And cut in half —
  It dies again —
  A sensate coffee cake!
SYLVIA: *(Curiosity mingling with terror.)* Beak — cake! Can you do that?
EMILY: *(Quivering.)* What a pleasure this is. I rarely get to greet a kindred spirit.
SYLVIA: Kindred? You and me? What do we have in common?
EMILY: *(Quivering with timid desire.)* A certain desire to — scratch the surface? Here, you dropped this. *(She pulls out a big razor blade and offers it to Sylvia, who reaches for it tentatively. Whispering.)* I'm so glad you'll be joining me. It's been so lonely being dead. I have no one to talk to and I've been looking for — *(She primps a little.)* — that Special "Anyone" for the longest time.
  (Sylvia drops the razor.)
SYLVIA: Special "Anyone"?
EMILY: *(Shyly.)* I've felt him so close, sometimes. But, oh, well, Longing is its own Rapture!
SYLVIA: If you are a hallucination, shouldn't you perhaps be gone?
  (Emily smiles at her.)
EMILY: Rapture. Now there's a word. From the Latin. To seize, pillage, plunder, rape. Mmmm. *(Shouting.)* Take me, Somebody! I'm not busy! *(Seems to be listening to something.)* They're playing with me, again.

SYLVIA: *(Afraid to know.)* Who?

EMILY: Ooh, that naughty Universe! Tell me. *(She comes closer.)* What did it feel like?

SYLVIA: No! *(She is convulsed by an electric current.)* Yes! That was a good one! *(Terrified.)* I want you out!

EMILY: You won't remember me when you wake up. But I'll remember you!

SYLVIA: Please go away!

EMILY: Not just yet.

SYLVIA: My head is splitting!

EMILY: *(Screams.)* — How else will anything get in? *(Pause. Emily is mortified at herself for losing her temper.)* I'm truly sorry. Want to meet my baby? *(She reaches under her dress and pulls out a shriveled, blasted little book.)* Isn't he beautiful? Guess who his father was. *(Lifting her arms.)* Lightning! *(Sylvia convulses.)*

EMILY: Poor thing. But I can't take care of him any longer. And I've selected you to be his mother! And now, you can have him! He'll bring you luck. *(Emily advances with burnt book.)*

SYLVIA: No! No! No! Sterility! Madness! Bone-bag! I want real children. I want a man to plunge his stake through my heart so that I can sleep at night! *(Emily tosses it on Sylvia's lap.)*

SYLVIA: I don't want it! It's a curse!

EMILY: Our duty is to SING. No backsies!

(She disappears, singing a wordless note.)

SYLVIA: *(Convulsing, gratefully.)* Yes! Yes! Yes!

Scene Four

A classroom at Wardwell College, a women's Ivy League school. Ted Magus is conducting a poetry seminar. Female students are taking notes. Sylvia walks into the classroom area, joining the other girls during Ted's story.

TED: Yes. The ending was a nightmare. I wrestled with it for weeks, like Jacob wrestling the Angel. Finally, I dreamed it. I saw the slug dying, covered with salt by the vicious housewife. As clear as day, I dreamed him, a big quivering mass of slop and mucus writhing in the rotted mulch . . . and I found the final lines . . . "And bubbling there, I'm left alone, a bitter pool of fragrance, shrinking in the sun."

ALL THE GIRLS: Wow. Oh, that's incredible. I cried when I —

TED: So. What have we learned? Don't be polite. Don't be small. Poetry is not all rose gardens and my cat with last year's dead leaves, you know. We're talking about the dark side. The unmentionable terrors. The unspeakable joys. What are yours? Show me. I know my fears are . . . shedding tears in public, showing affection for other men . . . in a physical way, hugging, wrestling, that sort of thing, and — Hah! Dancing! — I mean why — dancing? It terrifies me. My own twisted ideas of manhood, I suppose, as passed down from one generation of small, cramped men to another, when — my God! The blood of our ancestors *thrummed* with the dance. A good jig, a leap under the moonlight — the hunt, the rites of mating or of death — oh come! Let's . . . tango! Who wants to jump in first?

GIRL 1: *(Played by female actor. A flirt. Comes up to front of class with notebook. Adjusts her sweater. She giggles.)* Um, OK. I'm a nervous wreck. OK. Should I say anything about this first? Or just go?

TED: I'm not your judge. I'm not your executioner.

GIRL 1: Oh, Time, why keep'st thine armies marching on
Destroying flesh and withering with age?
The swelling breasts of happy girlhood droop, and —

TED: Yes, yes. And all that. I can tell you've faithfully studied the form. I commend your hard work. I recommend . . . a naked swim with a boy you love in a rock quarry in the blaze of a hot afternoon.

GIRL 1: I'm not sure I understand . . .

TED: Good, good. That's a start. Who else? Come, come, come.

GIRL 2: *(Played by male actor. A grind. She comes to front of class with notebook. Very nervous. Adjusts her glasses. Suddenly levels a passionate gaze at Ted.)*
The azure Mediterranean
Leaps against the chalky cliff
My skin scorches in the hot Greek sun
I left my sunblock at American Express
Dmitri sticks his hand inside my dress
Why, oh, why do they overload these donkeys so?
(Pause.)

TED: Someone else? No one? Oh, come, come. Don't make me talk about dancing, again.
(Sylvia gets up. Recites.)

SYLVIA: It is again the place of nightmare.
Hot breath surrounds me, rich and reeking
Brambles tear the skins from my thighs —

As I run, my blood excites.

Oh, rip from me this borrowed hide.

Teach me my skin.

(Girls look at each other.)

TED: Excellent.

SYLVIA: Omigod. Really? Thank you.

TED: I mean, profoundly usual, but excellent.

SYLVIA: Excuse me?

TED: You know, girls, it's interesting, that this last being one of the best, it's also one of the worst. Ha! That feels like the beginning of an insight! So? What. Class dismissed. Assignment! Assignment! For next week, I want everyone to go out and — spend a night — on a park bench. And write a poem about it. *(Pause. Consternation in the class. Thundering.)* Or don't. It doesn't really matter, does it? *(Student puts up her hand.)* No, I'm not taking any bloody questions! Just *do* it!

(Students leave. Ted collects papers. Sylvia walks over to him. He looks up.)

TED: What's up, Miss — Fluellen? Is it?

SYLVIA: I have a little bone to pick with you.

TED: Oh? What?

SYLVIA: "Profoundly usual"?

TED: *(Packing books, not looking at her.)* Oh, you know, the Tarzan meets Rima the bird girl fantasy stuff, the typical Junior year ambivalence about fellatio, the underlying hatred of your mother. But other than that, it's very well crafted. One of the best.

SYLVIA: *(Choking with fury.)* Tarzan? Rima the bird girl? Junior year ambivalence about — How dare you? How dare you? You — standing up there bullying all the girls all week in that filthy black sweater! Well, how about you! How about your boring male performance anxiety that's so rippingly evident in "Afternoon of a Slug!" Talk about profoundly usual!

TED: *(Laughs.)* Oh, what nonsense.

SYLVIA: Oh, come on! After the evil housewife puts salt on the poor old slug and you say "And bubbling there, I'm left alone, a bitter pool of fragrance, shrinking in the sun . . ."

TED: Don't be idiotic. "Afternoon of the Slug" my dear girl, is about the agony of the creator, writhing in the fleshy bondage of his own creation. An artist must come to terms with agony. The bubbling of a salted slug on a summer morning . . . *(Pause.)* Oh, my God.

SYLVIA: Ha Ha Ha! I'm right, I'm right, I'm right!

TED: I don't believe it.

SYLVIA: I caught you out! I —

TED: Be quiet! I'm thinking. "Short, thick, white bellied worm, I have not the vertebrate advantage . . . "

SYLVIA: "Flesh-helmeted, despised — "

TED: Shut up, will you?

SYLVIA: Hah Hah Hah.

TED: *(Mounting concern.)* " — the boneless one that will never stiffen — oh, where are you, Muscle for my Dreams . . . for my ramping will . . ." Oh, God. I can't believe it! It is! It's about my DICK!

SYLVIA: See, I told you, I was —

TED: I can't believe it. It's so bloody obvious. I sweated BLOOD over "Afternoon of a Slug." It was a death struggle. I pursued that poem like Ahab chasing after Mm — .

(Pause.)

SYLVIA: I am. So. Attracted to you.

(Ted looks at her.)

TED: Don't fuck with me, Miss Fluellen.

SYLVIA: I'm going to.

TED: I'm death to Little Girls.

SYLVIA: I'm not a little Girl.

TED: And I hate Women!

SYLVIA: Not as much as I do!

TED: *(Crossing to her.)* I'm trouble. I'm a filthy rucksack of a man in the dungheap of existence. I want a great muck of a woman, not a bright little coed. I need Big Ugly Woman! — to wake me up. When we have each other in the dead of night, it won't be full of sticky tenderness. It will be with the ancient frenzy and the FIRE ants that Couple and Kill.

SYLVIA: You don't frighten me!

TED: Such an all-American girl. With your big white teeth, red painted lips and — *(Grabbing her arms — she gasps and tries to break away.)* bandages all over your arms. *(He laughs.)*

SYLVIA: Take your hands off me, you sick bastard!

(He releases her easily. She stares at him for a moment, then suddenly pulls him to her for a passionate kiss. He mounts her as she lies back over the desk top. Her head hangs upside down, face toward audience, hair streaming downward. A tableau. Ted remains frozen in position as Sylvia speaks.)

SYLVIA: *(Face front, ferocious, joyful.)* Off! Sticky Mother Pot!

I throw my saddle shoes at your head

And dance barefoot with a goat-footed giant

We are laughing at you, he and I
My lips are red and my hair fills the forest.
(A metered laugh.)
HA HA HA HA HA!

Scene Five

Anne's house. Anne is in her bed. She is in a state. Her husband, Tito, is with her.

TITO: What can I do? I just don't know what to do for you!

ANNE: Get Dr. Dickter on the phone! I want to go back to the bin! I want to go back to the bin!

TITO: Please, Baby, no. Shall I call one of your lovers?

ANNE: It doesn't help. Nothing helps.

TITO: *(Reluctant.)* Do you want — to have sex with me?

ANNE: *(Anguished.)* I might as well masturbate! I mean, c'mon, Tito, we've become the same person! *(Pause.)* Oh, I've hurt you, Baby, my love. I'm a big mess. Make me a milkshake? I want the big sweet mama I never had. I want it with a straw.

TITO: Chocolate?

ANNE: *(Screams.)* Vanilla! Don't you listen?

TITO: All right! *(He leaves.)*

ANNE: Mommy's feeling crazy! Kit-Kat! KIT-KAT!!!
(Anne lights a cigarette, fussing for a moment, Kit-Kat enters, apprehensive.)

ANNE: *(Sweetly.)* Oh, it's so good to be home again with my Bunny-girl. Let's cuddle up. Give me your hands. Baby Bunny, do you believe that Mother loves you and what happened has nothing to do with you?

KIT-KAT: *(Reluctant.)* I guess so.

ANNE: *(Taking her hands.)* I'm so sorry, Kit-Kat, that you had to find me like that. Never again. Believe me?

KIT-KAT: I guess so.

ANNE: Do you really, Kitty? 'Cause part of our healing is to say what we really feel. *(Pause.)* What is it, Baby?

KIT-KAT: Oh, Mom. It was so gross! I had to clean everything up, all the puke and the pills — and all the kids coming over for my Sweet Sixteen party! Why'd you have to try and kill yourself on my birthday!! You hate me!!!

ANNE: I do not! Shut up you little bitch! Are you out of your mind? I said I was sorry!

KIT-KAT: Sorry!   TITO: *(Entering with milkshake.)* For Christ's sake, Anne!

ANNE: Oh, God, Tito — I could die! — this waste of my life — forced early into marriage (that prison routine of pancake breakfasts and chicken pot pies) — scrubbing toilets instead of fighting to save myself, singing idiot songs to an insomniac infant, whose little red face could only reflect my own fury back to me —

TITO: *(Furious.)* First of all, we eloped. Secondly, you don't cook, I do. And Kit-Kat has done all the housework! Ever since she moved back from Foster Care!

ANNE: You are undermining me! Do you give a shit if I survive or not!

TITO: Of course —   KIT-KAT: Oh, Mommy what's wrong! What did I do? Stop crying —

ANNE: Then support my truth!

TITO: *(Leaving so he won't hit her.)* Excuse me. I've got to check the roast.

ANNE: Oh, shit. *(Pause.)* Mommy loves you, baby. Forgive me.

KIT-KAT: For what?

ANNE: I'm grudging my blooming baby her day in the spring sun. Look how beautiful you are. I'm sorry I missed that darn party.

KIT-KAT: It's all right, Mom.

ANNE: No, it's not all right! I wanted to give you something my mother never gave me. Trust in yourself. In your body. Listen. You are beautiful. Your vagina is beautiful.

KIT-KAT: Mom, please, you're embarrassing me.

ANNE: Don't be. Everything you are, everything you feel, is right, love. Kitty, are you padding that bra — that can't be YOU — is it? Let Mommy feel — *(Swiping at her.)*

KIT-KAT: No!

ANNE: Listen. I know how it is when you're young and your whole taut little body is singing the song of sex. Is there anything you'd like to ask Mommy?

KIT-KAT: I've got to go. Some of the gang is waiting.

ANNE: I want you to never feel ashamed, baby.

KIT-KAT: I'm not.

ANNE: I love you!

KIT-KAT: I know you do.

ANNE: Mommy wrote a new poem, in the hospital. It's going to be in *The Atlantic Monthly.* Isn't that exciting?

KIT-KAT: Cool.

ANNE: Don't you want me to read it to you?

KIT-KAT: *(Exiting.)* Yeah, but not right now.

ANNE: All right, my angel. Some other time when you have the time. Jesus.
   *(Sighs. Reaches for her last cigarette and crumples the empty pack. A silence.
   Then, as a prayer, or a poem, or something she sees in the curling smoke.)*
   Jesus — God — Baby —
   What would you do with an old crazy lady —
   Can you smooth this old piece of worn brown wood —
   With your carpenter's hands —
   Can you make something out of me?
   Anne is finally ready for you, Jesus —
   A holy man with holes in his hands –
   A man in a white dress with a kind, kind face —
   Sweet old ghost that blesses all our adulteries —
   'Cause we *are* all adults now, aren't we?
   Except I'm not, Jesus, God, Baby —
   I'm just little Anne
   And I need a Big Kind Daddy to help this old girl home.

Scene Six

*Dr. Stoner's house. Preparation for a surprise birthday party is under way. Vera
is hiding party guests. Stoner comes in with dry cleaning in a plastic bag.*

STONER: I'm sixty-five years old and every word I ever wrote is a lie. Fuck everything. *(He rips out the clothes and puts the dry cleaning bag over his head.)*

EVERYONE: SURPRISE!

STONER: AAAHHH!

EVERYONE: Happy birthday to you, happy birthday to you, happy birthday
   dear Daddy-Bob, happy birthday to you.

VERA: Honey, blow the candles out and make a wish.

STONER: You blow them out. I don't give a shit.

VERA: Bob, people came from all over the country for your birthday.

STONER: Why? Oh, I'm so depressed. I'm dead already. Why didn't they just
   send flowers.

OTHERS: Oh, Daddy-Bob, no. No, that's not true. We love you, Daddy-Bob.

VERA: C'mon. Sweetie. Things aren't so bad. Blow out the candles.

STONER: I went out on the street, and the clouds were jeering faces. A dog pissed on my leg while I waited for a light to change. I was going to be the long-awaited messenger for my time. Arriving bloody, half dead, but bearing the olive branch of hope! All I am is half dead. I want a scotch on the rocks.

EVERYONE: Noo, noo, noo.

STONER: I keep trying to remember something.

(Pause.)

VERA: What, Honey?

STONER: *(Angry.)* Anything, goddammit. I'm hollow. An old shell. I can't finish a sentence anymore let alone a poem!

(Ted and Sylvia enter.)

STONER: And here's my young friend Ted — the bold new voice that makes my life's work a pile of shit.

(Pause.)

TED: Happy birthday, Dr. Stoner. So good to see you again.

STONER: Who's the little Miss?

TED: This is Sylvia, Dr. Stoner —

SYLVIA: *(Brightly to all.)* Wife!

STONER: 'Spleasure.

SYLVIA: Dr. Stoner, I just can't *wait* for the Cotton Mather poems!

GUEST: Jesus!

STONER: *(Sobbing.)* Oh, God, God, God — I wish I was dead!

SYLVIA: What did I say?

SOMEONE ELSE: No, Daddy-Bob. Please —

TED: Now, now, Daddy-Bob, what's all this?

STONER: I find that weeping fills me like a great storm, and all I can do is cry until I can breathe again. Ahh! *(He sobs while everyone waits. Abruptly, he stops.)* That's better. Really, I'm clear, again. Let's have cake! How are you all, all my young friends?

EVERYONE: Oh, we're fine, Daddy-Bob. Martha's play was reviewed in *American Quarterly,* the *New Yorker* took "Winter in Narragansett" —

(Stoner and Vera sit on the couch with cake, as guests chatter.)

STONER: *(Howling.)* Can't somebody kill me?

(Silence.)

SYLVIA: Well, Ted, I don't know about you, but I'm ready to —

STONER: Vera, I want a scotch!

VERA: No, Baby, no! And that's final!

Girl: How about a little —

STONER: Do I look like I want any damn cake?!

(Anne enters.)

ANNE: *(To Vera.)* I don't know if he'll remember me, it's been so long — I was in his workshop ages ago . . .

VERA: Hello, dear. Hang on to your hat. Do you two know each other?

SYLVIA: Oh, hello.

ANNE: *(Kissing her.)* Baby! Mwaa! How well you look! Have you —

(Stoner falls to his knees, arms outstretched.)

STONER: *(Sings.)* Oh Faith, most fragrant oil

We yield it up to You!

Essence of the lily mild —

The gift of rack and screw!

(Pause.)

Does anybody know what I'm talking about?

TED: *(Quietly.)* Yes, Dr. Stoner, yes.

(He crosses to him. Stoner stays on knees. Looks sideways at Ted.)

STONER: I once sensed the hard promise of God like distant chords of scary music. I've been sitting on the moon like a good little boy my whole damn life. Trying to be grateful for my fucking lunacy. One of God's special presents. I was promised a message and I've been so patient! Well, I've lain forty years on my right side and all I'm getting is bedsores!

(Guest snickers. Stoner lunges for him. Others hold him back.)

STONER: You think that's funny?

SOMEONE: He's really gone.

TED: Oh, no, he's not.

STONER: We'll talk about it in hell, you and I!

VERA: Robert? Oh, please, Bob —

TED: Let's admit what's happening, here. This man is crying out for help. Please. Can we all join together in a ritual of healing?

(Murmurs of assent.)

TED: You need a brother in the lonely walk, Bob-Doctor. We're all here with you. Would you like to hold my hand?

(Ted offers his hand to Stoner under the table. Stoner considers and then takes it, allowing himself to be led to the living room floor like a dog.)

TED: Please! Everyone. Join us on the floor. Leave your cake. Robert is in crisis. *(He test-drums on the floor.)* Dum dah dah dum!

MAN: All right!

STONER: *(To Ted.)* Where did we meet? I've forgotten . . .

TED: On the radio, Dr. Stoner. Last fall? I read from "Songs of the Fen" . . . we worked on the Mather poem together . . .

STONER: . . . shack shacka shack . . . ?

TED: That's right, that's right! Please, Robert, you must trust me. I'm with you. I hear you. And I understand your torment with the great hard Father. Listen to me. He's not home. He never was. *(Pause.)* But the Mother is. *(Reaction from guests. Wow. Yes. The Mother is.)*

STONER: What in hell are you talking about?

TED: Don't think — !
(Stoner starts to respond.)

TED: Look where it's led you. Don't talk! Words can't heal a heart.
(Some of the guests are nodding, starting to get weepy. They press each other's hands in support.)

TED: Try with me. I know it's hard, I know it doesn't make *sense*. Let's drum for healing, Dr. Stoner . . . I've seen miracles happen. Let's break a sweat!

VERA: He's on a new medication . . . I don't know if he should —

MAN: Let's all get naked together! I'll go first!

VERA: No!

TED: *(Drumming softly.)* We call for healing . . . hear us great Mother!
(Some drum. Stoner is confused. He drums.)

SYLVIA: *(To party guest.)* Take your hand off me — Ted! That man just —

TED: Shhh!
(Sylvia goes and stands behind Stoner in a huff.)
We're asking for the healing of our friend brother Robert . . . when the spirit moves you, let him speak through you.

GIRL: I love everyone in this room. Why not? Why shouldn't I? There's no shame in love!

TED: Good! Yes! Dum dah dah dum, dum dah dah dum. I can feel it. We are starting to invoke something. Name the unnameable — put words to the darkness —

STONER: Ahh! Someone's here! An evil spirit . . . I sense her presence — she's standing next to me with a look of anger and disapproval . . . she hates me! And I'm only a little boy!

TED: *(Hissing.)* For Christ's sake, sit down, Sylvia. *(Beating on the floor.)* Dum, dah dah . . .
(Sylvia shoots Ted a furious look and sits down huffily.)

STONER: Dum dah! Dah! Ahh! Ahh! *(He stands up, suddenly. Disoriented.)* Where am I, where am I?
(Anguish from Vera, excitement from group.)

TED: *(Intense.)* What do you see, Robert? Take us with you —

STONER: *(Terrified — backs into a hostile houseplant.)* A jungle as green as a lemon! The leaves are sharp and glowing! *(Hides behind it, peers through the foliage.)*

TED: The primeval lap of the great mother!

(Ted gestures to the guests who are waving their arms soothingly — as they try to corner him. They look like Pygmies on a hunt, increasing Stoner's scrambling terror.)

STONER: *(Horrified.)* Insects hanging upside down — with eyes as big as hubcaps! Everything is chewing everything!

TED: Yes! Yes! Accept! Don't be afraid! The great circle of creation! It is the dance of being!

(The guests begin to writhe and frisk. Ted pounds on ottoman.)

GUESTS: *(Euphoric.)* Go into it! Go into it! We love you, Daddy-Bob! We're WITH you Daddy-Bob! Let it GO, man . . .

(Vera is distressed. Sylvia, repulsed. Anne watches Stoner with increasing alarm — gets to her feet.)

TED: The great circle of CREATION!

STONER: *(Clutching torn leaf at groin — realizing.)* I'm Adam! The first man! Oh, poor Adam! Naked and alone! I wish for death, but it hasn't been invented yet! GAAAH!

(He crumples. No one knows what to do. Group falters. Suddenly Anne cuts decisively through the group, cuffing a lone drumming guest into silence as she goes. Assertive, sure.)

ANNE: But Love has! It's me, Baby, Eve.

(The group hushes.)

STONER: AAhh! Adam's senses thrill. His skin ripples.

ANNE: I'm here for you, baby, my old Adam baby! I'll keep you warm. Come creep into my arms and rest.

STONER: Could you love a bad, bad man like me?

ANNE: Oh, Doll, all men are bad. Eve just loves and loves her bad little boy.

(Stoner moves into her arms. She holds him. Vera sits in corner quietly.)

TED: Astonishing. Beautiful. She's stepping into his undermyth.

SYLVIA: What?

GIRL: Wow.

SYLVIA: Did you say his "undermyth"?

TED: Be quiet, or leave.

ANNE: It's all right now. Everything is all right now.

STONER: I think I know you. Oh, my, it's not Little Annie from my Tuesday night class at Boston College! Look how you've changed!

ANNE: Yeah, I know.

STONER: You used to be a morsel and now you're the whole three layers! Isis! Cleopatra! Betsy Ross! Come with me and be my love, we'll face the dark together, you and I!

ANNE: Oh, you lovely man! But you have your good Vera and I have my dear, boring Tito.

STONER: Oh, no, don't send me away now that I've found you. Beautiful Mother! It's you! It's you! Love me! Love me or I'll die!

VERA: I think he might, too. This has happened before. The Air-India stewardess, the Jamaican nurse, the lady from the IRS — *(Earnest.)* Oh, please, Miss Bittenhand, don't turn him away.

ANNE: Oh, really, I couldn't . . .

VERA: I'm begging you as a wife. Help him. I can't. Take him with you . . . he will make you feel so cherished . . . for a while.
(She exits.)

GIRL: And to think I almost stayed home tonight.

STONER: Come live with me and be my love.

ANNE: Where would we go, you Great Wonderful Mad Daddy?

VERA: *(Reentering with checkbook.)* We have a cabin near Indian Lake. You could be there by tomorrow evening if you —
(She tries to put checkbook in Stoner's pocket.)

STONER: Who the hell are you, bothering my love and I? Keep your money, strange woman. We don't need your money.

ANNE: Hey!
(Vera passes checkbook to Anne behind Stoner's back.)

VERA: Bless you, Honey, oh, bless you. I thank you and America thanks you. Take good care of him. Call me when he's himself again. Does this put you out very much?

ANNE: Put me out? I don't think so.
(Vera and Anne embrace.)

ANNE: C'mon, Papa-Doc.

MAN: *(Quietly.)* Daddy-Bob.

ANNE: Let's you and me go play house.

STONER: In Xanadu, did Kubla Khan
A stately pleasure dome decree —
(As he and Anne exit.) — my inspiration is coming back to me . . . my Angel, you restore me to myself!

(Guests stand around uncertainly.)

GIRL: Let's celebrate, anyway. Let's celebrate that we're here, we're alive, we have warm flesh, awake minds, there is love in this room —

TED: *(Smiling at her.)* Absolutely — let's all —

VERA: Do you mind! Thank you all for coming, but I think I'd like to be alone, now.

EVERYONE: Good night, Mrs. Stoner — call me if you just want to talk, shall I stay and help you clean up? Good night, good night, good night —

(Guests leave.)

TED: Are you going to be —

VERA: No.

TED: Would you like me to —

VERA: No.

SYLVIA: Are you sure that you —

VERA: No.

TED: Well, uh, good night, then.

(He and Sylvia exit. Vera sits alone onstage.)

Act II

Scene One

A cabin at Indian Lake. Anne and Stoner have just arrived.

STONER: I'm frightened. Woman. Woman!

ANNE: I'm here, Honey.

STONER: I'm really in for it now. Oh, I can feel it coming on. I'm feeling very, very sneaky, and so much smarter than everyone else.

ANNE: But you are!

STONER: No, you don't get it. I'm harboring these little epigrams. Like . . . this one . . . occurred to me, just as we came in the door. "Insouciance is Dominion's Ticket." It means nothing to me yet, but soon it will and then I'll be lost, lost, lost, and back in those dreadful arts-and-crafts rooms, making ashtrays and moccasins, the laughingstock of ghosts. Soon, I'll feel those awful giggles come upon me, and I'll be a laughing Jack, a balloon of grotesque euphoria! Oh, I hate my enthusiasms . . . afterwards. I love them when they're happening, though.

ANNE: You just keep talking to me, and I'll rub your shaggy old head, and I promise you my damnedest that we're never going to find out what your little epigram means.

STONER: Annie. How unbearably lovely you are. That is something that I can still see.

ANNE: Want to go to bed?

STONER: You'd let me have at you?

ANNE: I don't see any problem with that.

STONER: I'm blinded, by your goodness. I may die, to gaze upon such beauty. Look at you!

ANNE: Don't look too hard. Let me —

STONER: Sweetness of my heart. Why are you afraid to be seen? The little places where you're crumbling are full of light. Tiny air bubbles are bearing your clay away and replacing you with helio-sycory.

ANNE: And what might that be, Crazy One?

STONER: Divine substance. I love your little sags and bags. It means the beginning is near, my Eternal Salamander, my Sun-Angel.

ANNE: You're nutty as a fruitcake, but I think I'm falling in love. Oh, you move me, you old madman. You're so different than when I first knew you. You were sour and respectable, then. Scary and oh, so learned.

STONER: I was trapped in the lower levels. The horrible sea-bottom of my special lie.

ANNE: You're losing me. Take me with you.

STONER: I was a lie! A false monster built of pretension and the desire to be admired. Why, my greatest poem was a fraud. The poem I once read on the White House lawn, "To a Confederate War Horse, Dead at Chattahoochee." Biggest fraud of my life.

ANNE: Oh, the horse poem? But I loved that!
(Jogging his memory.)
There you lie . . .
Dung and honor smeared, inseparable —
In the clotted strands of your tail . . .

STONER: *(Slowly.)*
— What did you know, Great Beast,
Eater of Oats,
Of men with beards in board-rooms of Washington
Or of a ringletted girl smacking her pickaninny silly
You carried her on your back,
Old Switcher of Flies —

ANNE: — Had you know, would you have run so,
Would you have burst your great heart
Willingly, for the Confederacy,
That harpy in the hoopskirt?

Look at me, I'm weeping. Lies, or no lies, no one did it like you, Sweetheart. You were the king.

STONER: Well, I did do a jolly good job of pirating Walt Whitman. He probably spun his way to China when he heard that one.

ANNE: What do we do now?

STONER: Go to bed and wait.

ANNE: Yes.

STONER: Lie down with me. I can't have at you, really, of course. All that's long gone with those salts and God knows what of Dr. Von Seyffertitz, but a little sanity is much sweeter to me now, except for those moments when I'd trade it all for sadness. But would you take a nap with me, Sweet Anne? It would mean more than anything else I could think of.

ANNE: You know, it's the funniest thing.

STONER: Yes?

ANNE: I was never one for naps, but right this minute, that seems like the best idea.

STONER: Crawl in.

Scene Two

Ted's and Sylvia's place. It is an old restored lighthouse with rough stone interiors and a dominant upstage window. Morning. Sounds of the sea. They sit across a Ouija board, hands on the planchette.

SYLVIA: This isn't going to work! I'm a fat, phony fraud!

TED: Shh. Shh. Go on. Ask him again.

SYLVIA: *(Intoning with great seriousness.)* I commme to the Spirits as a tonngue-less Mute. I seek my Voice. What strange grip chokes me and leeeves me silent? For mmmany mmmoons now, I have lingered in an aimless malaizze. Why cannot I write, Mr. Pandora?

TED: Why cannot you speak normally?

SYLVIA: Mr. Pandora — there is a force that stifles mmee. Throttles this song-bird so she cannot sing — sheee that once sang free. Would it be so hard, Mr. Pandora, to speak to me, and tell me what am I supposed to do? It is I, the true seeker that comes to the spirits in her hour of need. *(Pause.)* Oh, just MOVE you FUCKER! Tell me something! Anything! Who do I have to FUCK to get an IDEA? *(Planchette starts to move.)* There! He moves!

TED: Look at him go!

BOTH: Go — t — wait you're pushing it — *(Slowly sounding out the words as Planchette moves.)* GOOO. TOOOO. HEEEEEELLLL.
(Pause.)

SYLVIA: *(To the board.)* You bastard. He just told me to go to Hell. I'm being rejected by the OCCULT! Oh, this is really too much!
(She gets up and crosses away from table.)

TED: You're overreacting. A certain amount of nonsense just comes up.

SYLVIA: *(Stung and furious.)* Oh, ho ho. No, no, no, Ted, I wouldn't call this NONsense. It's calculated to WOUND — Mr. Pandora is aiming his advice right for where it HURTS. Go to HELL. That's been the message of my life. "Go to HELL" is what they said when I tried to join the SWIM team. "Go to HELL!" is what they thought when I asked them to my BIRTHDAY party. Oh, yes, they came all right, but only to laugh and sneer, while Mother played the piano and sang in her peculiar voice, PAR-LOR songs from the wrong CENTURY! Go to HELL!! I LISTENED to those voices, and finally I WENT to hell, my Sophomore YEAR, when I tried to cut off my HEAD with an AX!

TED: What?

SYLVIA: I couldn't tell you the whole truth. After I slashed my WRISTS I became afraid I hadn't done the TRICK. I tried to cut off my HEAD with an old WOOD-AX!

TED: God!

(Seeing his horror, she quickly shifts gears.)

SYLVIA: *(Suddenly playful.)* Fooling! Fooling! Oh, Silly, just my wrists. *(Kisses his head.)* Mwaah! *(Furious again.)* I know all about Hell!

TED: Then WRITE about it! I've got to go. I'm due at the station at two.

SYLVIA: Oh, Baby, good luck! I'll be listening! Oh, wait, your manuscript! Silly!

TED: Try and do a little work, huh?

(Ted kisses her, grabs manuscript, exits. Sylvia waves. Goes to table and, disconsolate, pulls out her notebook.)

SYLVIA: *(Signs.)* Go to Hell. Hmm. Hell . . . Hades . . . the dark underworld from which Demeter, the mother of the earth, returns. Astarte. Inanna. Gaia.

Hmm. "The bee-struck blossom, nods,

Heavy in the pregnant honey-scented breeze —

It is waiting for her —

She is coming, she, dressed in a gown of grain —"

(She is defeated. Starts to idly wiggle her pencil in front of her face to make it look like rubber. Falls into a stupor. Her head drops. Emily enters through upstage window, shivering, compressed, overwrought. May be covered with ice and fairly crackles with her hunger for the Living.)

EMILY: *(Eagerly.)*

The little MAID snug in her cot

The sun poked in his head

And lifting up the coverlet

He saw that she was — DEAD!

SYLVIA: *(Jerking upright.)* Oh, my God! Who are you?

EMILY: The TOOTH that circles in your soul

And carves its basement out!!

SYLVIA: *(Terrified.)* AAUGH! *(Pause.)* That's — not very good!

EMILY: "Perpetuity" has made me sloppy. Don't think I don't know. Anyway —

I can't maintain much longer, Everything is pulling at me from Everywhere, and later . . . or sooner . . . I've an appointment with —

SYLVIA: What?

EMILY: Oblivion! Ahh! Now there's a word to lift your HEAD to!
(She pantomimes lifting her head off her shoulders. Sylvia screams.)

SYLVIA: How did you get IN here?

EMILY: Oh, no, no, no. I'm not. Here. In that sense. I'm your imaginary friend. You might say. That's the degree before psychotic. That's when YOU become MY imaginary friend.

SYLVIA: What?

EMILY: Don't worry. That's a ways off yet. Months! *(Laughs.)*

SYLVIA: What do you want?

EMILY: Company! A chance to hear your verse? Maybe later, a little game of knucklebones? Oh, never mind that — look. You seemed stuck. I can help. I really BELIEVE in you.

SYLVIA: Oh, no, I don't think that —
(Emily assaults her, wrestling her to the floor.)

EMILY: Just spit it out!

SYLVIA: The honey-scented breeze ripples the branch —

EMILY: *(Quivering, delighted.)* — And everyone was DEAD!

SYLVIA: Galloping sunrise scatters its tangerine largess —

EMILY: *(Horribly helpful.)* And everyone was LONELY and dead.

SYLVIA: *(Desperately.)* Long-legged hares clip-clop their legs together — they joy at the meadow's newness — they are bringing her to herself — !

EMILY: *(Beside herself, dismounts Sylvia and raves around the room.)*
And we tried to get out of our coffins but we couldn't!
Ha ha ha! And we tore our nails out scratching at the ceiling! And we screamed and screamed but God couldn't hear us! Yes! Yes! Yes!
(Pause.) But that's just me talking!

SYLVIA: Stop it! This is horrible!

EMILY: Horrible! Oh, where I am now is so far past horrible! Horrible was the last report of land — what I wouldn't give for merely horrible — I'd give my eyeteeth, if I had any!

SYLVIA: Where are you . . . ???

EMILY: *(Howling as some undertow sucks her back out through the window.)* Where you belong — !!

SYLVIA: Wait — !

EMILY: *(As she disappears from view.)* Out! Of! Time!
(Sylvia, shell-shocked, picks up her wooden spoon and mixing bowl.)

Scene Three

Afternoon. A radio station. Ted is on air with Interviewer. Something looser, more dangerous, ripe about him. This reading could scarcely be called a reading — the atmosphere is volatile, immediate.

INTERVIEWER: If you're just joining us, we're chatting with poet Ted Magus. Exciting to have you with us. Ted! How would you describe your direction in these new poems?

TED: Basically what I'm trying to do is rip a new asshole in a dead language.

INTERVIEWER: Umm. That's really interesting that you should say that — because I found that I literally couldn't sit down for hours, after reading some of them. I just had to pace, I was disturbed.

TED: Good for you. That's very good. It means you're open. It means you're more than just a suit with an English degree from some death-mill bullshit university.

INTERVIEWER: Ha! That's interesting.

TED: The Spider.

> The light through the window is green with rain.
> The dust lies thick — upon the sill.
> The schoolboy in me becomes unstuck.
> I write my initials and then write "Fuck."
> A buzzing draws my eye.

> A spider is squatting on a fly.
> Her eight hairy legs unknot his — tie!
> He was HAPPY just an hour ago
> Dreaming of DOG-SHIT!
> Now eight hairy legs —
> Root — and find —
> His green heart's shell
> And his SCREAMS become her DINNER bell —
> As EIGHT. HAIRY. LEGS. Beat.
> . . . in time.
> *(Pause.)*

INTERVIEWER: — God! You know, it's so odd. I'm sweating!

TED: You're a man. You're alive. You're simply a man who's alive.

INTERVIEWER: *(Fighting tears — quietly.)* — I'm sorry — God! It's just —

TED: I know. I know. I know.

(The men look into each other's eyes. Ted pats the Interviewer on the back.)

Scene Four

Evening. Ted's and Sylvia's house. Sylvia is cooking as Ted enters.

TED: Sweetheart, did you hear that! Were you listening? He asked me back for next week. Ha ha!

SYLVIA: Terrific. Let's eat.

TED: I wasn't nervous at all. I felt calm, like I had a right to be there, just simple. Sharing who I am and what I think. How'd I do? Was it all right?

SYLVIA: Eight legs? Eight hairy legs!! You utter FUCK? Is that what you think of me?

TED: What?

SYLVIA: You think I don't know that's ME?

TED: What I want to know is are you really crazy, or are you just pretending?

SYLVIA: Because if you think that was me, we can just end this here and now. I will not be humiliated on national radio as some kind of big, rubbery, Venus Fly Trap! Is that what you think I am, some kind of big, rubbery, Venus Fly Trap?

TED: Actually, you're more medium sized and chalky.

SYLVIA: Medium sized and chalky!! I deserved that. Oh, Ted. You have a laughter in you that heals my heart. Thank God we found each other. Let's eat. You were wonderful. Absolutely thrilling. I've married a giant. You stimulate me! When I'm with you I feel like I'm teeming with new life, new ideas. I see a bean sprout in a jar, and I hear a villanelle, a cat asleep on a porch step . . . I still can't seem to get much down on paper, however.

TED: Do we have any beer?

SYLVIA: *(Thoughtfully.)* My man wants mead to wash down his meal . . . the bubbling joy-nectar of the distant spit of bees now dry and dead.

TED: You're a little over the top tonight.

SYLVIA: Over the top! Excuse the shit out of me. I'll subside. *(She is silent.)*

TED: I know what's going on with you.

SYLVIA: Oh, you know what's going on with me. You know what's going on with me.

TED: You're angry because you don't have a dick.

SYLVIA: What?

TED: That's not completely true. You're angry because you don't have a dick, and you can't write. I have a penis, I have a pen. I can piss for yards and yards. You know, I could write poems on a highway divider. I don't wear out Ouija boards and consult fifteen horoscopes before *not* writing all day. I just write down what's on my mind, I guess you could say I'm alive.

SYLVIA: Well — gee, everything's about ready.

TED: Did I hurt your feelings? *(Pause.)* Then why are you smiling!

SYLVIA: *(Screams.)* Stop yelling at me!!

TED: Yes, there! Just, BE there, in — that! place. That hurt place. Breathe from there.

(She starts to cry.)

TED: That's right. It's all right. I'm here. Come here.

(She gets in his lap.)

TED: Better?

(Pause. She nods.)

TED: Sorry. I just sensed you needed to be lanced. Like a boil.

SYLVIA: Honey. Is it tame? Our life, I mean?

TED: No.

SYLVIA: *(Earnestly, sweetly.)* Because, if you want something different, just tell me. I can be other things, for you. I mean, I can't be one of your eighteen-year-old students, but then, they can't read your work with any discrimination, with any critical insight. They can't see where it starts to be less than honest, where you're bluffing, where it starts to suck. See, I can.

TED: Give it a rest, huh?

SYLVIA: Let's do something completely unexpected. Let's make love. Right here in the mashed potatoes. Here and now.

TED: *(Surprised, pleased.)* Big silly slut —

(He reaches for her.)

SYLVIA: I'll just put some newspaper under the dish.

(She gets up.)

TED: Well, then. That isn't exactly here and now, is it.

SYLVIA: It will be here and now in just a second.

TED: But the here and now you wanted to jump into is dead and gone.

SYLVIA: Oh, don't be so pedantic.

TED: I'm not pedantic! How dare you call me pedantic!

SYLVIA: Well, you're not UN-pedantic, I mean, it's not an insult —

TED: *(Exploding in frustration.)* Aggghhhhh!

SYLVIA: What. What's the matter?

TED: Nothing.

SYLVIA: Don't you want to tell me?

TED: I'm going out for a walk.

SYLVIA: You are not! I will not have you walking out on me!

TED: Get out of my way.

SYLVIA: *(Swiping at him.)* Noo! You stay here and fight me man to man!

TED: I can't fight with you man to man!

SYLVIA: Yes, you can. Yes, you can, yes you can! Do it! I know you want to do it! I dare you. Do it, you bastard! *(She starts pushing him. He grabs her and pins her arms.)* Ow, stop it, you're hurting me!

(He rushes her and they start to tussle. He bends her back over the table. They have sex. They do not hear each other's fantasies.)

SYLVIA: I cannot SCREAM

You have cut out my tongue

Nazi scientist!

TED: Too young for a stewardess, who can she be?

This red-headed one who wants me —

SYLVIA: My Jew blood sinks into the slate

Hey SS Mister, take my —

SYLVIA: Sister!   TED: — Sisters?

My shaggy flanks burn —

For a bottle of beer and a long fuck —

SYLVIA: It is the time of the gouge and pluck

I tremble and curse my luck —

TED: There are no names here —

That way seems truest —

SYLVIA: I am no name to him, just Jewess —

TED: We three, happy, in the long tall grass —

Just me, two jolly sisters,

Balls and ass — !

(He comes. Pause.)

SYLVIA: *(In a terrible level voice.)* He has slit me open

In this place where Jack gutted his sluts —

(Ted gets off Sylvia. Buttons himself up.)

TED: Baby, I'm so sorry. Look at you. I'm an animal. I don't know my own strength. You have mashed potatoes in your hair. Oh, spinach on your white blouse. Now, that was great. *(Silence.)* Baby, what's the matter? I said that was great! I forgot you were my wife! *(Silence.)* Oh, get over it.

What's the matter? Look, I'm not going to apologize. Oh, Baby, say something. Please say something.

SYLVIA: Look what you did to my arm. It's all purple.

TED: Yeah.

SYLVIA: And my skirt's ruined!

TED: I'll buy you a new one. As soon as I get a job.

SYLVIA: Oh. God. I feel — really — *(Stops. She slowly looks up. Wonder.)* GOOD. Really — good. . . Ted!

Scene Five

Outside Ted's and Sylvia's. One month later. Stoner and Ted are walking on the bluffs.

TED: And this is the wisdom of wolf —
In the beginning was the howl —
In the middle was the owl pellet —
And in the end will be the memory of meals.

STONER: *(Entering.)* What the fuck is that supposed to mean?

TED: What does it sound like?

STONER: Nothing!

TED: That's right. Cold freezing nothing . . . out of which we must invent ourselves from a stone and a fart. Like Wolf.

STONER: That's the most insidious crap I ever heard.

TED: *(Crestfallen.)* Oh, really? Do you think so?

STONER: Save it for your students, Son. I wrote the book on bullshit.

TED: Hah. Marvelous! Marvelous!

STONER: Hah hah hah! You actually SNOW people with this shit. I like you, young Ted. I want you to call me Bob-Father. I've never invited anyone, before.

TED: Bob-Father! Do you mean it? I never had a proper father, Bob-Fath —

STONER: "I walk through the chill New England copses, wearing Vera's hand knit sockses." That's the only verse I've written all year, and I have the feeling that I didn't write that, either. I think maybe I heard it somewhere. You know, this is the very coast where perhaps Mather himself walked, wrestling with his God, and all I hear is the mocking hoot of a distant garbage barge.

TED: *(Excited.)* But, that, what you just said, about the mockery of a distant garbage barge! There it is! You're meeting the great emptiness, just as he did! Now, that — is powerful!

STONER: Who do you think I am? Fucking Robert Frost? Meet the great emptiness! That's too damn easy, my boy. You small, sorry men! — (don't be offended — I'm very fond of you, personally) — you small, sorry men! You've gone and pulled God down from the sky to shape Him to your own devices.

TED: Well, He didn't put up much of a fucking fight, did He?

STONER: Aha ha ha, aha ha ha! You have no idea how funny that is.

TED: What do you mean?

STONER: As if He has to try and fight! He's laughing while he waits, quiet and slack as a pussycat as you do what you want, rewriting him to fit your beast-nature.

TED: I think we'll find instinct a better God than some old man with a beard and a stone tablet.

STONER: You'll have to kill me. We can't both be right.

TED: Oh, not so. Not. So. The world to come embraces contradiction. Why look at you, Old Calvinist like you, you've left your wife again.

STONER: I'm a miserable old bastard. I can't wait to die. Except that I feel all right, just now. And it's true. I am in love, one last time. Isn't a woman just a wonder?

TED: Once a woman throws her legs over your head you're finished.

STONER: Ah! Aha ha ha! You put me in such a good mood, Teddy Bear. It's so refreshing to have changed women. You'd think that sex wears off when you stop having it. But it doesn't. It just keeps getting better.

Scene Six

Meanwhile. Interior. Sylvia's kitchen. Sylvia and Anne are making dinner, rather Sylvia is. Anne smokes and nurses her drink.

ANNE: *(Dreamy.)* Baby, if you had it to do over again . . . would you still use a razor blade?

SYLVIA: I don't know if I could, again. That was almost an accident. I didn't know I'd cut myself till I saw blood. Like a gorgeous blossom.

ANNE: Sylvia, I just admire you so much. I could never cut. I'm a big coward. Booze and pills. If I didn't have my kill-me pills, I wouldn't have even tried once.

SYLVIA: I could drown. The great welcoming arms of the sea — .

ANNE: Hah! Virginia! Dazzling.

SYLVIA: Jumping off a bridge, falling in front of a subway car, what else — what else — pass me the spatula? That's a whisk.

ANNE: Swallowing lye? I mean, it's always right under the sink — it's there — oh, no. No.

SYLVIA: Yes! Yes! Yes!

ANNE: God, you're something. I just don't think I have it in me.

SYLVIA: Eating fire, like the daughter of a God?

ANNE: No, I mean — all this — pie crusts — Look at you go!

SYLVIA: Oh, it's easy. Oh, I know, I know, gas!

ANNE: Gas, yes!

SYLVIA: Jumping?

ANNE: Are you nuts?

SYLVIA: Burning alive?

ANNE: God! — Your whole skin rolling up like a big garage door!

SYLVIA: Intestines roasting before your eyes, like the Indians used to —

ANNE: Oh, Sylvia, Sylvia — we have fun together! The little sister I never had!

SYLVIA: My new dark Auntie!

(They hug. Sylvia breaks off abruptly.)

SYLVIA: That's enough. Oh, I'm sorry. It's just I —

ANNE: You don't have to explain anything to me! Do I need manners! Fuck manners! Mother impeccably pleasant to the help, and then she went and douched me with carpet cleaner!

SYLVIA: My God, did that really happen?

ANNE: Doctor and I were never totally sure. But if it didn't, I must have felt it necessary to invent. And why? Tell me what you feel and I will never punish you! "Back off, Annie! I don't like to be touched!" Yes! Give me that! What are you working on?

SYLVIA: Perhaps a chanty about a woman lit like a wick by the hot quick flame of a man. Oh, I know one! Gun — blam!

ANNE: No, I couldn't take having my face spattered all over. I mean, it's happening all ready! *(Feeling her chin, anxiously.)* I used to have a profile like a Greek coin!

SYLVIA: Oh, no, you look wonderful! For your age!

ANNE: Honey, I don't care. In a way, I mean. Do you know what Daddy-Bob said to me? He told me that decay sets in so that divine love can get in the cracks! Isn't he mad and marvelous? Oh, I still believe in death, more than ever, but I'm becoming much more wholesome. Where did you put that scotch? It's all Stoner, cracked old minister. And we go to all the best parties! Dinner at Allen Ginsberg's next week! Just with him and Peter!

Scene 7

Same. Ted and Stoner approach from outside.

STONER: *(Entering.)* I'm not going.
(Ted enters behind him.)
TED: Look, Sylvia, we found a horseshoe crab!
SYLVIA: Not on the table. Put him outside.
ANNE: Oh, look at him! Isn't he marvelous! Like a big ugly spiky shoe! Can I touch it?
(A moment between Ted and Anne.)
STONER: *(To Anne.)* I said I'm not going!
SYLVIA: *(To Ted.)* Porch! Quick march!
ANNE: *(Crossing to Stoner.)* Of course you're going, Lover. Ginsberg's the big new thing.
STONER: Well, I'm the big old thing, and I won't go. I hate his work.
TED: *(Getting drinks.)* Why, Bob-Father? Don't you think it's remarkable in its power, its anger, and the purity of its vision?
STONER: I think it's a sad day in hell when a big fruit like that provides the defining voice of his generation.
ANNE: Lover, it doesn't matter if he loves ladies, boys, or pussycats. Love is love.
STONER: Men don't matter? Women don't matter? Destroy the principalities of creation themselves?
SYLVIA: But Dr. Stoner, you write all about adultery and pills and being insane.
STONER: Well, I write that it's a damn shame, too, don't I? I don't put it forth as a new damn religion, do I?
TED: Daddy-Bob, I think you fail to understand something. Old dualities are over. Read Jung! Freud! For instance, the Communists, are they the devil? They think we're the devil! Hysteria! We do it with everything! Take sex!
ANNE: Yes! Please!
TED: The good, clean wisdom of the body, the ecstatic, the defining experience! Dirty *that,* now *that's* pornography!
ANNE: Yes.   SYLVIA: Now, I don't know about —
TED: Ah, Ah, Ah! And is it also coincidence that the people that are the most sexually terrified are the most rabid anti-Communists?

ANNE: Ah. So true!   SYLVIA: That's complete nonsen — !

TED: No, no, think about that. It's true, it's true, it's —

STONER: The world is turning. I'm sorry to see it. The destruction of species. This constant intermarriage of Italians and Jews. Ancient identities are being lost. The foundations of manhood and womanhood disappear. And God is no longer speaking to us.

SYLVIA: God never spoke to us!

(Pause.)

STONER: Well, that's true. But we always listened anyway. And out of that listening came everything wonderful. But we don't need him anymore.

ANNE: So gloomy! So gloomy! I think we're missing the celebration that is lurking just around the corner! That nothing's really wrong, anymore! Except the really wrong things, of course . . .

STONER: And you say that as if you've said something simple.

ANNE: Look, it's like . . . I don't need to write in rhyming couplets. You know how hard I word to find new meters, and once I do, I stick to them, but it's play, not fear, that gives me my structure. And I think that's a damn good metaphor for living.

TED: Play, not fear. I like that. Like marriage. It's a choice, not a jail sentence or a coffin.

SYLVIA: But it's serious play. I mean we take its limitations seriously. We took an oath, I mean. To care for each other exclusively and eternally. That's not all that playful. It's more like sacred.

TED: Can't the sacred be playful? I mean look, as long as the impulse is there, then the oath is a true oath. But once it's gone, the truth of the emotion, then who cares if there was any bloody oath or not?

SYLVIA: But if we knew emotion was always there, then there wouldn't be any such thing as an oath. An oath before God is to give you strength for those times when —

TED: When what?

SYLVIA: When the emotion isn't there.

TED: Look, if something's dead, bury it!

SYLVIA: But *marriage.* It's inevitable that the flesh lose its luster. *Literally,* it does. *You* know about that, Anne, I mean, we were talking about that before. Without some kind of, well, moral commitment, sex is disgusting.

TED: It's supposed to be disgusting. That's what it's about, being disgusting. My God, if you can't embrace the wonderful, obscene, disgustingness of sex, you might as well not bother.

SYLVIA: I've been trying!

TED: It's not a matter of trying. Either you respond to the great howl of life in death . . .

ANNE: Or you don't. I know what you mean, Ted. I had to learn to love words. But boy, I always loved to fuck!

(She laughs, Ted laughs, looks at her. Sylvia starts to speak. Stoner bursts out.)

STONER: I walk down the cobbled streets of Old Boston

Litter fills the gutter —

A vicious drunk accosts one —

His red face frightens with its yellow eye —

Its stained grizzle —

Until I see —

Oh, my Christ — it's me!

ANNE: You old monster! No one says it like you do!

STONER: Reflected in the night-time windows of Filene's.

"On Sale" shrieks the sign.

Our souls are what's on sale

What ever happened to the City on the Hill?

The silence makes my heart bleed,

But I bear the wound as mine.

TED: Bear the wound as mine . . . yes!

STONER: Stinking drunk and puking in the alley, I'm —

Just like every Puritan before there was valium!

You, Ted. Go, Sonny-Ted! Spit out your beliefs! Dare them out!

TED: A baby lemur's eyes —

Big as headlights —

They swing this way and that.

ANNE: Oh, poor thing, I bet he wants his mama!

TED: His big lamps strain

For any sight of his vanished Mama —

Two weeks since she disappeared

He looks over his branch

And into a howling void.

In anguish bites off head of snail

Suddenly, he feels much better —

So much for milk — !

STONER: Hah! So much for milk . . . Annie Fannie! It's a regular happening like asshole Thornberg's! Go! Go! Say the true thing!

ANNE: What's that noise?

Ooops, just one of my chins hitting the floor —

Let Mama sleep a little later —

She's been out all night with her little

Blue, yellow, pink lovers again —

TED: Hah!

ANNE: Or a man or two still shows up when I hold up my steaming bowl

of grapes —

(The men may support her with sound, or percussive rhythm as her poem

builds.)

TED: Yes! Yes!

ANNE: *(Shutting her eyes, swaying.)*

But I'm no dummy, and tell truth,

The game just ain't the same . . .

Now, I'm starting to believe, that it just might be

You, Jesus —

Making my skin crumble,

Making my teeth get these tiny cracks —

As long as it's someone, Sweet God, Baby,

As long as it's only You,

Well, I can be gallant to the bitterest, see if I can't!

(Men laugh and applaud.)

Sylvia, Baby, share with us . . . can you do a little something?

SYLVIA: Oh, I, gee, there's nothing I really feel comfortable . . .

(Emily appears in the window. Only Sylvia, terrified, senses her presence. The

others are momentarily frozen.)

EMILY: I've got one you can have!!

The *freezing* can extrapolate

Just what a Glacier —

Be —

When ice skates race across your

Heart

You murmur —

That is He —

(Emily disappears.)

STONER: What's that smell? Like wood smoke?

TED: Come on, Honey, what about the myth poem you started?

SYLVIA: Myth poem?

TED: You know, the thing, where she used to be the goddess but now she's

going cheap on the docks?

SYLVIA: Oh, no, that's not ready . . .

TED: "Your ritual wound is a price tag now, snot-face German schoolboys suck on your serpent curls —" It's good!

SYLVIA: *(Screaming.)* I've got a soufflé! It's got to come out!
(Shocked silence.)

ANNE: *(Covering.)* Well, damn, let's get it on the table then!

STONER: Why did we stop? We were having fun, dammit! Fun!

ANNE: Come sit at the table, Honey.

STONER: Sylvia? Can I help you?

SYLVIA: Look. I'm perfectly fine.

Scene Eight

After supper. Stoner is asleep in a chair. Sylvia is at the table. Anne and Ted are outside in the moonlight.

ANNE: God forgive me. But He always does.

TED: Don't talk. Don't think.

ANNE: She can't ever, ever know. You must protect her.

TED: Don't worry.

ANNE: What about him.

TED: If a tree falls in a forest . . .

ANNE: I'm falling.

TED: So am I.

ANNE: This will never happen again. And I am only weak because I'm dying.

TED: We're all dying.

ANNE: Yes. Yes. Oh, yes.
(They kiss and slowly move down onto the ground. Lights up on Sylvia at table, writing. Emily is hovering in the window frame behind her, watching quietly.)

SYLVIA: *(Reads slowly.)* The . . . moon . . . drags her pus-bag over the marsh.
Scabs crackle, and old wounds
Part their thighs, again . . .
(Begins to write. She tastes the images as she struggles to finish the poem.)
When he touches my face, he feels a fine white dust.
We bury our fear in each other,
Like dogs humping in a midnight boneyard . . .
(Slowly.) I don't know. Something like — that?
(Sylvia turns to Emily. Emily nods, thoughtfully.)

Act III

Scene One

Ted's and Sylvia's house. Ted is hypnotizing Sylvia.

TED: Breathe into my hand. Let your face soften. Heavy, soft, thick, and fleshy.

SYLVIA: My face feels like an old potato. I can feel actually feel my lack of bone structure. Yuuch.

TED: Let go judgment. Let go the critic. That's your mother. That's your mirror. You are going to meet your guide. I am going to count from one to five. You are going deeper and deeper into the spirit world. The world of the ancestors. One. Two.

SYLVIA: Aaahh! Aaahhh! You're scaring me!

TED: Don't be afraid. What are you seeing? Three. Four. Close your eyes and wait. Go deeper and deeper into your blackness. Five. *(Something happens.)* Where are you?

SYLVIA: I'm hearing —

TED: Mmm . . .

SYLVIA: A jingling — a tramping — oh!! They are CARRYING something!

TED: Who?

SYLVIA: It looks like . . . these little men. They are wearing these skirts made of skins, and bones . . .

TED: Yes?

SYLVIA: They are chanting and murmuring.

TED: What do you hear?

SYLVIA: I can't make out the words.

TED: Forget words. What do you hear? The sound, the sound.

SYLVIA: It sounds like . . . tsimpapa, managuwe, tsimpapa, managuwe, awiah, awiah, awiah . . . tsimpapa . . .

TED: What do you see?

SYLVIA: They are dancing into a clearing. Tsimpapa, manguwe, tsimpapa, and then another group of them come staggering in. They are carrying something —

TED: Yes?

SYLVIA: A kind of cage . . . on their shoulders. It's braided with all these big flowers, like poinsettas, maybe, or hibiscus. Inside there's this big fat, huge, brown woman. Her hair is long and oily, kind of blue-black. She's naked, and her breasts are like gallon jugs, but all flattened out. Her thighs are so big that there's only a V down there. Just a triangle, no hair. She's smiling and smiling, and her smile is all gums! What happened to her teeth? Her mouth is bloody. Oh Ted, they pulled out her teeth!

TED: Ritual purposes. Blow jobs or something. It's all right. Now what's happening?

SYLVIA: They're putting the cage down on the ground and opening the door. She's smiling, and she's lying down. A little man is going to her. He's getting on top of her. Oh, I can't look at this anymore. It's repulsive! All that brown greasy fat! Her feet are so little, and the soles are black with dirt! They are all chanting!

TED: What! What!

SYLVIA: Bab-weh, bab-weh, bab-weh! He's going up and down on her, and everyone is smiling. Some of the men are masturbating. I'm going to throw up!

TED: Get through it. This is your vision. What's the woman doing?

SYLVIA: Her eyes are rolling back like an idiot. She's not happy, not sad, just lying there. Her arms are around the man. Her legs are around the man.

TED: Good. Yes. Good. Now what?

SYLVIA: Oh! *(Surprised. Perhaps pleasantly.)* Oh. Oh!

TED: What do you see?

SYLVIA: Oh, Ted! She's breaking the man's back with her legs! She's folding him!

TED: Really? Are you sure?

SYLVIA: *(Intensely.)* Yes! She, it looks like she's inhaling him, or something, it's like a whirlpool, or a blender! He's getting broken!

TED: Are you positive! How are the other men reacting?

SYLVIA: They are dropping their musical instruments! The ones that were playing with themselves just stopped. Some of them are running out of the clearing. Some of them are on their knees. What could this mean?

TED: How about the little fellow?

SYLVIA: She's, oh my God! She's swallowing him! His head and his arms and legs are sticking out, but they are getting pulled into her! It's like watching a birth, but in reverse! This is fantastic! Oh, Ted, I wish you could see this!

TED: My God.

SYLVIA: Her face! It looks different. She's not frightened. She's big as a house, she's getting bigger! Ha ha, yes! Yes! Yes! OM BALALA, MEHYAH!

TED: What? What's that you're saying?

SYLVIA: I didn't say anything. All the men have run off now. The little man is gone, almost. There's just one little finger sticking out from her, oops, now that's gone too. She's just lying there. She's humming.

TED: That's enough. I'm bringing you back up, now. You are swimming back to the here and now. Into your body, into this room. You are swimming into the present. I'm going to count from five. When I get to one, you will be with me. Happy, alert, and ready to fix dinner. Five, four, three, two, one.

SYLVIA: Wow! What happened?

TED: You had a vision.

SYLVIA: Oh, I did? Oh! That's wonderful. Did you tape-record it?

TED: No. But I made some notes.

SYLVIA: *(Reading them.)* It's starting to come back! Was I speaking in tongues?

TED: Yes, you were. Good for you.

SYLVIA: Did I bypass my intellect?

TED: I think so. Yes. Definitely.

SYLVIA: Oh, I can use this! This is so exciting!

TED: Terrific.

SYLVIA: What's the matter? Are you sulking?

TED: No. Of course not.

SYLVIA: You are. You are sulking. Is big sulky Ted mad wif his Syvie?

TED: Don't be ridiculous.

SYLVIA: Oh, Baby. I really had some kind of vision. I really did, you know. I went out!

TED: All right, all right. You needn't go on and on about it.

SYLVIA: Sweetie. You're frightened!

TED: *(Savagely.)* You just had a little experience, a badly needed one, a little jaunt in the unknown, and, well, I'm delighted!

Scene Two

Ted's and Sylvia's house. Ted, Stoner, Anne, and Sylvia are at dinner.

ANNE: Attention, everyone, Robert has some big news. Honey?

STONER: I've finished it. The defining Mather poem. I broke that fucker's back. Hah hah.

TED: Oh, marvelous!

ANNE: — And when he read it to me I just started to weep! It is an utter masterpiece!

TED: Bravo, Bob-Father — after your long incubation in darkness —

SYLVIA: Well. Gee. Can we hear it?

STONER: Oh, well.
> *(Clears his throat.)*
> In Old Nantucket, the drugstore boys spit phlegm-slick wads
> Of gin-soaked Bazooka Joe into the cobblestones.
> The relentless sea flickers its withered tongue
> Over the ragged rocks.
> A gray drizzle coats the shabby house where Cotton Mather
> Died with greasy rain.
>
> Its slick rot reflects the pink and green lights
> Of the new Burrito Bell.
> The corpse of a drowned Nantucket Indian bangs restless
> Against the sea-bell,
> Alive again with every undulation of the tide.
> Dead for more than a century, he'd still like to sink his
> Tommy-hawk into a white bonnet.
>
> I have a floater in my eye.
> It dogs me everywhere.
> It curls like a dried-out tail of a Confederate horse.
> I think I'll dry out again.
> *(A silence. Anne gets up and kisses his head.)*

ANNE: You magnificent man. You've made me weep. Again!

TED: Really, Dr. Stoner. I don't know what one can say. It's wonderful. You've put your finger on something. On a number of things, actually.

STONER: It costs, my boy. It costs. To bear witness.

SYLVIA: I think it's Taco Bell.

STONER: What?

SYLVIA: You said Burrito Bell. I think it's Taco Bell.

ANNE: *(Whispers.)* He needs a B word.

SYLVIA: But it doesn't work as a symbol of New America if it isn't the right —

ANNE: SHHH!

STONER: What's she saying, my dear?

ANNE: Nothing, she loves —

SYLVIA: *(Loudly.)* It's Taco Bell. There is no such thing as Burrito Bell.
> *(Pause.)*

STONER: Are you sure?

ANNE: Now, wait a minute. I'm sure I've seen a Burrito Bell, they have all sorts of —

SYLVIA: And Cotton Mather's house was in Boston. I'm pretty sure. But other than that, it's, gee, just a great poem. So unexpected, about the floater at the end. I can tell how you got there, it was kind of unconscious, right, you were talking about a corpse of a drowned Indian, well, a drowned corpse is a floater, and floater in your eye, floater and floater, and there you were, weren't you? And there was so much water in the poem that, naturally, you wanted to dry out! *(Pause.)* Anybody ready for more coffee?

ANNE: Bob, do you want some coffee?

STONER: *(Quietly.)* Is that how I got floater? I'd like a brandy, please, Ted. That *is* how I got floater. Floater and floater. Oh, God. How transparent.

ANNE: Ted, he doesn't drink —

STONER: I'd like a brandy, please.

(Ted gets him one. Stoner drinks it and subsides into a sort of sulking coma.)

SYLVIA: Well, my God, did I say something wrong? It just occurred to me that he might want to be accurate. Everyone just goes along with everything because of his reputation, and they just let him just be wrong, and —

ANNE: *(Aside to Sylvia.)* You've destroyed his confidence for no reason at all! It's the best new poem he's written in ten years!

STONER: It's the *only* poem I've written in ten years. And she's right. I can't stand her, but she's right. It's drivel.

TED: No, Bob-Father, no! It's free, it shimmers, it marries the great hard New England undermyth with the shifting, slimy flicker of the new Godlessness . . .

STONER: Who do you think I am? Matthew Arnold?

SYLVIA: Exactly, yes, Daddy-Bob. How silly, you, posing as some kind of a college existentialist when you're really a renegade Calvinist, or more recently, a failed Catholic —

TED: It is Catholicism that has failed us —

SYLVIA: Oh, how the fuck would you know, you've never been to a church where they didn't kill a chicken.

ANNE: Now hold on a minute — I think we're forgetting that God spelled backward is Dog! Good, real, shaggy, warm Dog! Not nearly as grand, but much more fun at the beach!

TED: Hah! Brilliant!

SYLVIA: Isn't it possible, Dr. Stoner, I mean this is just a thought, that God is punishing you for your sins by reducing you to free association — ?

STONER: Aaaghh!

ANNE: Hey, every thing I *write* is based on free association!

SYLVIA: I know.

TED: *(Suddenly.)* Oh, why can't we all stop talking, and — and — sing! Or — fuck! Or build a barn, plant a tomato plant, anything but think our dead, tired thoughts. We need a wordless anthem for our lost time, a . . . koan. A new reality. Let's all . . . shut up and look inside ourselves. *(Pause. They all look inside themselves.)*

STONER: *(Brooding, upset.)* When I try to look inside myself all I find that's left is a craving for nicotine and a handful of unspeakable sexual fantasies about, you know, nurses. *(Humbly.)* I'm sorry. But since we're being honest.

TED: Good for you, Bob-Father! I'd rather hear about nicotine and your strange longings than all the sacred, petrified wisdom-turds of our dying civilization. Maybe I'm mad — but some nights, when I walk in the fields, I listen to the weird star-struck language of the night-birds — *(He makes a bird-call sound.)* and I feel that the wall of illusion is about to dissolve — the bird-speak is about to become clear, that I'm on the verge of the miraculous.

ANNE: *(Moved, quietly.)* Yes. Marvelous.

STONER: Idiot! You idiot!

TED: Daddy-Bob?   SYLVIA: Hah hah hah!

STONER: Understand the language of the birds? I've woken up to hear them plotting on my life! Miracles! You fool! You don't know the utter horror of miracles! I take 3,000 milligrams of lithium a day to keep me from walking on water, and sometimes I do it anyway!

TED: I'm sorry — I didn't mean . . .

STONER: You think all creation's some big Hindu illusion? You wing-growing bastard. Turn yourself into a goddamn bald eagle. And I hope some teenager pops you with his daddy's shotgun.

ANNE: Testy! Testy!

STONER: Think you're the first man to dream of wings? You've never experienced the horrible freedom of the winged mad. You want a miracle? Try this one! One and one make two! But you won't stop till they make three! Or cat!

TED: Bob-Father, you're excited. I think you misunderstood what the Zen masters are saying.

STONER: I'm saying have the guts to call a spade a spade, recognize the cold hard law of gravity for what it is, which is the grace of God — recognize how many angels are at work each day insuring that Newton's apple continues to fall down, down, down, not up into the ozone with all your Zuni medicine men flapping around as bats and hoot-owls along with *me* when I forget to take my pills! Have the guts to give glory to the truth!

(*Quietly.*) If only that, we should have the guts to give glory to what truths we can.

SYLVIA: (*Odd, avid.*) Like what, Daddy-Bob?

STONER: Like —

SYLVIA: Go on.

STONER: Like the truth that I'm an old washed-up has-been and ten years past being any kind of man at all.

ANNE: Oh, Lover, what are you talking about?

STONER: You're very sweet, my dear, and very slick. And I've been slick, too, haven't I? I never let on that I know of your little recreations, do I?

ANNE: Oh, Baby! What an idea!

STONER: You know what? I sneak around. I follow her. The Poet Laureate of the United States of America. I dog her like a spy. To doctor's offices and shabby student apartments, and once, oh, once, she betrayed me with her own husband! I know! I'm an old bastard, but I'm not a complete fool!

ANNE: Robert, we agreed to trust each other!

STONER: But that was when I thought you'd stick with me.

ANNE: Honey, I have my own way of sticking with you. We didn't make rules.

STONER: Bad enough that I'm washed up, but to be such a sorry old cuckold in the bargain, bewitched by an aging vixen!

SYLVIA: (*Delighted.*) "Aging Vixen"! Now what's the point of saying things like "Aging Vixen"!

ANNE: (*Angry.*) Baby, you don't get to be a cuckold if you can't stick it in. (*Pause.*)

STONER: (*Devastated.*) Oh, Anne. Once you told me that you loved our naps and cozy lie-downs. That I delivered you from yourself! That our love was carnal in the best of all Platonic worlds!

ANNE: Well, maybe the best of all Platonic worlds doesn't make it when you need a man's warm love-stick in you, stirring away your troubles!

SYLVIA: You are disgusting!

TED: There's nothing disgusting about people trying to carve some kind of comfort out of the howling blackness that calls itself life.

SYLVIA: Oh, please. The only howling blackness around is you. What would you know about comfort.

ANNE: He comforted me pretty good, once.

SYLVIA: What?

ANNE: Gee. Me and my big mouth.

STONER: *(Anguished.)* No! No! No! You did it with him? My adopted son
  Tedipus?
  (Pause.)
SYLVIA: What?
TED: I'm not quite sure . . . what is going on, here —
SYLVIA: What's going on is it's out and you can't stuff it back in.
TED: But it's not true!
ANNE: Baby, it's no use. Truth is out and truth will make us free, and I think
  we need a healing, here.
SYLVIA: Shut up. Ted, I want you to tell me. Say it!
TED: All right! All right! You asked for it. I know this sounds — try to un-
  derstand this. It — allowed me to bring — more of myself to you. And
  I never thought you'd know. If a tree falls in the forest —
SYLVIA: It hits the ground all the same, you bastard!
TED: I won't apologize for nothing! It was *less* than nothing!
ANNE: Oh, really?
SYLVIA: Nothing, nothing and nothing.
ANNE: I said I'm sorry and I meant it.
SYLVIA: I said shut up.
TED: Don't make such a big fucking deal about it! One bloody time in our
  whole marriage!
STONER: Oh, Son, it was wrong. You should have left her to me. You had all
  those students and actresses already, you could have left me this withered
  Jezebel for my dotage!
SYLVIA: Students! Actresses!   ANNE: Withered Jezebel!
TED: All right! Yes! What! I've got a hunger in me — it's who I am, see? This
  is my life!
ANNE: Robert!
SYLVIA: *(Swivels her head to look at Anne.)* You abomination!
ANNE: I'm leaving. Bob, are you coming? I say are you coming with me?
STONER: No, strumpet! I could have borne the rest, but to shame me with my
  adopted son! I want to go back to Vera! What's her address?
TED: Bob-Father —
STONER: No!
TED: Look, Sylvia — I know you don't see it this way right now, but I
  think this will be very good for us, this coming forward with —
  Bob-Father — forgive me.
STONER: I'm not your Bob-Father! Meet the great emptiness! You and your

Buddhist crap! *I'm* the great emptiness! Let's meet! I told you you would have to kill me!

(*Gets up and starts swinging at Ted.*)

TED: I said forgive me.

(*Stoner picks up a wine bottle.*)

ANNE: Stop it! Stop it! Put that down!

STONER: (*Throws it into the ceiling.*) Firestorm! Rejoice!

ANNE: Help! Help me, Sylvia!

(*Stoner throws wine glass into the ceiling.*)

STONER: Hailstorm!

SYLVIA AND STONER: Rejoice!

(*Stoner breaks out of murderous hallucination in terror.*)

STONER: Annie, Annie, come and get me! I'm so afraid!

ANNE: I'm here, lover, I'm —

(*She tries to get close to him.*)

STONER: (*He swings at Anne, frenzied.*) Painted Harpy!

(*She leaves, devastated.*)

STONER: (*To Ted.*) Bastard of a Rat-Son!

(*Seizes Ted and drags him over to the window, forcing him out. Hangs him out over the drop by his arms.*)

TED: Shit! You're breaking my fucking arm!

STONER: — Him the almighty power
Hurled headlong flaming from the
Ethereal sky — aha ha ha!

TED: Let me up! You old shit!

STONER: — With hideous ruin and combustion down
To bottomless perdition, there to dwell —

Now show me *yours*, pretty Boy! Do the shak shaka shaka one! Do it!

TED: Shak shaka shak shaka —
Sylvia!
Shaka shaka shaka shak
Call the police!
Shaka shaka shaka shak!

STONER: — in Adamantine Chains
and penal Fire — who
durst defie th'
Omnipotent to Arms!!

STONER: How do you like them apples! Now *that's* a piece of work! you free-associating, jingle-writing wife-stealing scribbler-dribbler! And that's just off the top of my fucking head!

TED: It's off the top of Milton's fucking head!

STONER: What's that you say?

TED: It's from *Paradise Lost!* Everyone knows that.

STONER: *(Concerned.)* They do?

TED: You can call me thin but I write my own ticket. Oh, go ahead. Let go.

SYLVIA: Do it! Smash him! Kill him! Let him fall!

(Stoner looks at her, pulls Ted up.)

STONER: I'm so tired.

(He pulls Ted inside. Ted drops to floor, holding his arm.)

STONER: Where the hell am I? Who opened this window? I'm freezing. Anne? Anne?

SYLVIA: She's gone.

STONER: Did I say something?

SYLVIA: Dr. Stoner, there's going to be a black mass in this room in about five minutes. I don't think you want to be here when the girls arrive.

STONER: *(Scuttling toward the door.)* Awfully decent of you. Thanks for the tip —

SYLVIA: Out!

(She opens the grate of wood-burning stove and jabs at burning coals with a poker. Picks up a bound manuscript from a shelf. Dumps it onto the fire.)

TED: My arm . . . is broken . . . what are you doing!

SYLVIA: Cold in here.

TED: My manuscript!

SYLVIA: Not anymore! *(Prodding the embers with poker.)*

TED: *(Staring into flames.)* You —

SYLVIA: Move please.

TED: You — cunt.

SYLVIA: *(Holding poker at his stomach. Screams.)* Get out!

Scene Three

Same. Sylvia is sitting at the table. She has an open notebook. Emily is with her drinking coffee.

SYLVIA: I say three magic words —
I hate you.
The sun just rose.

My first haiku.

EMILY: I admire that. I could never say that.

SYLVIA: Would you like some more coffee?

EMILY: Oh, no. It goes right through me.

SYLVIA: Most of them are about my husband, but this one is for my mother.

Old red bladder, eyes like foreskins

I am sick to death of your love-tentacles —

EMILY: You're scaring me.

SYLVIA: It was you in the root cellar, Mommy —

With your nuzzling suction cups —

EMILY: I can't stay very long today. I have a feeling that Someone . . . might show up.

SYLVIA: You just don't get it, do you?

EMILY: *(Heading for the window.)* I'll just slip out while you're having such a wonderful hot streak. You remind me of me in 1862. What a year I had — *(Sylvia swivels her head to look at Emily.)*

EMILY: I won't bore you.

SYLVIA: Hey, not so fast — *I* invited *you.*

(Emily, cowed, slinks back to her seat.)

SYLVIA: Haven't you figured out that there's no one out there? You've been wandering around in the dark for a hundred years. No one's even lit a match.

EMILY: You can be awfully mean.

SYLVIA: I'm going to be joining you soon.

EMILY: Look before you leap!

SYLVIA: All roads lead to Rome. This collection is going to make my name.

EMILY: W-what are you going to call it?

SYLVIA: *(Lovingly stroking her notebook.)* "The Blood Tide."

(Sylvia puts on a pair of red gloves and crosses into Interview area with her notebook.)

Scene Four

A radio program. Interviewer is sitting with Sylvia.

INTERVIEWER: Good evening, and welcome to "Pot Shots." We're visiting with poet Sylvia Fluellen, author of the recent runaway best-seller, *The Blood Tide.* "I don't read poetry, but I read Fluellen" is a comment that we've heard again and again in the past few weeks. Sylvia Fluellen, reading from her extraordinary new collection.

SYLVIA: You liked to feel a flutter on your tongue.
Or you complained that dinner was overdone.
I tried to please you, to keep you
In live insects, terrified prawns,
Things that would resist your teeth,

But then you wanted sucklings,
And I prayed and plucked a kitten from behind the stove,
Sleepy at its mother's dug.

My kitchen was a chamber of horrors!
Piglets shrieked as you bit their heads off.
After the sow, which you ate in fifteen minutes,
I knew that I was next.

I packed my suitcase, I could hear you on the stair.
I threw the family spaniel at you —
You bit him in two.
I jumped out the window!

I managed to distract you in the lane by pointing out the
Neighbor's cow —
The last time I saw you,
You were squatting in the moonlight,
With a legbone in your jaws.

I've changed my name, and I move every week.
I wear a strong perfume so you can't snuff me out.
The papers are awash with your atrocities.

No one knows what's going on
There is a crime wave in this city.
And I'm unmasking you!

Scene Five

Later. Anne's bedroom. Anne sits on the bed. Her nightstand holds her vodka bottle and a multitude of prescription bottles. She's drunk, but steady.

ANNE: Most gals would dress in their best black for the most important date of their lives. Not me. For you, Honey, I'm putting on the softest blue dress with a mauve scarf. I've always known that you like the most tender colors.

(She begins to dress and make up her face.)

Just make yourself comfortable. I won't be long. The think I like about you is, I don't have to maintain any mystery. We've been intimate for years. I've always thought you were a real softy. The one that loved a girl for what she was inside. You really want to get inside. Not just inside the way most guys want to, but you want to tear a girl apart the way other men only dream of. And I'll tell you what. I don't think it will be so bad. Men all say I'll love you when you're old, but they only like to say it to you when you're really young. They can't do it, poor things, they'd like to but they just can't. But you. You've been gentle, you've been slow. But you've rained your constant acid kisses down on my poor flesh since the day I first bloomed. And now I understand that it's because you love me. You love me so truly you've been sucking me out of myself. Blasting my body so that I'll leave it finally, to be with you. You want to eat me. Well, I surrender. I don't know what it will be like. But I think maybe you know more about this than I.

(Starts swallowing pills by the handful.)

Scene Six

Later. Sylvia's kitchen. Sylvia is alone, wiping dishes.

SYLVIA: It's almost over, I can feel it.
EMILY: *(Rushing in.)* I've been doing some thinking. Don't throw in the towel.
SYLVIA: Throw in the towel? You misunderstand.
EMILY: You are just about to break.
SYLVIA: Oh, yes.
EMILY: *The Blood Tide.* Wow. I could never have written that. *(Her greatest*

compliment.) It was — *appalling!* And I'm a tough audience! Now, I know how upset you are about, well —

SYLVIA: Marriage is forever. He's about to find out.

EMILY: Don't get me wrong, I'd love your company. I'm just . . .

SYLVIA: Afraid? That I'll walk all over you? I just might.

EMILY: *(Desperate.)*

I cannot think you dead —

That sunshine smile —

Those —

(Emily slaps herself in the face at a look from Sylvia.)

SYLVIA: I'll be going home, now.

(Sylvia carefully selects a frying pan and a wire whisk. Holding her implements like sacred flails, she climbs up into the window ledge and stands, the backlit image of a sacred domestic Goddess. She whistles shrilly to attract attention from the road below.)

He pushed me!!!

(She falls out of the window. Emily runs to the window and bends out, watching.)

EMILY: *(Hand to her mouth. Looking out the window.)* Oh, my! Now that's what I call guts.

Scene Seven

Later. A classroom. Ted is teaching.

TED: When the poet writes, "Dead leaves to where there are no roses are . . ." he's talking, isn't he, about the passing of beauty into mulch, and there is the suggestion that the mulch is the bed from which beauty will evolve again.

(One of the students puts a bloodstained veil over her head.)

VEILED STUDENT: As in, for example, the girl that was beauty turns into the mulch of the abandoned wife.

TED: Possibly, Miss . . . Margolis, is it? And we all know you were cast in *The Bacchae* and we're very happy for you, except that when we're talking about the decay of female beauty, the mulch just turns into slime, and gradually into more and more corrosive elements.

(Another student throws a plastic bag full of something slimy and green. It bursts on the wall by Ted's head.)

THROWING STUDENT: Elements like truth, like the daybreak of anger, like the light of realization. Corrosive like honesty, like the power to shriek for justice!

TED: Listen. How dare you judge my life by rumor and innuendo!

(Third student stands up, wearing a pig mask.)

PIG STUDENT: No, you listen. I'm sure there are some women here who would rather hear about truth than to listen to a pedantic sadist nattering about beauty!

TED: Pedantic! I'm no pedant, young lady. I've lain eye to eye with a she-mamba, and she's the one who blinked!

THROWING STUDENT: Blinked! She jumped out a window! The blood tide is rising, Mr. Magus.

PIG STUDENT: It's licking your ankles, cocksucker!

STUDENTS: *(Chanting softly.)* Shak shak shak shak shaka

Shaka shaka shak

Shak shak shak

Shak shaka shaka shaka shak —

TED: What do you want!

PIG STUDENT: We want to go everywhere with you!

THROWING STUDENT: We want to be your companion!

VEILED STUDENT: Till death do us part!

PIG STUDENT: Yours!

CLASS: Shak shak shak shak!

TED: I'm going to meet my agent. And I can tell you you're not going with me. This class is fucking dismissed!

(Girls surround him. He fights his way to the door and exits. Girls follow him, chanting.)

STUDENTS: Shak shaka shaka shaka shak!

Scene Eight

A summer evening. Vera's and Stoner's cabin. Vera and Stoner are sitting on the porch. Vera is reading a newspaper. Stoner is sunk in thought.

VERA: *(Delicately.)* I see where your young friend Ted has got some very sturdy reviews for his new book. " — Finally found his voice. Like a cloud of poisonous gas holding itself erect in shaky dignity over a cosmic abyss." Does that make any sense?

STONER: *(Sad. Quiet.)* Oh, who gives a shit. There's nothing to be said anymore, and I'm not the man to say it. I'm cured of my enthusiasms, and here I am, all old and gray with my old gray wife. I'm blurred, small, and soggy, ready to play model trains for the rest of my life. *(Pause.)* Are you sure you want me back?

VERA: I've forgiven you.

STONER: *(Confused.)* For what?

VERA: Oh, Robert! You know, I really think in many ways this was just the worst. Of your many, many spectacular betrayals. What are you looking at? My old baby. You used to be mad for justice, like some beautiful Greek. Then you were just mad. It's really just —. Boy, I'm chilly out here. Honey, do you want me to get your sweater?

(Pause.)

VERA: What is it, Baby?

STONER: Someone just walked over my grave. I'm tired, my dear. Let's go up to bed and curl up together like soup spoons.

VERA: My old darling.

STONER: It's so quiet tonight. The girls are underground.

(They sit in silence for a moment.)

VERA: Look at that old pus-bag of a moon.

END OF PLAY

The Dianalogues

By Laurel Haines

For my parents, who brought me to the theater.

PLAYWRIGHT'S BIOGRAPHY

Laurel Haines has lived in New York, Arizona, and, most recently, Chicago. In addition to *The Dianalogues*, she has written plays about documentary filmmakers, cryogenics, and a two-hundred-pound baby. Recently, First Stage Children's Theatre commissioned her to write the book and lyrics for *Stones of Wisdom,* a musical puppet extravaganza presented at Milwaukee Summer Fest 2003. Her play *Raw Footage* won the Yukon Pacific New Play Award at the 2000 Edward Albee Last Frontier Theater Conference and the AriZoni Award for Best Original Script from the Arizona Production Association. Ms. Haines also teaches playwriting and directs new plays. She earned an MFA in playwriting from Arizona State University and is currently a member of the TBC Musical Theatre Writers' Workshop in Chicago.

ORIGINAL PRODUCTION

The Dianalogues was developed at WordBridge in St. Petersburg, Florida. Earlier versions of the play were performed by Sirens Theater Company in Seattle, Third Circle Theater Company in Chicago, Abstract Productions in Portland, Oregon, and the Bloomington Playwrights Project in Indiana. This version of *The Dianalogues* was first produced by Stray Cat Theater in Phoenix, Arizona. It was directed by Ron May, stage managed by Marcos Voss, and dramaturged by Will Hare, with sound design by Ben Monrad. The cast was as follows:

Carly	Amanda Kochert
Diana/Mary	Seth Bogner
Doreen	Lisa Pletsch
Arlene	Jessica Flowers
Shari	Alicia Sutton
Candy	Cameo Hill
Starlet	Christy Little
Jean	Nina Kulhawy
Miss Bickworth	Angela Calabrasi
Mother Teresa	Paulina Glider

PLAYWRIGHT'S NOTE

I never expected to write a play about Princess Diana.

But one day I found myself at WordBridge, a writing workshop in Florida, faced with a dilemma. I had been invited there to work on a play about women who kill their husbands, but every time I sat down to write, my mind wandered. Each day I would try to focus on murderous women and instead the characters would babble way off topic. And for some reason, they loved to talk about Princess Diana. I had a choice of letting them go where they wanted or coming up with nothing, so I wrote *The Dianalogues*. It's funny what comes out of one's subconscious.

From this unlikely conception, *The Dianalogues* has gone through a number of transformations, and I have many people to thank. The play would not exist if not for WordBridge and its director, Richard Rice. Guillermo Reyes and KC Davis gave important guidance in the early stages. All the actors and directors who have worked on the various workshops and productions have given me insight, especially Emily Petkewich and Ron May. And Rich Perez revealed the possibilities of *The Dianalogues* in drag! Finally, I am ever grateful to my partner in life and theater, Will Hare, who has supported me every step of the way.

CHARACTERS
The Dianalogues is a series of eleven monologues, which may be cast in a variety of ways. The characters are:
> CARLY: An eight-year-old girl.
> MARY: A Diana impersonator. Late thirties.
> SHARI: A high-powered lawyer. Thirties.
> ARLENE: A nice mid-western woman. Forties.
> DOREEN: A fifteen-year-old girl.
> CANDY: A cabdriver — any age.
> STARLET: A Hollywood starlet. Twenties.
> JEAN: A housewife. Fifties to sixties.
> MISS BICKWORTH: The head of a finishing school. Any age, but seems much older.
> MOTHER TERESA: Mother Teresa.
> CARLY 2: The first Carly, now an adult.

SETTING
The set should be minimal and flexible. The puppet stage may be indicated with a set piece, lights, video, or any other creative means.

NOTE ON TRANSITIONS
The transitions are performed with dolls and can be played by any actors who are free at that time. Transitions may also be eliminated or videotaped to allow for a smaller cast.

The Dianalogues

DOLLS

5 AM. A darkened basement. Carly, an eight-year- old girl, sneaks downstairs and turns on the TV. The royal wedding comes on. She watches for a minute, then hears a voice.

CARLY: *(Yelling.)* No, Mom, I'm fine. I'm just watching TV. I don't know, I guess I just got up early. No special reason. Nope, I'm just watching cartoons. No Mom, don't come down here, don't come down here don't come — *(She quickly switches the channel to cartoons.)* See, just cartoons. What are you doing up this early? Couldn't sleep either, huh? No, I don't mind changing the channel. *(She switches the channels. An infomercial comes on.)* There's this. *(She switches again. A Spanish lesson comes on.)* And this. *(She switches again: The royal wedding.)* Oh! And this. Sure, I don't mind watching this.

I guess she's just riding through the streets right now. Pretty boring. How come she's riding by herself? Well, why can't he? What would happen if he did? So if nothing bad would happen why can't he ride with her? Huh Ma? Huh Ma? Huh? OK.
(Silence, watching.)

Mom, when you got married was it just like this? A lot different? But that's a big dress. How could your dress have been bigger than hers? Oh! *(pause, watching.)* Did you and Daddy ride to the church together? Oh. Did you ride to the courthouse together? Did you ride there on horses? OK.
(Silence, watching; then a burst of questions.)

How come it's taking so long? Do you think her arm is getting tired? What kind of cake are they going to have, will it be chocolate? *(Pause, listens.)* Sure, I can play with something.
(Carly finds two dolls. One doll is Prince Charles and the other is Princess Diana.)

Oh Prince Charles. I love you. Oh Diana, I love you. Kiss Kiss Kiss. *(Voice of Queen.)* Prince Charles, it's time for bed. *(Voice of Charles.)* OK, Mother! Come on, Diana. Time for bed. *(Voice of Diana.)* Oh Charles, I'm scared. I'm a virgin. *(Charles.)* Don't worry, this won't hurt. I'm just going to breathe on you. *(Diana.)* Oh dear, Charles, then I'm not a virgin. I've been breathed on before by lots of people. *(Charles.)* Yes, but not like this: *(Imitates heavy breathing.)* Ha ha ha. Now you breathe on me. *(Diana.)* Oh Charles, Ha ha ha *(Charles.)* Ha ha ha *(Diana.)* Ha ha ha —

Huh? It's not? But you said . . . Well then how do you . . . ? Oh, it's starting? *(Distracted, she looks at the TV.)* She looks pretty. He looks . . . weird. Mom, when I grow up will I have to marry Eddie O'Neill? That's what Jennifer told me. She told me that she was going to marry Chris Williams, because he's the cutest boy at school, and Lisa's going to marry John Chillemi, because he's the second cutest, and I would have to marry Eddie O'Neill, because he's all that would be left. No, he's not the third cutest boy, he's not cute at all. You remember him, he's the one who follows me home after school. I don't? Good. No! I think he's weird. But I think he likes me, because he keeps giving me gum. Mom, if I don't marry Eddie will I have to marry a girl? But that's what Trina's mom did. She got divorced and had to marry a girl 'cause there weren't any men left. That's what Trina said. But there have to be enough men, because Uncle Terry lives with his best friend Mike, so —

Oh look! She's saying her "I dos."
(They listen.)

Did you hear that? She messed up his name. She said, "Phillip Charles Arthur George." Oh my gosh. They're not gonna go back. But she said the wrong name. Mom, does that mean she's not really married to him? Like, if she decided she didn't like him, she could say, "Well, I didn't really marry you, I married someone called Phillip!" What do you mean it's not that easy?

Well, I'm sure she's not gonna say that, I'm sure they're gonna get along just fine. Just like you and Daddy. Right? Mom, when's Daddy coming home? When's soon? But I thought he was only gonna be gone for a week. What's he doing? What kind of stuff? How can you not know, is it a secret? Well, he'd better get back here soon because we're supposed to go camping next week, so he'll come back before next week, right Mom? Mom? Mom?
(Looking at television.)

Well, that was pretty boring. I don't think I want to get married that way. Too much waiting. I want to do it like you did it, Mommy, fast! OK, not that fast. But I want to do it my way. I want to have a chocolate cake, and I want to wear overalls, and I want to marry somebody who looks a lot better than that. And I want to live happily ever after!

What's the matter, Mom? Just tired? Yeah, me too. It's still really early, I guess this is gonna go on for longer. It's gonna take them about ten years to get out of the church. Boring. You don't? Yeah! I don't want to watch this anymore either. Let's watch cartoons!

(She turns on cartoons. Fade out.)

TRANSITION 1

Lights up on the puppet stage. The Princess Diana doll is pregnant. The Charles doll is reading a newspaper.

DIANA: Charles? I need to talk to you about something.

CHARLES: *(Still reading his newspaper.)* What?

DIANA: Well, I thought you might have noticed by now.

CHARLES: Uh-huh?

DIANA: I'm pregnant!

(Charles throws down his paper.)

CHARLES: You are? Good God!

DIANA: Yes, isn't it wonderful?

CHARLES: *(Catching himself.)* Ahem. Yes, well, it's quite good.

DIANA: Charles, I thought you'd be more enthusiastic.

CHARLES: I am. This is me. Very enthusiastic.

DIANA: Oh.

CHARLES: Is it a boy or a girl?

DIANA: I don't know. But I hope it's a —

CHARLES: Right then. Well, let me know when it comes out.

(Charles goes back to reading his paper.)

DIANA: Right.

(Lights down on the dolls.)

PRINCESS FOR LIFE

Princess Diana is moving through a crowded party, talking to different people.

PRINCESS DIANA: Oh hello. It's a pleasure to meet you. Charmed, I'm sure. Excuse me. Pardon me. Why thank you. Thank you very much. Yes, the children of Africa are dear to my heart. Excuse me. This gown? It's a Versace. A Versace! No, no canapés, thank you. Excuse me, can you tell me how to get out of here? How to get out? Out! Out!

(Diana is pointed in the direction of a door and bursts through it. She opens her jeweled purse and takes out a cigarette. She looks for her lighter.)

Shit. Shit, shit, shit.

(She hears a voice behind her and turns around.)

Oh, it's nothing. I just can't find my lighter, that's all.

(The figure lights her cigarette.)

Why thank you, Elton.

(She turns around again and takes a long drag on her cigarette.)

Every once in a while I need to take a drag on a cigarette and remember who I am. You know what I mean? Of course you do, you're Elton John. I swear to God, if one more person tries to kiss my hand I think I'll scream. I shouldn't complain. It's a good living. It's just that I get in the middle of these parties with everybody wanting something from me, and wanting me to be something I'm not, and it used to be fun, but now it just tires me out.

(She looks around.)

Is anybody looking? *(She takes her wig off.)* There. That's much better. Yours must be a wig too. That's all he wears anyway, right? Jesus. I can't stop talking in this stupid accent. Bleah!

(She shakes her head. Her voice changes.)

You know what just happened in there? I got propositioned. They think I'm a hooker. I guess they figure if I'm willing to dress up like this I'll do anything. He was a short man. Kept trying to jump up and grab my tiara. It's hard to stay demure and British when somebody's ramming their head into your breasts. So I had to get out of there. He wanted me to come home with him and play Royal Court. Believe me, there was a time I would have taken him up on it. In leaner years. But I've gotten rich off this gig. I couldn't stop, even if I wanted to. I can't do anything else. Oh, I can act, but nobody wants me to do that anymore. Just her.

I mean really, do you ever forget who you are? Sometimes I look in the mirror and I'm not sure what I see. I've played this woman every weekend for the past eighteen years. I think I might play her for the rest of my life. I walk like her, I talk like her, I dress like her. I have more of her clothes than my own. Of course some day I'll get too old to play her. That's the problem with impersonating someone who's dead. You change while they stay the same. You're lucky. You'll never have that problem. Oh I bet you might have been worried during the eighties, but he's cleaned up a lot. I don't know what I'll do when this is over. I figure I have another five, ten years in me. Dead icons are the best business. Marilyn, Elvis, you wouldn't believe it, but Nixon is a big one. I heard about a woman in Bel Air who will hire six or seven Nixons at a time, just for herself. Don't ask. I guess I could go back to temping. *(She shudders.)* Or telemarketing. I'll still have her voice. Maybe there's a 900 number that would hire me. *(Breathy and British.)* Oh, yes, baby, you really move me, you make me feel so wild, so unrepressed, so Scandinavian. Be my Master of the Horse. Be my Master of the Horse! *(Back to normal voice.)* And then I'll take out my dentures. You know what they should do? They should make an old folks home just for us. So people can come and laugh at us as we get old. Sure, I'm sure there's some freaks out there who want to see what Diana would have looked like at seventy. Or James Dean at ninety. Not to mention everyone who thinks Elvis is still alive. There's probably weirdos who would take care of us for free. They can come and feed us creamed corn and push us around in our golden wheelchairs. *(She is half-laughing, half-crying.)* Oh God, that's sick.

You know, you really do look like him. I'm surprised I haven't seen you around. I know everybody in this business, I thought I'd met all the Elton Johns. Where do you work generally? Oh, England. That explains it. You're here for a special gig? Uh huh.

I'm Mary. Mary McGuire. What's your name? Elton. Oh, all right, if you don't want to break character that's fine. I understand. I mean, I should put my wig back on anyway. I could get fired for this. *(She puts her wig back on.)* Hey you know what? We should go back in there and sing *Candle in the Wind* together. That would blow their minds. What do you say? I think it might cheer you up. It might cheer me up too. Oh, come on. *(She goes back into her British accent and coy Diana persona.)* Come on Elton. Elton? Come, darling.
(She takes his hand. They exit. Music.)
Wow, you do have a good voice.

PRINCESS FOR A DAY

A recorded message on an answering machine plays.

ANSWERING MACHINE: Hello, you've reached Fantasy Wedding Planners, where we make every girl's dream come true. For a Camelot Wedding, press one; for an Arabian Nights Wedding, press two; for a Helen of Troy Wedding, complete with abduction, press three; for a Royal Wedding, press four . . .

(There is a beep. Lights up. Shari, a lawyer dressed in an eighties power suit, is in her office, on the phone.)

SHARI: Look, I don't know what's going on. I was supposed to have my wedding dress fed-exed to me today, and all I got in the package was a robe and two buns. *(Holding up the contents of the package.)* They look like cinnamon rolls. A hairpiece? But I didn't order a hairpiece. There should be a veil, and a gown, and whatever else she wore. Well Princess Diana, of course. I ordered a Princess Diana Fantasy Wedding, what other princess would I be talking about? Leia? I don't understand. *(Looking at the package.)* Oh no. No! I ordered a Royal Wedding, not a Star Wars Wedding! Oh for chrissakes, the incompetence!

(Yelling.) Amber? Amber, pick up the line! *(She gets back on the phone.)* All right now, my assistant is on the phone with me and we're going to straighten this out. Amber, when you called the wedding planner, what did you order for me? A Royal Wedding. Correct? Do you have the receipts to prove it? Can you put hands on them? Good, Amber, you're learning. See, we have the receipts! Get off the phone now, Amber. So you see this is your fault not ours. I want a new gown in my hands tomorrow. And don't think I'm paying to have this one sent back. You can take care of that yourself. Excuse me? Well how long would it take? Three months? Are you joking? I'm getting married next Saturday. Excuse me. *(She presses it again.)* Could I speak to your manager, please? *(She presses the hold button and screams.)* AAAAAAAAAAH!

(Pleasant but firm.) Hello, this is Shari Sissman, that's Shari Sissman *Esquire*, and I've just been speaking with one of your subordinates. There seems to have been a mix-up on your end. My secretary has been arranging a Royal Wedding with you, and some idiot at your company ordered some kind of sci-fi wedding instead. Now I'm generally a very pleasant person, but ONE WEEK BEFORE MY WEDDING THIS IS NOT WHAT I NEED TO HEAR!!! Yes, yes, I see. Well yes, I've been very involved in the process. God knows my future husband isn't doing anything. Information? I've been getting your information packets. I haven't been opening them, I'm a very busy woman, but I've been getting them. I have them right here. *(She looks around on her desk.)* Well what are you trying to say? That something in these packets should have . . . *(She opens the packet and looks inside.)* Oh my God. This is all wrong. You need to change this. No, you don't understand. You need to change this or I will sue you for

every corsage and centerpiece you've got. There is no way I am going to get married by fucking Yoda! Hello? Hello? Oh God. Redial. Redial. *(A busy signal fills the room.)*

What am I going to do? Amber?
(She lies down on the couch and closes her eyes.)

Amber, is that you? Shut the blinds, please, I think I'm getting a migraine. No, I'm not angry at you. You did your best, even if you do have the brain of a snowpea. I'm sorry, Amber, that wasn't very nice of me. I'm just feeling a little stressed out. Yes, *Sounds of Nature* would be nice right now. I need to be soothed. Put on rain. *(Sound of rain fills the room.)* No, brook, brook. *(Sound of a brook.)* No, ocean. I need ocean. *(Sound of an ocean.)* Ahh. *(She relaxes to the sounds of the ocean for a few moments.)* Shut it off, please, Amber, it's making me want to kill someone. No, not you, Amber. I could never kill another woman. We need each and every one of us to take over the world. Even women like you. You'll need to get some flats for the street fighting. I'm sorry, Amber, that wasn't nice either. Really, you've done a good job. You've managed to keep everyone in the Women's Bar from finding out about my fantasy wedding. You even managed to keep the Radical Feminist Association from finding out I was getting married at all. And now you don't need to keep anyone from knowing because it's never going to happen. No dress, no train, no horse-drawn carriage. I'm going to be transported to my wedding on a Death Star! No, that won't happen either. Call the guests, Amber. Call the whole thing off! No, wait, I need you with me right now. I need to talk to another woman. You are another woman, aren't you? Sometime I can't tell beneath all that makeup. I'm sorry, Amber, I can't seem to help myself. I think I'm having a little breakdown.

Is this my punishment for wanting something I can't have? Is this how God or Gloria Steinem laughs at me? *(To the heavens.)* I didn't mean it, Gloria. Honest. I just got tired, that's all. I got tired of being called a bitch just because I know how to run a firm. I got tired of having to work twice as hard for half the credit. I got tired of shoulderpads and power suits and shoelifts. I just wanted to be pretty, was that so much to ask? I just wanted to be a princess for a day. For one lousy day!

What do you think of me, Amber? Do you think I'm a bitch? Really, be honest. We're talking woman to woman here, not boss to... slave. Tell me the absolute truth. We're in a "time out" right now. *(Listens.)* Well, that's sweet of you, Amber, but I know you do think I'm a bitch. I listen in on your phone calls to your boyfriend, if you haven't figured it out by now. Oh Amber, no. Don't cry. Please — There goes your eyeliner.

Did I cross a line? Perhaps I did. You know why I'm so mean to you, Amber? It's because you remind me of myself at your age. Oh, I know there's only ten years between us, but when you're on your way to splattering your guts against the glass ceiling, every year counts. I was once young and pretty, and I didn't have this crease between my eyebrows that comes from screaming at everybody all the time. I was sweet, like you. I thought I could stay sweet. You can't. Well, you can, but be prepared to get laughed at. Especially in those heels. What are those? Christian Dior? Uh huh. I saw them in *Vogue*. Every three years I pick up a *Vogue* and then burn it.

Do you have any guilty secrets? Victoria's? Well, that's a start. This is good, Amber, we're sharing. That's what true feminism is all about — women bonding with other women, even if one of them can't seem to understand that push-up bras bring down the entire gender. Oh I know there's all kinds of feminism, but some of us need to stay orthodox, don't we? Otherwise, we'll just assimilate.

Thank you, Amber. Thank you for listening to me. I feel much better now. All right, I'm ready. Call the guests. Wait, call my fiancé first. I suppose he might want to know. And then call the Radical Feminists. I need to go through reentry therapy. You may go now, Amber.
(She closes her eyes again.)

What's that? Another guilty secret? Well, of course you can share it with me. You sew? How 1950s of you. That's all right, I won't tell anyone. You could sew me a dress? You wouldn't happen to have access to horses, would you?

TRANSITION 2

Lights up on the puppet stage. Charles is whispering on the telephone. He hangs up when he sees Diana.

DIANA: Charles, who were you talking to?
CHARLES: Nobody.
DIANA: Nobody?
CHARLES: Just an old friend. No one you know.
DIANA: Really? What's his name?

CHARLES: His name is . . . Bob.

DIANA: How exciting! I didn't even know you had any friends! Can we have him over for dinner?

CHARLES: No.

DIANA: Why not? I'd love to meet him.

CHARLES: Well we can't! He's . . . diseased.

DIANA: Diseased! How tragic!

CHARLES: Yes, he can't leave the house.

DIANA: Oh that poor man! *(Pause.)* My goodness!

CHARLES: What?

DIANA: I just realized there are people in the world less fortunate than we are! Oh Charles, could we visit him?

CHARLES: No. Out of the question.

DIANA: But he's probably lonely!

CHARLES: Absolutely not!

(Sound of a baby crying.)

DIANA: That's the baby. I'd better go.

(Diana leaves. Charles reaches for the phone.)

ESCAPE TO SPAIN!

Arlene, a nice midwestern woman, sits in a travel agency, wearing a Princess Diana sweatshirt. She is surrounded by travel posters.

ARLENE: So I'm thinking, Denise, somewhere along the southern coast of Spain might be nice. How about Acapulco? Oh. See, what I'd really like to do is start at one end of the coast and work my way toward the other. How long do you think that would take? Well, I'd probably spend a day or so in each town. In each and every town. And I want to go to all of the beaches. Yes, every single one, including the private ones if possible. Hmm, you think that would take longer than two weeks, huh?

Oh this? *(Looking at her sweatshirt.)* Yeah, I made it myself. Do you like it? I bet you've never seen this photograph of her before, right? That's because I took it with my own camera! It was when she came to Chicago a few years back. Yeah, I had it silkscreened on the shirt. Pretty neat, huh? Oh, that's OK. Oh no, I'm not upset. There's nothing to be upset about.

Oh, you're not the first. A lot of people asked me if I was upset when she died. I mean, it's kind of gotten around that I'm a fan of hers. The day it happened, Phyllis and Georgia came over and brought me a pie. A pie! And I said, I don't need a pie. I'm fine. And they thought I was in shock, so they sat me down in the recliner and explained that, Arlene, there's been a car crash in Paris and so and so and so, and I just sat there with a big smile on my face. Because what they didn't know, which is what I knew, is that she was still alive. She faked it! It's so obvious, I can't believe everyone hasn't figured it out by now, but I was always smarter. I see things. I could have been a detective.

There was a white car. A Fiat Uno. They know this because they found chips of white paint on her cracked-up Mercedes. They spent three weeks looking for that car all over France. They never found it. Uh huh. Well, don't you get it? Do I have to spell it out for you? They never found it because it wasn't there. Diana and Dodi escaped in that car to some other country. And that country would be . . . *(Waiting for an answer.)* Spain, she was partial to Spain. And there they started a new life.

I mean, it all makes sense. You're thirty-six years old, you're hounded by the press, you're trapped in this life you don't want to live. What's the obvious solution? Stage your own death! Very canny to stage the crash scene in a tunnel, too, a very smart move. And what happened to the only passenger who "survived" the crash? He got "amnesia" and couldn't talk. Hah. Whoever believes that is an idiot. Well, I shouldn't say that. I mean I could figure it out, but that's me. They fooled the rest of the world. It was brilliant, just brilliant.

You see, I understand her because I relate to her. I know what it's like to be trapped and want to escape. *(Gradually getting hysterical.)* I mean, she was in this grind of parties, and press conferences, and royal functions, and I'm in this grind of working, and taking care of the kids, and the house, and the yard, and Steven. And sometimes you just want to smash your car into a bridge and walk away from it all!

So that's why I want to go to Spain. Oh I don't want to bother her. I just want to tell her, hey, sister, I'm proud of you, you did it! And if the press ever catches on that she's in Spain, then I want her to know that she has a nice home waiting for her here in Duluth. I've got the guest bedroom all set up for her. And she doesn't have to worry about me spilling the beans. I'd be quiet as a mouse. She would like it here, I think. Oh, I know she's used to fancier things, but that's why she got away from it all in the first place: to live the simpler life. She could take walks by our lake, and use the stairmaster in our exercise room, and she could even come to church with us, because the people at our church are good people. They wouldn't say anything. She once said, "I'm more like the people at the bottom than at the top." Not that we're at the bottom, Steven and I make a good living, but we're down-to-earth people. The kind she's looking for.

So you think it might take more than a couple weeks, huh? I mean, if I find her right away, then I can go home, but if I don't . . . No, Steven won't be coming. Not the kids either, they're in school. Just me. I've never been abroad. But I'm not worried. I can figure it out. I know a little Espanol. See the thing is, I've got two weeks of vacation saved up, but if I take more than that it comes out of my pay. Could it really take more than two weeks? I wish there was a way I could just go there and not have to worry about coming back. You know what I mean?

FAT CAMP

Doreen, a girl of fifteen, enters wearing a bathing suit, shorts, a crown, and a sash that reads, "Miss Camp Bluebird 1985." She knocks on the door.

DOREEN: Ms. Petersen? You wanted to see me? *(Doreen enters and sits down. She is overly cheery.)* Oh, I'm fine. I'm great actually! I've never been a role model before. All the younger girls are coming up to me and asking me how I did it. I tell them, well, hard work and discipline, and a little less time with Mr. Snickers Bar! I think some of my bunkmates are jealous, especially since some of them actually gained weight, can you imagine? But I just tell myself, only one person can lose the most weight in the first week at Camp Bluebird, and this year, it just happened to be me! Ten whole pounds! I mean, it's always been my dream to be Miss Camp Bluebird. Before I came here this June, I told myself, I'd do anything to win. Anything! So, what did you want to ask me?
(Pause.)

Sabotage? What do you mean? Well, no, I would never! How dare you suggest . . . ? I won this contest fair and square. I am Miss Camp Bluebird 1985! The scales prove it! Evidence? What evidence? I have no idea what you're talking abou — *(She looks up.)* Oh. Yes, that's mine. No, I can't explain it. Could I call my lawyer now? I guess they don't have lawyers for these kinds of things. My parents? No, please don't call my parents. They'd kill me. They'd be so ashamed. All right, all right. I'll come clean. Yes, it's true. That is my tub of lard. And yes, I have been putting it into the mashed potatoes. Oh, God. It feels so good to get that off my chest. That's not all, you know. I've got twelve more of those hidden around the mess hall. I've been stirring it into everything — the pancakes, the Egg Beaters, the tuna wiggle. I asked for kitchen duty just so I could do those things. It's an elaborate ruse I've been planning all year! I'm a horrible person, I know. I just wanted to win so badly. Yes, I understand that what I did was terrible. Terrible. Just unforgivable. I mean, there is no way you can let something like this slide. I must be expelled, mustn't I? Something like this is just too heinous to overlook. All right, I'll pack my bags.

(She gets up to leave.) What? Another chance? No, I don't think so. I've been bad and I need to be punished. There's nothing worse you could do than make me leave Camp Bluebird. I need to learn the hard way. Please, call my parents. It's in my best interest. Send me away.

(Beat.)

You're not getting it, are you? Look, you seem like a nice counselor. At least, you're the only one whose thighs have three dimensions. Can I tell you the truth? I don't want another chance. I want out. That's why I sabotaged the beauty pageant. I want to be expelled. Please. Help me get out of here. I've been coming here for six summers and I can't take another minute of it. This place is crazy. I mean, a beauty pageant for fat girls? Who are they kidding? We all prance around in our sensible one-piece suits while the judges try not to laugh at us. We know. Look, I don't mean to be disrespectful. I tried to follow your program, I really did. I ate the fruit cup and the square of toast you put in front of me every morning. I spent my afternoons doing aerobics to "It's Raining Men" and "Oh, Mickey!" And at night I closed eyes and tried to visualize myself shrinking. None of it worked. In fact, your program isn't working for anyone. The rest of my bunk survives by smuggling in Snickers bars and throwing them up at night. The PeeWees are popping Ex-Lax. They hide it in their training bras. And what about Judy, who went away for that mysterious week six to a "wedding"? Yeah, right. Try *liposuction.* Who comes back from a wedding with eggplant-sized bruises on their thighs? She said it was from waterskiing, but smart people know better. I mean, how can you reward that? You might as well put a crown on the vacuum!
(Beat.)

So can I go now? Please? I mean really, you don't want to keep me around here. I'm dangerous. Who knows what I'll do? *(Pause.)* Can't you just chalk me up as a hopeless case? A loose cannon? A bad seed? *(Pause.)* OK. Fine. But you know what? From now on, I'm going to eat whatever the hell I want. Oh, I have ways of getting food. Many, many sources. And by the time this summer is over, I'll be the first Miss Camp Bluebird who will have gained fifty pounds. You can put THAT in your ad in the *New York Times*. Oh yeah? What are you gonna do about it? Deny me the crown? Oh, I'm so upset. Crowns are for princesses. I'm just Doreen. You can keep your crown.

(She takes off the crown and exits.)

NEW YORK

A New York cab. Candy, the driver, picks up a passenger.

CANDY: Where to? Around? Lady, I don't just drive around, I ain't a sightseeing tour, you know what I'm saying? This is a cab. I go from here to there, I don't just . . . *(Turns back to audience holding a wad of bills.).* OK, you got it. I'll drive you around.
(Drives.)

You from out of town or something? *(Pause.)* OK, not the talkative type. You know, you really don't need to wear those sunglasses, my windows are tinted. Only people I know who wear sunglasses indoors are movie stars and my Uncle Rick. He got an eye shot out. Hey, wait a minute, you are a movie star! I know I've seen you before. Wait, wait, don't tell me. Melanie Griffith! No? OK, give me another chance. You're not a porn star, are you? Holy shit! I know who you are! You're Princess Diana! Holy shit! I've got Princess Diana in my cab! *(She turns fully around in her excitement.)* What the hell are you doing here? Huh? *(She faces forward and jerks the wheel.)* Hey! Watch where you're going! Oh my God. OK, OK, I'm cool. Princess Diana! *(Listens.)* Yeah, sure you're not. I know Princess Diana when I see her, and you're her. OK, fine, you want to pretend like you're not who you are, that's cool. I can do that. I won't say another word.
(Silence.)

So, like, what, you just wanna get out of the castle for a while, see a few sights? Figured you'd come to New York for some action? *(Pointing.)* Bet you don't see freaks like that at Buckingham Palace, do ya? OK, OK, I'll stop. I know what it's like for you royalty, always getting bugged by people. You probably just want some time alone. Hey, that's what's going on! You wanna get away from that husband of yours. Yeah, it's been all over the news. He's having an affair with that lady, whatsername, Camilla! Calling her on the phone and shit. Oh man, let me just say he must have his head up his ass. I mean, she is one ugly bitch! And you, you're beautiful, and glamorous. You're like, a princess! Hey, you're not thinking about getting back at him, are you? I mean, that's not why you're cruising around, is it? Because there are some real weirdos in New York; you should be careful who you pick up. Some guys look real nice, but they're psycho. The Wall Street types especially. It's always the clean-cut looking guys who turn out to have bodies in their refrigerators. I won't pick 'em up. And in this part of town, forget about it. Drug dealers and whores, that's all you got on this street. Hey, wait a minute, that's my cousin Denise! Denise!

(Turning her head, she nearly runs into a truck and slams on the brakes.) Whoa! That was a close one. What were we talking about? Oh yeah, I mean, what guy gives up a princess for some butt-ugly broad? But you know something, it don't surprise me. I mean, men will *(Gestures.)*, you know, anything that moves. You got to keep your eye on them. I got a lot of experience with that. My guy, James, when we first met he was like, oh Candy, I love you, you're so beautiful, you're my queen, right? And every day, he's going on about how gorgeous I am, and how I should be a model, and I'm like, yeah, you're beautiful too, James. And he's like, no baby, I got my face burned in a fire, I ain't beautiful, and I'm like, yeah, but James, you're beautiful inside. And he's like, no Candy, no, you, you're beautiful, you are, you, *you are beautiful.* And I'm like, OK, I'm beautiful. So we move in together, and we're in love, and we decide we're gonna get married as soon as I can get a divorce from my last husband. Well you can guess the rest of the story. One day, I come home from work, walk in the door, and he's on the floor with the deaf-mute girl from the dry cleaners. And she is a dog. I mean, worse than Parker-Bowles. This woman's face looks like scrambled eggs. And I'm so confused. Because I thought I was supposed to be so beautiful, and here he's been banging a circus freak. And he's like, oh baby, I'm sorry, I don't know what happened, please forgive me, and I'm like, oh no, no you don't. *(As James.)* But baby, baby, *I* can explain. *(As herself.)* Oh no, baby. I can explain. And I got my knife and — huh? Oh no, I didn't kill him. I just cut him up a little. Not a lot, just enough to scare him. That's what you gotta do with men, scare them. He don't fool around no more. *(Beat.)* That's what you gotta do with your husband. Just cut him a little. I bet he won't be expecting it from you. That's what'll make it twice as good. Dontcha think?

Yeah, like one time when the two of you are eating your tea and crumpets and shit, and he gets up to make another phone call, you just go chk chk chk *(Makes stabbing gesture.).* He won't be making no more phone calls after that, believe me!

(Horn honks.)

Oh go screw yourself!

(To the passenger.)

Huh? You wanna get out *here?* Oh no, you don't. This is not a good area of town. Believe me, you don't want to be walking around here at night, especially a gal like you. They'll eat you alive. No. I'm sorry. I can't let you out. I cannot be responsible for your certain rape and death. Or worse, one of these pimps might decide he likes you. "Princess Diana found turning tricks on Avenue C." No way. That's not gonna be on my shoulders. Well, yeah, by law I have to let you out wherever you want, but that don't mean I'm gonna. Yeah, you paid me. It's your ride. OK. OK, I'll let you out, but on one condition. You gotta take this. *(She holds out a knife.)* For protection. And whatever else you wanna use it for. Come on, take it. Yeah, there you go. *(To herself.)* Jesus.

(She rolls down her window.)

Hey, good luck, you know? I'm rooting for ya!

TRANSITION 3

Lights up on the puppet stage.

DIANA: Oh Charles, how could you do this to me!

CHARLES: Stop it Diana! You're acting like a child!

(The Diana doll throws herself around in anguish.)

DIANA: Oh, Charles, if you don't love me, I'll kill myself.

CHARLES: Good heavens, Diana!

DIANA: Are you having an affair? Tell me! Tell me!

CHARLES: Why, uh, er, no.

DIANA: Liar! I found the cufflinks!

CHARLES: Uh, oh.

DIANA: They have your initials on them. And . . . hers.

(She starts to cry.)

CHARLES: Now Diana, it's not what you think . . .

DIANA: I know everything, Charles.

CHARLES: You don't understand.

DIANA: I understand that you don't love me anymore.

CHARLES: That's not true!

DIANA: It's not? Then say it! Tell me you love me.

CHARLES: I — I —

DIANA: Say it or I'll throw myself down these stairs!

CHARLES: *(Having difficulty.)* I llllll . . . ooooo . . .

DIANA: Noooooooooo!

(Diana throws herself down the stairs, landing at the bottom with a thud. Charles looks at her.)

CHARLES: Oh, dear. Mother?

BEACHES

Cameras flash. A red carpet. A starlet in sunglasses stops to speak to the reporters.

STARLET: Thank you! Thank you all so much! I couldn't do it without you!
(She blows a kiss to the cameras.)

My opinions? Why yes, I have many opinions on the subject. As you may know, I've been an advocate of privacy and stalking laws for quite a while. I mean, celebrities have rights too. You might think that just because you see me on a magazine cover I'm not real. I am real! I have thoughts and feelings just like you. Feelings that get hurt when someone snaps a photograph of me and prints it under the caption, "Who's Getting Flabby?" And by the way, I gained that weight for a role. *The Life of Gertrude Stein,* my next film, opening Friday at a theater near you. And as you can see, I've lost every single ounce of it. So snap away!
(The cameras go mad.)

Oh yes, this new law had a tragic beginning. It's just terrible that Diana had to be killed in that car crash. But as my yogi says, out of tragedy comes tranquility. I think she would be happy to know that because of her death, others are able to live in peace. Why just the other day I was on the beach at my new vacation home in Malibu, and I realized my towel boy had a camera strapped to his thong. Thank God I saw it before I took my top off. I felt so violated! Well of course he said it was just for his mother, how many times have I heard that one? It's just such a comfort to know that because of this law, I can throw him in jail for six months instead of having my bodyguards hold his head under the surf. They're big men, but their arms get tired.

(As if answering a question.) Well, I relate to her, I really do. It's awful to be wanted all the time. People just don't understand. I mean I can't go anywhere without people looking at me, following me, telling me how much they love me. When I became an actress, I never asked to be the center of attention! And I am an *actress*, I'm tired of you reporters identifying me as a "former adult-film star." I haven't done those movies for years. At least two years, and I've gone through the same training as Marilyn. All I want is respect. We celebrities work hard to get to the top. Do you have any idea what I did to get here? Well, of course you do, you've all rented the videos, but do you know what I went through *inside?* The pain, the suffering, the loss of innocence? Yes, innocence! Even I was once just a little girl in Kansas, growing up on my parents' farm, when one day they were killed in a horrible tractor crash and . . . wait a minute. Is that my story? No, that's my publicist's story. My story is . . . Where did I grow up? Oh right, New Jersey, but isn't that bad enough? New Jersey! The details aren't important. What matters is that I suffered. I was working at the mall! At Hot Dog on a Stick! And then when some man with a greasy mustache comes out of the blue and tells you he'll pay you $200 to . . . well, what was I to do? What would you do in that situation? No, don't answer that. You'd probably turn it down. You probably think you're better than me. And you'd be right. I'm just a cheap little whore! *(She starts to break down crying, then stops and looks up.)* A cheap little Oscar-nominated whore, so HA HA HA HA HA!
(She gathers herself together.)

Well, that's enough negativity. I'm going to release it now.
(She does a yoga pose.)

Aaaah. Well, they're calling me. I must be going. All right, just a few more photos.
(She strikes a few poses while the cameras flash.)

Oh you. The press. I love you, but I hate you. And I know you feel the same way about me. It's such a teasing relationship. You dig at me, I slap back at you, and then we all get in bed together and fuck like crazy! So I know you won't take this new law the wrong way. It doesn't mean I don't love you anymore. It just means you'll have to work a little harder to love me. But absence does make the heart grow fonder, and that's why I'm so glad I'll be able to take my next vacation to Malibu in peace.
(Beat.)

That's Malibu, on the South Shore. 1191 Coconut Lane. It's a private drive, but if you sneak through the service entrance no one will see you. *(Winks.)* I'll be waiting.

PALMS

Jean is being escorted into a police station, her hands behind her back. She speaks in a soft British accent.

JEAN: Can't you take these off? I mean this is ridiculous. Look at me, I'm built like a bird. I couldn't hurt anybody. I can't even take the lids off jars. *(She releases her hands, as if the police officer has taken off her handcuffs. She sits down.)*

Oh, thank you. Finally someone's being reasonable. Please listen to me. You're making a big mistake. I loved my husband, I would never hurt him. Well, yes, I suppose I did, but it was an accident! I didn't mean to do it. You have to believe me!

Where do I start? Well, there was a plant, and there was Carter, and . . . oh, that's not it. If you understood, if you only understood . . . Have you seen the royal wedding? Of course not, how old are you, twenty? I want to make you understand. Sometimes the beginning doesn't seem like the beginning, if you know what I mean. Sometimes you have to go a little farther back.

Carter was a royalist. He made us watch the wedding, the one between Prince Charles and Princess Diana, every single Sunday afternoon. I wanted to watch *60 Minutes* once in a while, but no, every Sunday I had to watch that damn wedding while I served Carter crumpets and tea. It's a long wedding. It starts with the procession through the streets. Then they get to the St. Hoo-hahs Cathedral, and Diana gets out with that twenty-five-foot-long train. What is the purpose of such a thing? I guess Prince Charles needed to have something to grab on to if she ever tried to run away. Then, finally, the ceremony starts. I know every word of it by heart, because I've seen it nine hundred and thirty-six times! *(Going a little crazy.)* "Phillip Charles Arthur George, Phillip Charles Arthur George, Phillip Charles Arthur George," get it right once for God's sakes!

The poor thing's dead now. One shouldn't speak that way about the dead. When she died, Carter cried. And cried, and cried for a week. Do you know what it's like to wash and iron a hundred silk handkerchiefs?

I bought him Kleenex, but no, he wanted silk, only silk. On the day of the funeral it was nighttime here, so Carter made us stay up until three in the morning to watch it. The procession for her funeral was almost as long as the one for her wedding, and it was so unbearably dull that the network started to intersperse it with clips from the wedding. Diana in a veil, Diana in a box. Well, they showed little Diana saying her vows under that mass of tulle, and I just lost it. I started screaming at her, "Don't do it! Run for your life! It looks like a fairy tale, but it's not. Just look at his ears. His ears tell the story. He's going to cheat on you with that horsey-faced woman, and then you're going to die in a car crash with a man named, of all things, Dodi!" Carter turned ashen. He didn't speak to me for a week.

Then, the next Sunday, Carter announced that we would continue to watch the wedding every Sunday afternoon, but we would also watch the funeral every Sunday night. He had decorated the house with com-memorative Diana plates. Shy Di, only nineteen years old. Sophisticated Di, wearing an off-the-shoulder Versace. Motherly Di, hugging her two big-eared little princes. I couldn't go to the bathroom without being watched by her.

That evening I decided to carry the potted palms back into the house for the winter. They're tender things, and they can die from just the slight-est cold. I love my plants so much. I think I like them better than peo-ple. I love the sound plants make, that quiet sound when they rustle in the wind. Anyway, I was carrying one of the palms through the living room, where Carter was setting up the videotape. "Bring me a hot toddy," he said, in that phony British accent. Oh, we're not British, we're from Queens, but Carter liked to speak that way, and he made me do it too. And now I can't stop! "Chop, chop," he said. I said, "Just a minute, dear, let me carry this plant upstairs," and when I got to the top of the stairs, it happened. The pot slipped out of my fingers. And that's the strangest thing about it, because I'm always so careful with my plants. I haven't dropped one in thirty years. But I dropped this one. Right on his head.

That's when you came in. You and your partner. I don't remember that, I don't remember anything after the plant fell. What happened, could you tell me? I was screaming? Well, of course I was screaming, I imagine I was very upset about Carter. I was saying what? "My palm? My palm?" No, that's not possible. That doesn't make any sense! I loved Carter! I tell you I loved him, I loved him, *(Her accent drops.) I hated him! I hated every-thing about him! I would do it again!*

Do you hear that? It's gone. My accent's gone. I feel so free. I'm sorry, what? Oh, yes. Yes I suppose you will have to book me. I don't blame you, I suppose I'd do the same if I were you. Just one question. Do they let you have plants in jail?

MISS BICKWORTH'S SCHOOL FOR GIRLS

A woman wearing a conservative dress and a string of pearls stands in front of a class. Next to her is an easel with photographs.

MISS BICKWORTH: Welcome to history class, girls. I trust you are all comfortable in the new seats that you reupholstered last week. Oh dear, Tina. Did you leave a pin in yours? Learn from the pain. Today we continue in our series on Notable Women of History. I graded your papers on Catherine the Great.
(Holds up a paper with an F *on it and thick black marks.)*
Wherever you see a black mark, that's something you shouldn't have written. Remember, ladies, and it is important to stress that we are all ladies here, if you don't write about something disgusting, then it didn't happen. And so we turn to our next Notable Woman.
(She reveals the first photograph: Princess Diana.)
The topic of today's lecture: Princess Diana: Fairy-Tale Princess or the Devil's Slut? What happened? Where did she go wrong?
Let us begin by tracing the path of her life. As some of you may know, a bust of Diana used to be in our role model hall of fame, along with Jackie Kennedy, Nancy Reagan, and Phyllis Schlafly. When she arrived on the scene, Diana appeared to be the perfect modern woman: virginal, dutiful to her husband and country, devoted to her children . . . until she fell from grace! Yes, she fell, and how did she fall? What was her first mistake? She strayed! And how did she stray? She began to hang out with the wrong sort of people.
(She reveals the second photograph: Diana and Elton John.)
This was the beginning of the end. From her perch on high Diana fell, tumbling down the stairs as it were, tumble, tumble, tumble, tumble, knocking her head on bulimia, then hitting her rear on depression, then down to adultery, then divorce, and finally death, death, death!
(She reveals the third photograph: The crash scene.)
Now children, there is a lesson here. And the lesson is, how can we

avoid such a fate in the modern world? Well, you've taken the first step by enrolling in Miss Bickworth's, the last finishing school on American soil and proud of it! Here you learn all the lost arts: table setting, doily placement, and of course, pretending to enjoy bad sex, which you must not have until marriage! Miss Bickworth's has never allowed a lady to graduate without her maidenhood intact — and we check!

But Miss Bickworth's mission is not just to prepare one tiny group of girls for the modern world. No, we want to prepare the modern world for us. And we want to change it. We must turn the tide! When you get out of here those feminists and lesbians will eat you alive, unless you eat them first! *(Beat.)* That's right, we must fight back. When you graduate from this school and go out there you will see horrors, my children, horrors!

(She reveals photographs illustrating all the horrors.)

Women fixing pipes, women running companies, women in the Senate! Women living with other women, divorced women, women living alone, and they're all happy about it! When you go out into the real world they will try to convince you that you are the crazy ones, but make no mistake about it children, you are sane! We graduates of Miss Bickworth's are a tiny island of sanity in a mad, mad sea. Other women wonder why they can't get husbands these days. Why the men are sending to Japan and Russia for mail-order brides. Well, you can't fight biology. You can't blame the men, oh no, they're not the ones who have changed. It's us rocking the boat. Well, not us, but all the other women! And it's time we stop it, otherwise we're all going straight to hell!

(She pats her face with a handkerchief.)

Well, I've broken my own rule about not getting angry. Remember, girls, a lady must always stay in control.

And that was Diana's final mistake. She got angry. She said, I'm not taking any more of this, I'm out of here. You're darn right she was. Out of there and into the Hospital de la Pitie Salpetriere and then death, death, death!

Girls, you've been very good today. Very quiet and attentive. Why there hasn't been a single question all period! I'm very pleased, you're learning. Your essays on Princess Diana are due next week, *(She holds up the paper with an F on it.)* and remember, be discreet. And now we'll all file into the cafeteria for lunch. Lunch today consists of burnt toast and sour milk. You will enjoy it — as you will learn to enjoy the burnt toast and sour milk of life. Class dismissed.

TRANSITION 4

Lights up on the dolls arguing. Diana is holding a suitcase.

DIANA: I can't take it anymore! I want a divorce.

CHARLES: We can't get divorced! We're the future king and queen of England!

DIANA: I don't care. I don't love you anymore.

CHARLES: Well. I don't love you anymore.

DIANA: I know! That's why I'm leaving!

CHARLES: Diana, please. Think about what people will say. Think about my mother!

DIANA: I don't give a damn about your mother! I want my own life and I am going to have one, no matter what anyone says. You can't stop me. No one can stop me. Good-bye, Charles.
(She storms out.)

CHARLES: Diana! Diana! *(To himself.)* Who will get the cats?

UNFORGIVEN

Sound of a choir of angels singing. Fade out as Mother Teresa approaches the podium.

MOTHER TERESA: Well, thank you. Thank you for this posthumous award. It's very kind of you to give me something. And thank you for the choir of angels, that was a nice touch. But while I have your attention, here's a question for you. Perhaps not a popular question, but a moral question. A question of importance: Why, in newspapers around the world, did the death of Princess Diana get top billing over mine? *(Imitating the headlines)* "PRINCESS DIANA DEAD AT THIRTY-SIX!" — "Mother Teresa also dies, see page 4." Didn't I do enough for you? What more do you want from me? You know, it's very painful to arrive in heaven and find the lobby TV tuned to "E!" and see Kevin Costner calling her a saint. A saint? What am I, chopped liver? What do I have to do? Wear a ball gown while I clean the lepers? Pause while spooning out the gruel to reapply my lipstick? You know, when I was young, I was quite the hottie. Hard to believe, maybe, but true. And when I took my vows, I thought, nothing could be more noble than giving up one's life to help the poor. All that youth and beauty, tossed to the wind. And now I find I should have just married royalty and hung around land mines.

Oh screw it, who cares anyway. I bet you didn't think Mother Teresa said screw it. Well, there's a lot of things you don't know about Mother Teresa. Do you know what it was like to arrive right behind her? All the angels weeping and singing at the same time, everybody coming out to get a look, snapping photographs, and then when I get there all they've got for me is a tray of donut holes. It hurts. It hurts.

At least my friends are here to support me. *(She waves.)* Nuns generally get to go to heaven. Except Sister Annunziata. I had no idea she had been impersonating me at parties. We always talked about how much we looked alike, I always thought she was a little jealous of me, but we were good friends. And then I get here and find out she had been borrowing my robes and smoking cigars with Richard Gere.

But I don't really like heaven so far. There's nobody here to help. Everybody's doing pretty well. All the lepers have their limbs back, and nobody is hungry because they feed you about five times a day. There's nothing to do here except go to parties, and *she's* always there.

I met her once. Oh, I met her on Earth, too, but I could care less about her there. But here, well, she's the center of the universe. *SHE* always has something new and exciting to wear. All I came with is this old robe, and it's hard to dance in. Anyway, I met her at one of these parties, she was talking to the rock-star table, of course, and I'm just trying to squeeze past her to get to the hors d'oeuvres (I still can only eat in small portions) and she says to me, "Mother Teresa! It's so lovely to see you." And I just nodded, which is what I do when I don't want to talk to people. They assume I don't speak English, or that I'm too weak to talk or something. And then she turns back to that table of idiots, most of whom don't even recognize me. And as I'm passing her I start thinking about how I have to spend the rest of eternity with this woman. For the rest of time, I have to look at her, tall and willowy and forever young, while I have to be old and wrinkled and . . . invisible. So I gave her a push. Just a little one. I had to do it really, to get by. But I guess on stiletto heels a little push can go a long way. How would I know about such things? And she loses her balance and falls right into the dessert tray. Face forward. It was very unladylike. It was very . . . nice. No one suspected me, of course. That's the one thing I like about heaven. I can get away with anything.

And while I'm up here, I've got a few words to say directly to the man himself. Is he here, by the way? Oh, right, he's "always" here. Why doesn't he ever show up to these things? Has he got something better to do? Like what, stopping poverty? Oh right, that's my job.

(Oscar-type music cue.)

Wait, I'm not finished! I've got some important questions! Like, if this is Heaven, why does it look so much like Club Med? I didn't bring a bathing suit. And what's up with us all still having our bodies? I thought we'd all be spirits whizzing around. I thought we'd all be equal. If I'd known I'd have to come here looking like this, I would have died at thirty-six too! I want some answers!

(Mother Teresa keeps shouting as the music drowns her out.)

TRANSITION 5

Lights up on the puppet stage. Charles is in bed with a toy horse.

CHARLES: Oh, Camilla. At last we're together.

(A phone starts to ring.)

CHARLES: Good God. Who could be calling at this hour?

(He answers the phone.)

CHARLES: Hello? Oh, Mother. It's you.

(To the horse.)

It's my mother.

(To phone.)

Heard about what? No, I'm not watching the telly . . .

(He turns on the television and watches.)

DOLLS, PART 2

The television is still on. The dolls are now lying on the floor, along with other Princess Diana memorabilia: a videotape box, magazines, etc.

CARLY: *(Offstage.)* Sara! Where are you? Are you watching TV?

(Carly enters, holding a child's dress. She is the same character from the first monologue, now an adult.)

CARLY: Sara, it's time to go. I don't have the patience for this right now. You need to put on this dress and get in the car! Daddy's waiting! *(Softer tone.)* OK, I'm sorry I yelled at you. Mommy's just under a lot of stress today.

It hurts Mommy's feelings when you say you don't want to go to Grandma's funeral. Grandma was Mommy's Mommy. Wouldn't you be upset if mommy died? Wait, don't answer that. All right, I'm going to sit here until you put on this dress.

(She waits a long time; then, as if answering a question:) You don't know who that is? That's Princess Diana. This is the story of her life. Uh-huh, she was a real princess. Just like in the storybooks. Well, not quite like in the storybooks. She wore a crown. And she married a prince. That's about it. But she was very beautiful, and everyone loved her very much. Except for some people, like her in-laws. And some other people, like the lady who wanted to steal away her husband. What? Oh, never mind, Mommy's said too much.

(Points at TV.) Look, there she's getting married. Yes, that *is* a big dress. I remember watching this wedding with Grandma when it happened. I was a little girl, and I had to get up early to watch it. That was a long time ago. Mommy took out the tape to remember that time. And these are Mommy's dolls from when she was your age. *(She holds up a doll with its leg chewed off.)* Mommy didn't take care of her dolls, either.

(Pointing at the TV.) That's the prince, right there. His name is Charles. Well, no, he doesn't look like the prince in the storybooks. Not many people do. But that shouldn't matter. Just because somebody doesn't look like a prince doesn't mean they aren't a prince. Inside.

(Horn honks, Carly yells out the window.) We'll be right down, Eddie! *(To Sara.)* Sara? All right, just a couple more minutes.

(She turns back to the TV.) That's her son. She had two sons, Prince William and Prince Harry. Someday Prince William will grow up and become a king. Her sons loved her very much too, and they were sad when she died. Well, yes, honey, she died. No, they did not live happily ever after. She died very young. No, a witch didn't poison her, she died in a car crash. Well, yes, I'm sure the prince was sad, but they had split up before she died. They got a divorce. Just like Grandma and Grandpa. Sometimes it happens that way.

(Pause.)

No, honey, she's not going to wake up like Sleeping Beauty. She really died. It doesn't matter that she was a princess. She died, and nothing can bring her back. See, this is her funeral. There are all the people who loved her, and those are all the flowers they threw. Yes, this is a funeral like Grandma's funeral. Well, not quite like Grandma's funeral. It won't be on TV. And it's just going to be us there, not thousands of people. And Aunt Harriet will sing, not Elton John. But it will be important, just the same. And Grandma would want you to be there. I know she would. And I want you to be there, because you're my daughter, and I was Grandma's daughter. And even though neither of us want to go, we have to. To say good-bye.

(She looks at her daughter.) Come, Sara. Let's put on the dress.

(She leads her daughter offstage. Lights brighten on the two dolls left on the ground. Lights fade.)

END OF PLAY

Daisy in the Dreamtime

By Lynne Kaufman

PLAYWRIGHT'S BIOGRAPHY

Lynn Kaufman is the author of twelve full-length produced plays. *Daisy in the Dreamtime* had its New York premiere at the Abingdon Theatre, its university premiere at San Francisco State University as the recipient of the Rella Lossy Playwright's Award, and a full developmental workshop at the New Harmony Project. *Fakes* premiered at Florida Studio Theatre, was optioned for film by Twentieth Century Fox and for television by Jean Doumanian Productions. *Shooting Simone* premiered at Actors Theatre of Louisville's Humana Festival and received six subsequent regional productions. Four of her plays premiered at The Magic Theatre including *The Couch,* which won The Glickman Award for Best New Play in San Francisco and *Speaking in Tongues,* which won the Kennedy Center/NEA/New Plays Award. Her play *Our Lady of the Desert* won Theatreworks "Best New Play in California Award" and premiered in its Palo Alto theater.

Ms. Kaufman's plays have also been produced by such theaters as Walnut Street Theater (Philadelphia), the Fountain Theatre and the Cast Theatre (Los Angeles), the Contemporary American Theatre Festival (West Virginia), and Horizons Theatre (Washington, D.C.)

The Couch is published by Dramatists Play Service. *Shooting Simone* is published by Smith and Kraus and by Dramatic Publishing. Before writing for the theater, Ms. Kaufman published dozens of short stories in such publications as *McCalls, Cosmopolitan, Ladies Home Journal,* and *Redbook.* Her first novel, *Slow Hands,* was published in June 2003.

ORIGINAL PRODUCTION

Daisy in the Dreamtime was presented at the Mainstage Theatre, Abingdon Theatre Arts Complex, New York City in March 2003. The production was choreographed by Karen Azenberg and directed by Kim T. Sharp. Cast and crew included:

Daisy Bates	Molly Powell
Spirits	Afra Hines, Carey Macaleer
King Billy	Jerome Preston Bates
Radcliffe-Jones	Larry Swansen
Jack Bates	Michael Chaban
Grandma Hunt	Pamela Paul
Annie Lock	Jodie Lynn McClintock
Didjeridoo player	Matthew Goff
Production manager	Jonathan Sprouse
Production stage manager	Emily Metz

Scenic designer . . . . James F. Wolk
Lighting designer . . . . David Castaneda
Costume designer . . . . Susan Scherer
Dramaturg . . . . Julie Hegner
Dialects . . . . K. C. Ligon
Assistant choreographer . . . . Lenny Daniel
Assistant stage manager . . . . Talia Krispel
Production assistant . . . . Serene Brisco

TIME
The 1920s through the 1940s.

PLACE
Australia, a tent in the Outback; a lecture hall in Adelaide; Ireland in memory.

PLAYWRIGHT'S NOTE
In 1913, an Irish émigré, Daisy Bates, pitched a tent in the Australian outback and lived there with the aborigines for thirty years. She fed them, doctored them, recorded their stories and rituals. She was the first white women to enter the dreamtime. Her only enemies were the Trans-Australian Railway and Annie Lock, the Lutheran missionary. Daisy's people called her Kabbarili, the great white spirit of the never-never. This is her story and theirs.

The play explores Daisy's life and why she abandoned her family and all the comforts of civilization to live in the bleakest place on earth with the most primitive tribe and proclaimed herself blessed. It examines a culture that is free of the two great obsessions of modern civilization: the pressure of time and the accumulation of goods.

CHARACTERS
DAISY BATES: A slender, wiry Irish woman, forty to fifty.
KING BILLY: An Aboriginal man, about forty.
JACK BATES: A handsome Australian, thirty to forty.
ANNIE LOCK: A stout German woman, thirty to forty.
GRANDMA HUNT: An Irish woman, sixties.
RADCLIFFE-JONES: An Englishman, sixties.

Daisy in the Dreamtime

Scene One

Lights come up slowly on a campsite in Australian Outback. It is dawn. A vast stretch of red sand and pink sky. Silence. Then . . . the sounds of the wind, a lizard slithering across dry leaves, finally the drone of the didjeridoo.

DAISY: *(Enters, dressed in a long cotton duster.)* South western Australia. 1930. The Nullarbor Plain. The Ooldea Soak. Kabbarli's campsite. Kabbarli's tent. *(A distinctive bird call, she listens.)* Kookaboro. My people say he sings the sun up.

KING BILLY: *(Enters, rolling a large canvas tent.)* At least he think so.

DAISY: And who's to argue? It comes up every day. My beautiful capacious tent. Thank you. King Billy. If you saw my tent from above, it would look like a tiny white sail in a vast red sea. My tent the only structure in miles of red desert.

    Most people can't understand why I'm here. How can I live like this? How can I live with them? With the blackfellas. Black as the ace of spades. They think I'm crazy. Or worse.

    A few think I'm a saint, a martyr. Giving up all the comforts of civilization to help the heathen. As for me . . . I wake up each morning in a world I understand. To a people where I belong. I have everything I need and nothing I don't.

    (Playful.) My casa, su casa. *(She gestures and the sides of the tent flip up to reveal the furnishings within.)* Fine strong canvas. Holds up in the sand storms. And opens to the stars. My stretcher bed. One blanket. One pillow. Two sheets. One to wash. One to sleep on. My food box. *(Opens metal box, peers inside.)* Rather low right now. Flour. Sugar and tea. Enough to get by. And a big sack of porridge for my people.

    My shower. *(Slips off duster; she is in long silk underwear. Takes out kerosene tin and basin, stands in basin, turns tin upside down, a tiny trickle of water, washes face and hands, catches rest in basin.)* Not a drop is wasted. I use the runoff for cooking. Scoop out the flies and boil it for tea. I carry that water three miles in one hundred and ten degree heat.

    (Opens trunk.) Four identical outfits. I do not hold with novelty. *(She dresses as she speaks.)* My corset. Not that I need it for girth. But a lady

always wears a corset. My shirtwaist. My skirt. It used to be black, faded to green now, but lined with silk. I must have silk next to my skin. If not, it burns like acid. My fine leather belt. I've always had a twenty-two-inch waist except for that one year . . . and then it went right back. My starched white collar. Jack said he married me just for the pleasure of removing it.

And here is the heart and soul of my house. My desk. *(She opens a black steamer trunk.)* My pens, my paper. My notebooks! Fifty-two of them packed with the stories of my people. And when I run out of notepaper, I tear open brown paper bags and stitch them together. Can't use the ones with food stains or the mice will nibble away at my precious words. I am the first person to write down these words. The words of my people. To record how they think, what they love. I have this frequent dream. This nightmare that the desert wind will come and blow my papers away and no one will know that once in this place maia was grain and beera . . . the night sky. *(Pause.)* King Billy . . .

KING BILLY: *(Enters.)* Kabbarli.

DAISY: Kabbarli, the great white spirit of the never-never land, is ready for her language lesson. *(She gets out her notebook and sits opposite King Billy.)* Name?

KING BILLY: Illi.

DAISY: Illi. *(Writes it down.)* And for digging stick?

KING BILLY: Wanna.

DAISY: Wanna. *(Writes.)* Wooden scoop?

KING BILLY: Dhagulla.

DAISY: Animals?

KING BILLY: Seru.

DAISY: For plants?

KING BILLY: Maia.

DAISY: And lizard? What do you call a lizard?

KING BILLY: Birant.

DAISY: Birant. *(Writes it.)*

KING BILLY: Also Yemerr.

DAISY: Yemerr?

KING BILLY: Is also lizard.

DAISY: What kind?

KING BILLY: Different kind. *(Points to his genitals.)* Me, birant.

DAISY: Oh, I see, a nick name.

KING BILLY: You. *(Points to Daisy's genitals.)*

DAISY: Me? Yemerr?

KING BILLY: *(Nods his agreement.)* What do you call it in your country?

DAISY: *(Hesitates.)* It has many names.

KING BILLY: *(Broad smile.)* Here, too.

DAISY: *(Smiles to audience.)* Sex is always a winner. The academic types call it gender studies, but it's really sex. As for myself, I'm not a trained anthropologist, no formal degree. Just instinct and experience. And passion. But they still send out pith helmets with Ph.Ds to validate my findings.

RADCLIFFE-JONES: *(Enters, with helmet, khakis, etc.)* Ready when you are, Mrs. Bates. Will you present the subject, please?

DAISY: *(Leads King Billy forward.)* King Billy this is Professor Radcliffe-Jones from Harvard.

KING BILLY: Nice hat.

RADCLIFFE-JONES: I'd like to know who is your mother?

DAISY: He wants to know who is your mother?

KING BILLY: The river snake.

DAISY: He says the river snake.

RADCLIFFE-JONES: His real mother.

DAISY: He wants to know your real mother.

KING BILLY: Real mother?

DAISY: The one who raised you.

KING BILLY: Ah . . . my mother's mother?

RADCLIFFE-JONES: Yes.

KING BILLY: The kangaroo.

DAISY: He says the kangaroo.

RADCLIFFE-JONES: *(To Daisy.)* That poor bastard doesn't know who his mother is.

DAISY: *(To King Billy indicating Radcliffe-Jones.)* That poor bastard doesn't know what a totem animal is.

RADCLIFFE-JONES: Can you ask him where babies come from?

DAISY: King Billy, can you tell the professor how babies come into the world?

KING BILLY: He doesn't know?

DAISY: He has an opinion.

KING BILLY: *(Steps forward to deliver the tale.)* Three worlds there are. The past. The present. The future. And they are all here at once in the Dreaming. When a woman wishes to have a baby, she walks to the rocks where the spirit babies live. She lies upon the earth and opens her legs wide. She lies all night long and she waits. If the spirit baby wants a new mother and she is the right mother, the spirit baby comes to her in a dream and enters her womb.

RADCLIFFE-JONES: So it's all sympathetic magic. He doesn't understand the first thing about the principles of biological conception.

DAISY: What about the man, King Billy? Does he do nothing?

KING BILLY: The man waits. The next morning, the woman finds him and tell him it is time to plant the seed for the spirit baby. He is so happy.

RADCLIFFE-JONES: Plant the seed! But the baby's already in her womb.

KING BILLY: Yes, of course. First there must be spirit. Nothing can happen in the world without spirit.

RADCLIFFE-JONES: What did he say?

DAISY: He said you're right.

(King Billy Exits.)

DAISY: Is that all?

RADCLIFFE-JONES: Well, there is just one more thing.

DAISY: *(To audience.)* Do I sleep with black men? They all want to know that. And then . . . how was it?

RADCLIFFE-JONES: *(Nervous laugh.)* I wonder if you'd be so kind as to look at these obscene drawings I've made. *(Pulls out a drawing pad.)* I've heard that the aboriginal male scarifies his penis in various ways. You'll note diagram one . . . the penis is cut along a diagonal path *(Gestures.)* abcd . . . . In diagram two, the penis is cut in a circular path *(Gestures.)* abcd and in diagram three *(Gestures.)* ab it appears to be two straight lines . . .

DAISY: Yes?

RADCLIFFE-JONES: Would you say the drawings are accurate?

DAISY: Well, the penis *is* larger than life . . . but that's a common male error.

RADCLIFFE-JONES: And can you attest to these variations, Mrs. Bates?

DAISY: I beg your pardon.

RADCLIFFE-JONES: Have you seen them yourself? Personally?

DAISY: It would be hard not to. My people do not wear clothing.

RADCLIFFE-JONES: It is said that the men mutilate their sex organs. As a display of courage?

DAISY: You'd be the expert on that.

RADCLIFFE-JONES: Eh?

DAISY: You've got the penis.

RADCLIFFE-JONES: *(Thinks.)* I imagine it would be extremely painful.

DAISY: Well, there you go.

RADCLIFFE-JONES: The scarified member is also said to provide increased sexual pleasure for the women.

DAISY: They do seem to enjoy it.

RADCLIFFE-JONES: Which would you say would provide the greatest pleasure . . . the lightning bolt, the mountain path, or the striped tie?

DAISY: The bolt, the path, or the tie? *(Thinks.)* I'd say the tie. Simple but elegant. You'll have to excuse me now; I've work to do.

RADCLIFFE-JONES: Just one more thing, Mrs. Bates. I've heard that the aboriginal women are willing to perform oral sex and sometimes even drink the semen of the men. Is that true?

DAISY: Sorry, professor, I'm saving those findings for my own book.

RADCLIFFE-JONES: Quite. *(Exits.)*

KING BILLY: *(Enters, laughs.)* Why does Kabbarli take no lovers?

DAISY: It would be unfitting . . .

KING BILLY: No, it fits. Yemerr always fits birant.

DAISY: It would not be wise.

KING BILLY: Is it wise to be lonely?

DAISY: There must be no tracks of a man in the sand around Kabbarli's tent.

KING BILLY: Do you not miss the weight of a man's body on yours? His breath in your mouth?

DAISY: I barely remember.

KING BILLY: But when you do?

DAISY: I try not to.

KING BILLY: But at night. When you dream? Who do you remember? *(Pause.)* Your husband?

DAISY: Yes. My husband. I remember Jack.

KING BILLY: Was he pretty?

DAISY: Yes, he was. *(Shows King Billy photo.)*

KING BILLY: Nice moustaches. *(Exits.)*

DAISY: A thick manly moustache and a wide white smile. Broad at the shoulders, narrow at the hips.

JACK BATES: *(Enters.)* And my boots, tooled leather, polished so you could see your face in them.

DAISY: A drover, a great horseman. It was at a gymkana that I first saw him.

JACK BATES: I brought in the wickedest horse, an unbroken stallion. I offered a prize of ten gold coins to anyone who could ride him.

DAISY: And each of the young men took his turn.

JACK BATES: And each was thrown. That devil horse scraped them against the rails and trampled them. No one could stay on for more than a minute.

DAISY: And then you strode into the ring, leaped on to that horse, and held on as if there were teeth in your thighs. And when you climbed down, that stallion was tame as a kitten. You gave the prize money to the saloon.

JACK BATES: *(Shouts.)* Drinks on the house, for everyone.

DAISY: Then you walked across the ring . . . thin and strong . . . straight toward me . . . and how you stared.

JACK BATES: *(Enter.)* And what may I offer you, Miss . . . ?

DAISY: O'Dwyer.

JACK BATES: Some wine, perhaps.

DAISY: A large whiskey.

JACK BATES: A pleasure. You're new to town, Miss O'Dwyer.

DAISY: Hardly, Mr. Bates. I've been in Adelaide for six months now. You're the one who's been away. On a cattle drive, I hear.

JACK BATES: From Adelaide to Sydney. Took almost a year. But we delivered most of them alive.

DAISY: And now?

JACK BATES: A few weeks break and then I'll do it again.

DAISY: A demanding life.

JACK BATES: And you, Miss O'Dwyer. What of your life?

DAISY: Currently I'm a governess for a family of six.

JACK BATES: Equally demanding. You need a break as well.

DAISY: What have you in mind?

JACK BATES: A ride into the desert. A picnic lunch. And dancing. Will you come?

DAISY: Yes, providing I get the stallion. *(To audience.)* I have been riding since childhood.

GRANDMA HUNT: *(Appears and disappears.)* Hands and heels down, Daisy. Head and heart up . . .

DAISY: Head and heart up.

JACK BATES: We ride together every morning until the day before I am to leave. That last morning, we ride into the desert to a small church I know.

DAISY: You open the doors of the chapel and we ride right down the aisle and there waiting for us are the chaplain and his wife. And you ask, "Will you" and I say, "I will." And we are married right there in my sweat-soaked riding gear atop that stallion.

JACK BATES: Our wedding cake is a buttermilk scone that shatters as we share it.

DAISY: You lick the crumbs off my fingers. *(Turns away, Jack exits, then to audience.)* Oh, God, how did that splendid cowboy become such a gross and uninteresting man?

KING BILLY: And your boy, Kabbarli? Will you talk to him today.

DAISY: No, not today.

KING BILLY: You think he is still angry?

DAISY: I was not a good mother.

KING BILLY: And why not?

DAISY: *(Quick annoyance.)* Some of us are not meant to run in double harness.

KING BILLY: End of talk.

DAISY: *(Conciliatory.)* For now. *(Pause.)* What say we have a bit of porridge, King Billy? I'll cook us up a fine new mess of it. I'm feeling quite puckish. Or would you prefer some bread? I saved you the center.

KING BILLY: No, thank you, Kabbarli, I have no hunger.

DAISY: No hunger. Since when? Are you ill?

KING BILLY: No. I am well. I have just eaten.

DAISY: Oh really. What? Where?

KING BILLY: A woman has arrived in the Soak. She has much food.

DAISY: What sort of woman?

KING BILLY: A white woman.

DAISY: White . . . like me?

KING BILLY: No, not like you. *(Teasing.)* There is no one like you.

DAISY: How is she different?

KING BILLY: Bigger. Not so old. And . . . *(Gestures toward head.)*

DAISY: Her hair?

KING BILLY: No hair.

DAISY: She has no hair?

KING BILLY: You cannot see.

DAISY: She wears a hat?

KING BILLY: Yes. A long hat.

DAISY: A long hat?

ANNIE LOCK: *(Enters.)* A wimple. Ah, Mrs. Bates. Sister Annie Lock, here. I have so much wanted to meet you and here we are at last. I know all about the work you have been doing and I have such admiration for you. You have been an inspiration to me for many, many years. I do hope we can work together in helping bring our black brothers and sisters to God.

KING BILLY: Only say "Thank you, Jesus" you get a belly full of food. I bet she give you food, too, Kabbarli . . . "Thank you, Jesus."

ANNIE LOCK: So this is your campsite. They told me you lived out in the middle of nowhere. And so far from water. Now that the mission is here, you are welcome to come and stay with us. You must miss your own kind.

DAISY: Thank you, but I am accustomed to living right here.

ANNIE LOCK: Of course, Mrs. Bates. Or may I call you Daisy?

DAISY: My people call me Kabbarli.

ANNIE LOCK: And what does that mean?

DAISY: Great white queen of the never-never.

ANNIE LOCK: I see. Well, I look forward to learning the language. In the meantime, *Mrs. Bates,* I do hope that you can join us for dinner and prayer session tomorrow. We are moving so quickly. Thanks to God's grace, we'll put the roof on the chapel this very afternoon. The kitchen is already up and next will be the schoolroom and then the dormitories.

DAISY: Dormitories?

ANNIE LOCK: For the people.

DAISY: Why?

ANNIE LOCK: Why? So they can live there, of course . . . If they like.

DAISY: They are nomads, Miss Lock. Their religion requires that they go on walkabout.

ANNIE LOCK: They can walk all they like.

DAISY: It's not a stroll, Miss Lock. They walk into the desert for weeks. *(Pause.)* They don't live in shelters. They sleep outdoors.

ANNIE LOCK: We are just giving them a choice, Mrs. Bates. I think you'll be surprised. The desert is harsh. Stinging flies that cover your body like a shroud. Ants that eat your shoes and socks and toenails if you let them. Blood sucking mosquitoes with trunks like elephants.

DAISY: You've noticed.

ANNIE LOCK: Half the natives have blurred vision from the wind driving the sand into their eyes. You, yourself, I've heard suffer from the sandy blight.

DAISY: It comes and goes.

ANNIE LOCK: It must be a terrible trial.

DAISY: *(Nods.)* I think of it more as a memento. A geologist could map the desert from the grit behind my eyes.

ANNIE LOCK: *(Laughs.)* Tomorrow then. You must come to dinner. So far, my little house keeps out the wind. And I've brought fresh vegetables from Adelaide. Beefsteak tomatoes. English cucumbers. And three kinds of lettuce. And . . . as a special dispensation . . . you won't even have to say thank you, Jesus.

KING BILLY: *(Enters, carrying two chairs and table.)*

DAISY: *(Puts on hat and gloves, carrying umbrella, enters.)*

ANNIE LOCK: A sun shade, Mrs. Bates. Very useful.

DAISY: Very special, Miss Lock.

ANNIE LOCK: How so, Mrs. Bates? If you pardon me, it looks serviceable . . . but quite ordinary.

DAISY: The gift is ordinary. The giver is not.

ANNIE LOCK: Oh?

DAISY: The umbrella was given to me by Queen Victoria.

ANNIE LOCK: You knew Queen Victoria.

DAISY: I met her when I was a girl. In the gardens of Balmoral Palace. I didn't belong there, of course. I must have slipped through the gates and then I saw this very distinguished woman in a large black hoopskirt walking towards me and I knew immediately who she was. I was terrified.

GRANDMA HUNT: *(Appears.)* Cat got your tongue, girl? What do you say?

DAISY: *(Curtsies.)* Good morning, mam. *(Grandma Hunt nods and exits.)* And then she reached out her hand and I took it. I shook hands with the Queen of England. And then this remarkable thing happened. She handed me the black parasol she was carrying. This very parasol. It is my most prized possession. I expect to be holding it one day when I am chosen . . .

ANNIE LOCK: Chosen?

DAISY: Officer of the British Empire and Protector of my People.

ANNIE LOCK: A great dream.

DAISY: I suppose in your line of work it's sainthood . . . But, you have to be dead first. *(Folds napkin.)* That was an excellent meal. Now I myself have no talent for cooking.

ANNIE LOCK: It's just a little hobby of mine. It helps me to relax. And I find that even my mistakes can be surprisingly tasty.

DAISY: How fortunate that food is so forgiving.

ANNIE LOCK: As opposed to?

DAISY: People.

ANNIE LOCK: Ah yes, people are much more difficult. Particularly intimate re-lationships. I suppose that's why I've never married. *(Pause.)* And you, Mrs. Bates? What about you?

DAISY: I had a husband and a son.

ANNIE LOCK: The outback is hard on marriages.

DAISY: It wasn't the country.

ANNIE LOCK: You grew apart?

DAISY: You could say that.

ANNIE LOCK: Do you must miss him?

JACK BATES: *(Appears.)*

DAISY: I killed him.

ANNIE LOCK: What?

DAISY: In my mind.

ANNIE LOCK: I know it's none of my business but . . . why?

DAISY: *(Moves center stage.)* Because he changed. Or I did. *(Shrugs.)* Because of the weather. *(Pause.)* It was so hot that day. The morning after the corroboree. I had watched them prepare for the celebration for days. The women painting their breasts with red ochre. The men feathering their thighs with white down. The wail of the didjeridoo. The oldest musical instrument in the world.

KING BILLY: How does the song come to be? *(Whispers.)* Listen! The cry of the bird, the flutter of his wings, the sound of his feet as they touch the earth, the wind shaking the tree, the water as it flows.

DAISY: The celebration had lasted all night. The dancing and the drums and the plants that brought visions. And I had so wanted to join them. To sit by their fire. *(Pause.)* And feel my life. Jack closed the shutters, barred the door of our house . . . but their songs beat in my veins . . . all night long. *(Pause.)* It was high noon. The help were sleeping it off.

JACK BATES: *(Enters.)* Where the hell are you, you lazy bastard? The cattle need branding.

KING BILLY: *(Enters, lies upon ground, snoozing.)*

JACK BATES: *(Kicks him.)* Get up.

KING BILLY: It's too hot, sah. I will do it when the sun is lower.

JACK BATES: You'll do it when I tell you.

KING BILLY: There will be a breeze soon. Now I am tired. *(Goes back to sleep.)*

JACK BATES: I pay you for working. Get up!

KING BILLY: No one works in the heat of the day . . . but a fool.

JACK BATES: Damn you! *(Seizes a branding iron, smashes King Billy on the head.)*

DAISY: No! *(Rushes to King Billy.)*

JACK BATES: Don't touch him, Daisy. Don't you dare interfere.

DAISY: He's bleeding. You almost killed him.

JACK BATES: They're wild dogs. If they snap at you, you shoot them.

DAISY: You're the one who should be shot!

JACK BATES: *(Raises his hand as if to strike her, she flinches; he stops, strides away.)*

DAISY: *(Kneels beside Billy.)* What is your name?

JACK BATES: They call me Billy. *(He struggles to rise.)*

DAISY: Wait. *(She removes kerchief from her neck, holds it to Billy's wound.)* I'll get some medicine.

KING BILLY: There is no need. I will return to my people.

DAISY: But your wound?

KING BILLY: My wound will heal. *(Pause.)* And yours?

DAISY: Mine?

KING BILLY: The hole in your heart. How will *it* heal?

DAISY: I left the next morning.

ANNIE LOCK: With your son?

DAISY: No. The outback was not a suitable place for a young boy. He needed to be in school.

ANNIE LOCK: And where is he now?

DAISY: We've lost touch.

ANNIE LOCK: What a pity!

DAISY: Yes, it's a terrible thing for a woman to leave her husband and child. *(Irony.)* Though many might wish to. *(Pause.)* Intimate relationships, Miss Lock. They can be very difficult.

ANNIE LOCK: "I love humanity, it's just people I can't stand." *(They smile.)*

DAISY: So is that why you're here, Miss Lock?

ANNIE LOCK: *(Pause.)* I'm here because I was called. To bring the gospel. The good news. The word of God. To give these people a chance to embrace our Lord Jesus and be saved. To live eternally in the everlasting light. It is my consecrated duty to bring salvation to these people. Praise the Lord. And you, Mrs. Bates? What is your mission?

DAISY: Mission? I have no mission.

ANNIE LOCK: But you have lived among these people for twenty years.

DAISY: I have been fortunate.

ANNIE LOCK: But to what purpose?

DAISY: To protect them. To keep their wisdom from passing away.

ANNIE LOCK: They are an old and a gentle people, Mrs. Bates but I take exception to wise. You yourself must admit they are not much advanced. They have no metals. No agriculture. No writing. Rather stone age.

DAISY: They have no word for possessions, either. No word for time. Do you know what they call us?

ANNIE LOCK: *(Dubious.)* What?

DAISY: People of the clock. They think we're mad. We are always in a rush. So afraid of losing time.

ANNIE LOCK: And they?

DAISY: They are the people of the dream. Time is infinite. Eternal. The ancestors are still here, alive, among them. In the rocks. In the soaks. In the animals. And my people are a part of that. Everyone and everything is connected. Spirit is everywhere. A man is counted rich by his dreaming. And by how he cares for others. "Lift a stick and I am there." *(Pause.)* Does that sound familiar?

ANNIE LOCK: If you're trying to equate these pagans with Jesus . . .

DAISY: How does that song go . . . *(Sings.)* "And He walks with me and He talks with me and He tells me . . ."

ANNIE LOCK: *(Sings.)* "I am His own;

> And the joy we share, as we tarry there
>
> None other has ever known . . ." *(Exits.)*

KING BILLY: Ancestor, ancestor . . .

DAISY: *(Undercut with King Billy's song.)* There's a song my people sing / of how after the rains / the flood waters rush across the land to meet the sea / and how the salt and the sweet roll together / over and over / in each others arms . . .

KING BILLY: Me now they are kissing /

> Again they are kissing / now they are kissing / again they are kissing /
>
> Falling over and over / Feathers and foam /
>
> Rolling over and over and over again . . .

DAISY: Sometimes I hear King Billy and his favorite wife Fat Guara making love. Through the thin canvas of the tent I feel them moving. I fall asleep to the sound of their laughter and in the morning Guara smells of . . . such . . . pleasure. *(Pause, to King Billy.)* You have so many wives. Many young and beautiful. Now, how do you manage that? *(Takes notes.)*

KING BILLY: Love magic. Everybody know how.

DAISY: How?

KING BILLY: Man make a clearing in the desert. He take white pipe clay, draw big circle on the ground . . . paint inside the circle with red ochre . . . all red . . . very red. Then he take a pole. Big strong pole. Paint pole red and cover top with white bird feathers. Like a flowing . . .

DAISY: Fountain . . .

KING BILLY: *(Nods.)* Like a flowing . . . birant . . . then he dance. Like this. *(King Billy rotates his hips.)* He sings Guraday lardimah, guraday lardimah. Gura binba. Binba.

DAISY: *(Writing.)* My body is strong and attractive. You will think sweet of me in your dreaming.

KING BILLY: Bulgary rumana mungeera grana.

DAISY: You will dream that I am making love to you.

KING BILLY: Then he rub himself with juice and goanna fat so the woman cannot stop looking at him in her dreams. She see him in the evening star. In the lightning flash. When she wake she is wet . . . like from love making. She know she belong to the man who sing in her dreams.

DAISY: And it always works?

KING BILLY: Oh yes, she cannot help but to fall in love. Even if she do not like him before.

ANNIE LOCK: *(Enters singing.)* And He walks with me and He talks with me.

KING BILLY: *(Joins Annie in the singing.)* And He tells me I am His own.

ANNIE LOCK: *(At pulpit.)* Heavenly father make me a powerful instrument of thy perfect will. Praise Jesus for whom all praise is due. Brothers and sisters our sermon today is taken from Chapter 19 of Genesis. The story of Lot. The Lord sent His emissaries into the cities on the plain, to Sodom, where Lot dwelled among the sinners. And Lot said unto the sinners, "I pray ye brethren, do not do so wickedly." But these sinners were heedless in their nakedness. And in their lust. And the Lord spoke unto Lot and said, "Get ye up out of this place of darkness. Cover thy nakedness. And come forth into a brighter land." *(Hands King Billy a pair of pants.)*

KING BILLY: *(Examines them quizzically.)* And he covered his nakedness and came forth into a brighter land.

DAISY: Every Sunday I can hear that mission bell ring. Twenty times like a jackhammer in my skull.

ANNIE LOCK: Noah had three sons. Seth and Japheth. And Ham. And everyone of us, black and white, red, and yellow comes from one of those three. It is our family tree. One day Ham, the youngest, found his father lying drunk on the deck of the arc. And Ham laughed to see his father so and called his two brothers. But the other two took pity on their father and covered his nakedness. And when Noah woke they told him of his youngest son's disrespect.

DAISY: Damn tattletails . . .

ANNIE LOCK: And Noah cursed Ham and Ham's children. "You will be slaves for ever and ever and he made them black." *(Sings.)* "And He walks with me and He talks with me . . ."

DAISY: *(Furious.)* He made them slaves!

KING BILLY: *(Nods.)* Slave part bad. *(Pause.)* But black part very pretty. "And He tells me I am His own . . ."

DAISY: She is a thoroughly useless woman.

KING BILLY: But her God has strong medicine, Kabbarli. It stops the sweats and the shaking. My youngest boy Wagarri; it saves his life.

DAISY: She has quinine for the malaria. I have no money for it. It is one good thing that she does. *(Pause.)* I decide to be charitable. It is almost Christmas. I invite Annie Lock to dinner. And I think . . . kangaroo would be nice. King Billy does the marketing.

KING BILLY: How to find the kangaroo? Dance the dance of the kangaroo. Sing his songs. Paint his picture. Fast for three days. Wait for the dream. Meet him in the dream. Listen to what he tells you. Take our best spear and walk into the bush and look. Look for where he leaves his footsteps. Stop at the rock, blow on the moss, see his track and follow. Think softly to him, "Ancestor, I am coming towards you to honor the purpose for which you were born." If you are worthy, he will offer himself to you. And when it is over, you thank him and bury his heart in the desert so he will come again. And then you bring the tail to Kabbarli.

ANNIE LOCK: *(Enters, sits on the floor by Daisy's tent, ties napkin around her chin.)* Oh, Mrs. Bates, your tent reminds me so much of home. Every Christmas the whole town, from the castle to the river, becomes a fairy land of tents and vendors and lights and oh . . . the foods. My favorite was the weisseworst, juicy white sausage thick as your arm. And you, Mrs. Bates, what are your Christmas memories?

DAISY: I remember the Christmas my father died.

ANNIE LOCK: Oh, I'm so sorry.

DAISY: Don't be. He was a terrible drunk and I got to live with my grandmother.

GRANDMA HUNT: *(Enters.)* We laid him out in the parlor. Father Boylan gave him his last rites. And when he left, we opened your Da's mouth . . .

DAISY: And put salt on his tongue.

GRANDMA HUNT: To keep the devil from lightfooting in and stealing his soul. *(Exits.)*

DAISY: *(Smiles, to Annie.)* Do you believe in the devil, Miss Lock?

ANNIE LOCK: I have seen him, Mrs. Bates.

DAISY: And God? Have you seen Him?

ANNIE LOCK: I pray every day that I will.

DAISY: I hope you do, too. *(Calls.)* Billy, may we have our first course, please. *(King Billy presents a platter of small canapés. Daisy and Annie take one, chew.)*

ANNIE LOCK: *(Mouth full.)* Delicious. What is it?

DAISY: I'm glad you like it.

ANNIE LOCK: It's quite complex.

DAISY: Yes it is.

ANNIE LOCK: Puff pastry around . . . scrambled eggs is it . . . with a lovely aftertaste of mushrooms. What do you call it?

DAISY: Whittchity grubs.

ANNIE LOCK: Whitticity what?

DAISY: Grubs. Caterpillars. They're in season.

ANNIE LOCK: *(Swallows with difficulty.)*

DAISY: We have a lovely meal planned. A holiday mixed grill. Filet of snake, cutlet of lizard, and the pièce de résistance . . . tail of red kangaroo. And to wash it down. *(Pulls out a bottle of brandy.)* A tipple?

ANNIE LOCK: *(Holds out her glass.)* Yes, please.

DAISY: *(Pours generous amount.)* Part of my special cough medicine. Grandma Hunt's recipe.

GRANDMA HUNT: *(Appears.)* One tablespoon lemon juice. One tablespoon vinegar. One tablespoon olive oil. *(Pause.)* Fill with brandy. *(Pause.)* Don't forget the brandy. *(Exits.)*

DAISY: Works wonders. Only problem my people want to keep taking it long after they've stopped coughing.

ANNIE LOCK: *(Downs her drink and extends her empty glass.)* Really?

DAISY: They think they're putting something over on me. Just like with my lizards.

ANNIE LOCK: Your lizards?

DAISY: My thorny devils. My mingaris; I love them. They are so fierce. The female is the hunter. She invades an ant hill and stands there for hours sucking up ants while the ant soldiers swarm all over her, looking for a bit of flesh to bite. Her only unprotected part is her soft lower lip and the ants attack. But she stands her ground, tossing her head like a stallion, and . . . she never stops eating. I have several tame mingaris. I tie a red string around their legs so I know they're mine.

KING BILLY: And when we want sugar, we untie the string.

DAISY: And sell them back. *(King Billy laughs.)*

ANNIE LOCK: Isn't that encouraging lying, Mrs. Bates?

DAISY: It's a game, Miss Lock. We enjoy it.

ANNIE LOCK: Well, yes, but it's establishing a bad pattern. Are we not here to teach them our way of thinking?

DAISY: Have you tried to learn theirs?

ANNIE LOCK: A bit. But it seems quite muddled to me. The whole idea of dreamtime . . . the past, the present, the future . . . all existing at the same time. No clocks, no calendars . . . it all runs together.

DAISY: It all weaves together. Billy, my sticks. *(Billy brings out sticks, lays them on the table.)* Now . . . *(She arranges them . . . in a group of three and two.)* Now Miss Lock, what do you see?

ANNIE LOCK: A group of three. And a group of two.

DAISY: Correct. And King Billy.

KING BILLY: A group of three. And a group of two.

DAISY: Excellent. *(She removes one stick from first group, holds it in her hand, so there are two groups of two.)* Now?

ANNIE LOCK: Me?

DAISY: Please.

ANNIE LOCK: Two groups of two.

DAISY: King Billy?

KING BILLY: I see a group of two and a group of two.

ANNIE LOCK: Exactly.

KING BILLY: And I see one stick that is three making.

ANNIE LOCK: Three making?

DAISY: *(Waves third stick.)* Process, Miss Lock. Potential. What ever was is and forever will be. If God is everywhere, God is everywhen.

ANNIE LOCK: What!

DAISY: Never mind. How do you like your kangaroo, Miss Lock? Sautéed or stewed? *(Pause, to audience.)* We didn't give up on her though, King Billy and I. Not yet. We tried to share what we knew.

KING BILLY: Everybody wants to know about this Dreamtime. They ask what it is? Where it is? How do you know if you are in it? *(Pause.)* You are always in it. Asleep or awake. Dead or alive. So not to worry.

In the beginning there is only the Earth and nothing on it . . . no mountains, no deserts, no plants, no animals, no people . . . no nothing. Until . . . the Ancestors leap up from under the Earth, brush the clay from their thighs, and begin to walk. And each step they take, they sing out the name of a living thing *(He demonstrates, slowly walking, lifting one foot after another, singing.)* . . . acacia tree . . . red rock . . . kangaroo . . . wallaby . . . water hole . . . whirlwind . . . honey ant . . . full moon . . . *(To Daisy with a twinkle.)* . . . yemerr . . . birant. They sing the whole world into being. And that, children, is the Dreamtime.

The ancestors lay the songs in the land and we follow them today. We walk the songlines. And dream the world again. Each of us is born into a dreaming and a song. And we learn it by heart, so it is always with us. And we pass the song from elder to younger. It tells us where we are and where we are to go.

ANNIE LOCK: That's what I've wanted to know. Always. "Tell me your heart's desire," I would beg my little friends. And they would say things like new ice skates and fur mittens. Then I would tell them mine. Eight years old and all I wanted was one thing . . .

DAISY: What?

ANNIE LOCK: *(Softly.)* To be Mary.

DAISY: Mary, the mother of God?

ANNIE LOCK: Well . . . like Mary. I thought it was like a club.

DAISY: Once you've had one immaculate conception . . . ?

ANNIE LOCK: By the time I found out that it wasn't going to happen again, I was committed to the church. To becoming a missionary. *(Pause.)* It's a hard life sometimes, but it does have its compensations. I enjoy the travel and I just love those darling little pickaninnies.

DAISY: *(To audience.)* God she was ignorant. She wrote me a letter once attesting to her tolerance, "I do believe in my heart, Mrs. Bates, that all human beans are equal." Beans! I imagined us all planted in a row, waiting to sprout. *(Pause.)* Oh, but sometimes she did try to understand.

ANNIE LOCK: Mrs. Bates, I have heard that the blackfellas can read the thoughts of a tribesman twenty miles away. Now how can that be?

DAISY: They have this gift because their minds are clear. Receptive. For them, everything is one.

ANNIE LOCK: And yet they do not understand the concept of the Almighty.

DAISY: They spend their day in worship.

ANNIE LOCK: Where, Mrs. Bates? I have yet to see it.

DAISY: *(To audience.)* So we take her, King Billy and I, to see the paintings. *(Daisy, King Billy and Annie thread their way through a simulated cave with projected paintings.)*

DAISY: You are deeply privileged, Miss Lock. This is a sacred place. These paintings are ten thousand years older than the caves of Lascaux.

ANNIE LOCK: What strange creatures? Are those halos around their heads?

KING BILLY: That is their dreaming.

ANNIE LOCK: And their organs. Like x-rays.

KING BILLY: It is how we see them in the dreaming. There is no inside. No outside.

ANNIE LOCK: And these hands? A forest of red hands?

KING BILLY: It is the mark each of us makes as we learn the dreaming.

DAISY: And then we take her deeper into the cave. To the heart of the darkness. To the holy of holies. To the beginning. To the field of creation. The flames of the torch dance upon a wall of shimmering dots. Of pulsating energy.

ANNIE LOCK: *(In awe.)* What is this?

DAISY: And she looks upon it, transfixed.

ANNIE LOCK: Mary Mother of God!

DAISY: She turns and flees. We run after her. In the darkness, she falls and fractures her arm. I try to help her, but she'll have none of it. Her arm never heals properly. *(Pause.)* So there are no more dinners, but we do keep close watch on each other. Through King Billy. *(Pause.)* The mission makes great strides. The drought is her ally.

KING BILLY: The dormitories are up, Kabbarli. Very fine. Corrugated tin. With wooden floors.

DAISY: *(Measured.)* And have you moved in, then?

KING BILLY: Some nights we stay, but not when it is cold. You cannot dig into the sand to keep warm and you cannot bring your dogs in to keep you warm. And when it is hot, you cannot lie under the trees and find the breeze. That house keeps hot when it is hot and cold when it is cold. *(Pause.)* And clothes. We now have clothes. Each woman has a dress. Each man a shirt and pants. Sista Lock says we must wear them every day. They get dirty and they tear. We tie them on with rope.

Sista Lock cuts the children's hair with big scissors and scrubs their bodies. So hard, Kabbarli, I think she means to rub their skin off. Sista Lock reads from the Bible every day. We call it the story of Thou shalt not. And we march. Do you hear us in your camp, Kabbarli? We sing loud.

(Annie Lock enters, cranks up old phonograph, grabs two metal plates, begins marching and singing, "Onward Christian Soldiers" followed by King Billy.)

DAISY: Despite the mission, my people are loyal. They come at night to sit by my campfire and I fill their pipes and rub the aching limbs of the old and they tell me their stories.

KING BILLY: The stories of the time before time began.

DAISY: Of the rainbow snake and the white dingo and the seven emu sisters. And then I put out a bit of bread and porridge and we eat. My people and me. Oh, I am no match for Annie Lock. Her cooking pot holds a whole month of my meager rations. And she has an entire building filled with government supplies. She has all the food. And all the water. *(Pause.)* It does not rain for months. The clouds gather, big black clouds heavy with rain. They hang overhead for days and then the wind blows them apart before they can drop their moisture. I think they do that just to torture me. Everything dries up. Suspends itself. All I can do is wait. *(Pause.)* And my mind turns on itself. And my doubts swarm like flies. What am I doing here? Who do I think I am? In my baking tent, in my threadbare skirt, scratching words in tattered notebooks that no one will read. And even if they did, am I getting it right? I crawl from my cot, take a stalk of cabbage and nail it on a post outside my tent, my eyes so long for a bit of green. And I dream of home.

(Grandma Hunt appears.)

DAISY: The smell of the turf fires, the black-faced sheep, the cows with tags in their ears, pretty as young girls. The green hills of Ireland.

GRANDMA HUNT: Look at yourself, Daisy Mae, you wild thing. Your hair's a bird nest. Sit still, now. Let's get the brambles out.

DAISY: *(Sits happily as Grandma Hunt untangles her hair.)* Owww.

GRANDMA HUNT: We can cut it all off you know.

DAISY: I wish you would.

GRANDMA HUNT: It's your best feature. It'll catch you a man some day. And that lovely swan neck. *(Examines it.)* If you could see it for the dirt.

DAISY: I don't want a man.

GRANDMA HUNT: You will in time. It's a natural thing.

DAISY: A husband to cook for. A house to clean. Babies! No . . . I want something else.

GRANDMA HUNT: And what is that?

DAISY: *(Pulls the comb away, cuddles in her grandmother's lap.)* Magic.

GRANDMA HUNT: And what kind of magic shall it be this time? Ghost and goblins? Witches and warlocks?

DAISY: Tell me about the fairy people.

GRANDMA HUNT: The fairy folk is it? As you well know, they used to live among us. A whole kingdom right under this very tree.

DAISY: And they made the grass green and the sky blue.

GRANDMA HUNT: And they made the cows to calve and the sheep to lamb and the horses to foal.

DAISY: And the mums and das to . . .

GRANDMA HUNT: *(Quickly.)* Do the same thing. *(Pause.)* But then the church came and the world wasn't big enough for the church and the fairies. And the people stopped believing in them and the fairies fled.

DAISY: To the fairy hills and we can't see them anymore.

GRANDMA HUNT: But someday the veils will drop from our eyes and we shall see the world again as it truly is . . . an enchanted, shimmering place where every brook can dance and every stone can sing. *(Exits.)*

DAISY: When the drought breaks, the wind comes first. A howling. A fierce flapping. I hear it in my dreams. I wake to such fear. My notebooks! But they are safe. Locked in my trunk. The wind seizes my tent like a sail and if it weren't battened down, it would fly like a great white bird through the sky and I with it. I hold onto the rafters all night long. And then the rain comes. The blessed, driving rain.

I run out of my tent. Open my mouth. Drink the rain. Feel it plaster my hair and nightgown. Run down my face. Fill my buckets and tins. And the next morning the desert is in bloom. It is as if every seed in the universe has been lying dormant, waiting for that moment to open and sprout. Trees grow thick green leaves, wild flowers bloom fuchsia and gold, frogs gulp and blink, and snakes shed their dry skins and dance in the gullies.

And it is all the more sweet for the waiting. *(Pause.)* It is the night after the big rain that I hear the drums. And the clicking of the boomerangs. My people have returned to me. *(Pause.)* I wake to see you standing beside my bed.

KING BILLY: *(Enters, his face and chest painted, wearing a feather headdress.)* Come, Kabbarli. It is time.

DAISY: And I rise out of my tent and see the circle of men.

KING BILLY: Fifty warriors. Holding spears.

DAISY: Oiled and naked. Headdresses of cockatoo feathers. Bodies painted white and red. Hair belts around their waists, the tassels dripping blood.

KING BILLY: Single file we walk along the cliff. Fires lit on each side.

DAISY: Boys beat the flames with green branches. Clouds of smoke. We come to a clearing. A circle.

KING BILLY: *(Shouts.)* Yudu!

DAISY: Everyone closes his eyes except for me.

KING BILLY: And each man in turn brings you his churinga.

DAISY: Nine feet tall, they are. Wooden shields, carved and painted with the totem of each clan. The teaching from the Dreaming.

KING BILLY: And each comes forward and lifts it above his head.

DAISY: The way a priest might lift the host. And carries it toward me . . . and touches the wood to my forehead, to my breast, to my belly . . . And there are present, the clan of the emu and of the kangaroo . . .

KING BILLY: And the dingo from Victoria Plains and the water lily from the Capel River . . .

DAISY: And the black snake and the silver fish . . .

KING BILLY: And the wild cherry and the sea eagle.

DAISY: And they are there as they were from the beginning. The men and the creatures. And a man becomes a fish and the fish becomes a kangaroo and the kangaroo becomes a mountain and the mountain becomes . . . And they whisper their secrets. *(Chants over the sound of the didjeridoo.)* There is no death. Only returns. There is no death. No death. No death. Only. Only. Only. Returns. And I am a part of them . . . the only woman, black or white, to ever see this ceremony. But I do not know why I have been chosen. And why . . . now?

KING BILLY: You are now the keeper of the sacred boards, Kabbarli. You must hide them from the white man. Bury them in the deepest cave. You must protect them with your life. *(Pause.)* The black snake is coming.

DAISY: The railroad is expanding. Soon the black steam engine will be tearing apart the bones of the ancestors. The people of the clock have declared war upon the people of the dream. The black snake and the rainbow snake are at war.

KING BILLY: *(Shouts.)* Nardooooooo. *(Wail of the didjeridoo.)*

Scene Two

DAISY: They bring in three thousand men to build the railroad. First the teams to break the rock with pick and shovel. And then the men to move the desert. Red sand for hundreds of miles. Each day the men push against the red waves and each night the wind blows the sand back. And each morning the tracks are covered. Some of the men go mad, walk around in circles, but the others, go on and on . . . like blind desert moles. Until the job is done.

KING BILLY: They call the railroad stations by the old names . . . . bookalo . . . woocalla . . . pimba . . . wirramina . . . kingoonya, but it does no good for there is a sadness on the land. There is no one to remember its history or sing its songs. It is like a child without a mother.

DAISY: And the young women follow the railroad and the white men make them prostitutes and gave them diseases and half-caste babies. And the young women kill themselves or do worse.

KING BILLY: They eat their babies.

DAISY: No!

KING BILLY: I seen them with my own eyes. Nardoo!

DAISY: Nardoo. Homeless. Losing your homeland. Belonging no where. *(Pause to audience.)* They would become beggars. The train and Annie Lock will make my people, once kings and queens, into beggars and tramps. The train stops and the passengers lean out from the carriages and pelt my people with bits of their leftover dinner and coins. My women take off their dresses to wrap the goods and carry them away and the passengers laugh at the show. I cannot bear it. *(Pause.)* There is to be a government conference in Adelaide on the State of the Aborigine. Everyone knows they are dying away. I must go there. I must save them. *(Annie Lock enters, Daisy walks toward her.)* You realize I would not come to you if there was anyone else.

ANNIE LOCK: My pleasure, Mrs. Bates. God provides. And quite well, I might add. A horse carriage to the train. A first-class ticket to Adelaide. I realize you're opposed to the train but under the circumstances . . . and a room in the best hotel with a private bath. And I do think an event like this deserves a new hat. *(Holds out a pink one with silk roses.)* Never worn.

DAISY: *(Puts on hat, walks forward.)*

RADCLIFFE-JONES: *(Silences applause.)* It is my great pleasure to present Mrs. Daisy Mae Bates. Many of you will remember her name from my article last November in Indigenous Peoples on "Genital Mutilation." Although Mrs. Bates has no formal anthropological training, I found her research among the tribes of the Ooldea Soak to be insightful and I say so, in my footnotes. Mrs. Bates.

DAISY: I am shaking when I reach the podium. I haven't seen so many white people in a long time. They smell strange . . . sweet and musky like rotting meat. Their hands when they touch me are wet, not like my peoples'. Black skin is dry and soft like paper. And my peoples' voices are low and deep. And there is a stillness as they listen. There is no stillness in the room.

A sea of white faces, white badges on their breasts, white paper on their laps, pencils poised. I breathe deep like the wind in the mulga trees. Lift my shoulders like the sea eagle. My people can sing their dreaming for three days without missing a note. I can do this . . . "Ladies and gentlemen, I stand before you not as Mrs. Daisy Mae Bates of Dublin, Ireland but as Kabbarli, the great white grandmother of the never-never. I stand before you to speak on behalf of my people.

The history of the white race and their subjugation and destruction of the aboriginal people of Australia is a deep tragedy. Captain Cook is the first to land on these shores. He writes in his journal, "These people want nothing of us but that we leave."

But we do not leave. We stay and we steal their land . . . "Terras nullius" we call it. No man's land, we call it. As if their occupation for one hundred thousand years is nothing. Because they build no structures, fly no flag, we steal their land. We steal the land from a peaceful and noble people.

Now I ask you to return it. It is sacred land and they are lost without it. They need a big area, at least two hundred thousand square miles so it will be possible to walk far when their hearts are hot. And it must belong to them exclusively. No whites. No roads. No trains. No alcohol. No prostitution. No syphilis.

My people need to live in their own shelters. They may look crude to us but they keep out the wind and let them watch the stars and the moon. They must have their dogs. They hunt with them and sleep with them on cold nights. The police raid their camps and shoot their dogs and my people are heartbroken . . .

We must build a big fence around the land to keep out the foxes and feral cats that destroy the animals that belong to the desert so there will be enough food. And my people could hunt and gather in the old way.

I ask to be their protector. In the ways of the world, they are like children. But they are wise children. In time I will teach them the ways of the white man and those who wish may enter the world of automobiles and cities. And the rest are free to stay with me and with the old ways.

(During the next speech we see King Billy playing a haunting alarm on the didjeridoo.)

Oh, my friends, the time is drawing near. We are losing the oldest and truest people on the earth. They are dying. Not of hunger. Not of sickness. But of sadness. Of profound sorrow. They are losing their home. Nardoo. Nardoo. My people call it nardoo. The only cure is to give them back their land.

RADCLIFFE-JONES: *(Enters, carrying two glasses of wine.)* Mrs. Bates, you're looking so well. Remarkably well for a woman of your age. And what a becoming hat.

DAISY: Thank you. But what about my speech?

RADCLIFFE-JONES: Excellent, Mrs. Bates. *(Hands her glass.)* People really enjoyed it.

DAISY: Enjoyed it?

RADCLIFFE-JONES: I did especially. I have a new theory, Mrs. Bates. I call it a passion for place. I postulate that men enter the primitive to tame it and women . . . to become one with it.

DAISY: What about my proposal?

RADCLIFFE-JONES: Your proposal?

DAISY: To give back the land.

RADCLIFFE-JONES: Oh, it will be considered, Mrs. Bates.

DAISY: When?

RADCLIFFE-JONES: We will form a committee. *(Clinks glasses.)* To your very good health. Mrs. Bates. Cheers! Like that hat!

DAISY: *(Takes off hat, crushes it under her arm.)* My mouth is filled with black ash. A chain of steel binds my chest. I had failed. I could not protect my peoples' lands. I cannot wait to get home. Yet, the moment I get there I know something is wrong. None of my people are there to meet me. I rush to my tent. It is still there. Everything inside just as I left it. My precious notebooks untouched. I race to the cave where I have buried the churingas. They are there. Oiled and beautiful. Waiting. But there is such a silence. Such an emptiness. And then I know. My people are gone . . . They would not leave without telling me.

KING BILLY: *(Enters.)* The police come, Kabbarli. With their guns and their clubs. They come for the children. They tear them from their mothers' arms. When we cling to them, the police beat us and put us in chains. I hear my boy Waggari cry, "Father. Where are you?" But I cannot go to him. They take him far away. Change his name. Forbid him to speak our language. Sing his dreaming. They tell him he has no father.

DAISY: *(Strides forward, holding a large blood-tipped bone.)* Where are you? You snake! You slime! You waited until I was gone. Coward, come out here and face me.

ANNIE LOCK: *(From backstage.)* What's that you've got there, Daisy Bates?

DAISY: A pointing bone and I'm schooled in using it. Don't think I won't.

ANNIE LOCK: *(Scoffs.)* Black magic.

DAISY: This part turns your belly to stone. The red sets your blood on fire . . . This is blackfella business. The oldest religion on earth.

ANNIE LOCK: Only if you believe it, Daisy. *(Comes out.)* And I don't.

DAISY: Then believe in this, you devil. *(Pulls out .32 revolver.)*

ANNIE LOCK: *(Runs for cover.)* Now, don't be hasty.

DAISY: Come on out here. Let your God protect you.

ANNIE LOCK: My God isn't magic. He can't stop bullets.

DAISY: He can walk on water. Give him a challenge. *(Shoots a bullet in the air.)*

ANNIE LOCK: You won't accomplish anything by killing me.

DAISY: *(Shoots again.)*

ANNIE LOCK: There'll be others. God's soldiers are legion.

DAISY: You sent me to Adelaide so you could steal my people.

ANNIE LOCK: They came willingly.

DAISY: *(Another shot.)* Liar!

ANNIE LOCK: Put that down and I'll tell you what happened.

DAISY: *(Lowers revolver.)* Come on then. Make it fast and make it true.

ANNIE LOCK: I didn't know about the police. That was the government's doing, not the church. Things were moving too slowly for them. I wouldn't have taken the children. Not like that. But the others, they came on their own for the flour and sugar, for the tobacco.

DAISY: They don't need those things.

ANNIE LOCK: But they want them.

DAISY: Because you tempt them.

ANNIE LOCK: It's not just the food. They want the new. We all do. Curiosity. It's irresistible. They've heard about radios, cars, movies. They want to see them.

DAISY: I haven't seen a movie.

ANNIE LOCK: But you can, Daisy. Anytime you want, you can pick yourself up and get on that train and go to the city and turn on the electric light and open a tap and have a proper bath. And they can't. You're here by choice. They are here by necessity. All I want to do is give them a choice. Teach them to read and write. Teach them a trade. So they can walk out of the desert as freely as you walked in.

DAISY: You will teach them to be servants. They won't know what they're losing.

ANNIE LOCK: And you do? You know what's good for them? Excuse me, Daisy, but if that isn't paternalism, what is?

DAISY: They have what we are searching for. They live in a paradise where everything is sacred.

ANNIE LOCK: Exactly . . . And that's what our Savior Jesus Christ came down from Heaven to teach us. Everything is sacred. Everything is one. So why not worship it at the Mission?

DAISY: *(Lifts pistol, points it at Annie.)* I'll give you to three. One

ANNIE LOCK: Pray with me.

DAISY: Two . . .

ANNIE LOCK: You cannot stop progress.

DAISY: Three . . . *(Raises pistol.)*

ANNIE LOCK: *(Flees.)* God damn you.

DAISY: It's a good thing she ran . . . for I would have shot her. I am that mad. Instead I lie upon my bed and cry like a child for the first time in . . . I don't know how long. There are no more visits from Annie Lock. In fact, there are no more visits from anyone. My people are at the mission now and the mission is their world. I stay in my tent with my photographs and my memories. I think perhaps I will die there. I hope that I can die there. I think about it often.

JACK BATES: we were riding through the desert in a storm, Daisy. A massive burst of lightning hit a hollow tree right in front of us. It cracked open and there stood the skeleton of a man. He held a spear in the bones of his hand. He stood tall for a moment before he fell.

DAISY: How long was he waiting for that storm to release him? *(Pause.)* I have seen many burials among my people. Many births. And many deaths. When someone is sick beyond healing, the people gather round. They wait, patiently, for days until the final hour when the breathing stops.

KING BILLY: The men will dance around you, crying in despair. And the women will beat the hard sand with the flat of their hands.

DAISY: They will make a nest of fresh green acacia branches. At the head a circle of white sand. Like a green bed with a white pillow.

KING BILLY: And you will feel the weight of our bodies as we throw ourselves across your grave and hold you like a lover.

DAISY: I had a lover once who licked the crumbs from my fingers. We had a child. It was a painful birth. And I wanted no more. So Jack and I slept apart.

JACK BATES: I never should have agreed to that, Daisy.

DAISY: Why did you then?

JACK BATES: I thought you'd change your mind.

DAISY: There's a story I want to remember tonight, King Billy. About a mother and a son.

KING BILLY: So many stories, Kabbarli, about mothers and their children.

DAISY: About a mother who leaves her son. Under a tree. While she goes hunting.

KING BILLY: *(Enacts the story.)* Ah, Bunbundoolooey! *(Pause.)* Not here. Not near. Not far. Not up. Not down. Now now. Not then. But once. Once upon a time. Bunbundooley, the mother feel a heat in her heart and she must go on walkabout. She put her child, a baby boy, Bunbundoolooey, who can only crawl, into her goolay sack and sling him on her back. She start out to hunt. She come to a clump of wattle trees. She see some fat whittchity grubs, which are very good to eat. She pick them up and dig with her yam stick to get more.

DAISY: She goes from tree to tree, finding grubs at every one. She wants to gather them all, so she puts down her goolay sack so she can hunt better. She wanders further and further away, never once thinking about her baby, until at last she reaches the far country.

KING BILLY: The baby wake up and crawl out of the goolay sack. First he only crawl about but soon he grow stronger. He grow into a boy and then into a man. And all the time he is growing he do not see his mother.

DAISY: But in the far country at last, one day Bundundooley, the mother, remembers the baby she has left. "Oh," she cries, "I must go to him. I must have been mad when I forgot him. My poor baby."

KING BILLY: And she run, fast as she can, back to the clump of wattle trees. When she reach the spot, she see the tracks of her baby, first crawling, then standing, then walking, then running. She follow the tracks as they grow bigger and bigger until she reach a camp.

DAISY: No one is in the camp but a fire has been made. So she waits.

KING BILLY: And then at last she see a man coming toward the camp and she know he is her baby grown to a man. As he draw near, she run to meet him . . .

DAISY: "Bunbundoolooey, I am your mother, the mother who forgot you as a baby and left you. But now, I have come to find you." And she runs forward to embrace him.

KING BILLY: But the son, no answer do he make with his tongue, but he bend to the ground and pick up heavy stone.

DAISY: And he throws it with such force that she falls to the ground dead. *(Pause.)* Why did he do that? *(Pause.)* He hated her?

KING BILLY: No, Kabbarli, he did not know her. He had no mother to teach him.

DAISY: Teach him what?

KING BILLY: Loving kindness. It is what mothers teach. *(Beat.)*

DAISY: When I left Ooldea, the government found me a room in a boarding house in Adelaide. I had no money. All I had was my doctoring kit . . . Grandma Hunt's remedies. The brandy was useful. The city was so confusing. I couldn't see the sky for the buildings. Sometimes I forgot where I was and just froze right in the middle of the street. *(Amplified sounds of car horns, trolley cables whirring, people shouting, clocks striking the hour.)* And I had to be rescued. A policeman came and took my arm and led me across the street. He talked to me real slow and loud like I was a crazy, "Here we go, little lady, nothing to be afraid of." And then they take me back to my room. I don't make a fuss. I like my supper. Tea and bar of dark chocolate. *(Pause.)* It is so lonely here. I was never so lonely in nature. Here in the city everyone locks their doors. In the desert I have seen my people making love and giving birth and dying and I was always a part of it. I can't bear to be shut up in these four walls. *(Pause.)* There's a shop in town that sells what I need tonight. As soon as I walk through the door, I recognize her. Even from the back.

ANNIE LOCK: *(Back to audience, takes a bottle of brandy from shelf.)* So how much is this brandy, then? I can't read the sticker. It's in such small print.

DAISY: It's the cheapest one you can get. But you'd best not take it straight though. It could kill you.

ANNIE LOCK: It's not for me.

DAISY: Of course not. Why would you be needing spirits? You've got the Holy Ghost.

ANNIE LOCK: *(Wheels around.)* Let it go, Mrs. Bates. It's over.

DAISY: Of course it's over. You won.

ANNIE LOCK: Hardly. *(Pause.)* The mission's gone.

DAISY: When?

ANNIE LOCK: Years. There's nothing left. If you go out there all you'll find are rusted water pipes sticking out of the ground like so many question marks . . . The chapel, the school house, the hospital . . . all buried. You can't keep the desert out. Mountains of sand, blowing through the windows, under the doors. There is no station any more. Not even a notice board. No one would know it was ever there.

DAISY: And my people?

ANNIE LOCK: The army took the men to fight. They make excellent scouts. They can look at an airplane when it's a dot in the sky and tell you what kind of plane it is, and where it was going and how fast. They've moved to the cities now. They can vote. They have jobs. They listen to jazz on the radio and go to the movies.

DAISY: Not all of them?

ANNIE LOCK: No, many of them become sick with drink.

DAISY: And what would you do if everything is taken from you? *(Gestures toward their own bottles, an ironic smile.)* Where are they?

ANNIE LOCK: Hard to say. They've taken white peoples' names and forgotten their own.

DAISY: *(Sadly.)* Nardoo.

ANNIE LOCK: What's that?

DAISY: Nothing.

ANNIE LOCK: Nardoo . . . yes? *(Daisy nods.)* Homeless. I'm trying to learn the language now that I have some time.

DAISY: No more missionizing?

ANNIE LOCK: Too old for that.

DAISY: You haven't given up on God?

ANNIE LOCK: No.

DAISY: Still hoping to see Him?

ANNIE LOCK: Well, yes . . . any day now. Age is an advantage there.

DAISY: Only one I can think of.

ANNIE LOCK: Yah! Everything hurts and everyone's gone.

DAISY: I thought you'd be living with your "community."

ANNIE LOCK: I live alone. Like you.

Daisy What do you know about the way I live?

ANNIE LOCK: I know a lot about you. I'm interested. Just the way you were interested in me.

DAISY: *(Indignant.)* What makes you think . . .

ANNIE LOCK: It went both ways. Through the same source. He thought we had a great deal in common.

DAISY: Like what?

KING BILLY: *(Appears but not to them.)* Two white women far from home. No husband. No child. Come to save what is not theirs. Two lonely women who will not join hands.

ANNIE LOCK: Oh, he never said exactly.

DAISY: *(Pauses.)* We came to the same place, all right. But for very different reasons. You wanted to change everything.

ANNIE LOCK: And you wanted to change nothing. *(Pause.)* King Billy said you kept notebooks.

DAISY: Fifty-two of them.

ANNIE LOCK: A lifetime's work. *(Pause.)* Where are the notebooks now?

DAISY: Safe.

ANNIE LOCK: Where?

DAISY: Under my bed.

ANNIE LOCK: Never been published?

DAISY: There's no money for that.

ANNIE LOCK: And if there were?

DAISY: From where?

ANNIE LOCK: From me.

DAISY: You have money?

ANNIE LOCK: Enough for a book.

DAISY: Why would you want to publish my notebooks?

ANNIE LOCK: It's the only record of the mission.

DAISY: Not a very favorable one.

ANNIE LOCK: But truthful. Well then?

DAISY: They're too big for one book.

ANNIE LOCK: We'll edit them.

DAISY: We?

ANNIE LOCK: You and I. After all, who knows as much?

DAISY: It won't work.

ANNIE LOCK: We're running out of time.

DAISY: I can wait.

ANNIE LOCK: The ink is fading. The paper shattering. The only record will disappear.

DAISY: You're not the only one who can publish them.

ANNIE LOCK: I'm the only one who's offered.

DAISY: Why you? You never understood them. You ran from them.

ANNIE LOCK: That day in the cave?

DAISY: Yes.

ANNIE LOCK: In the mouth of the snake?

DAISY: Yes?

ANNIE LOCK: I saw something.

DAISY: What?

(Annie Lock is silent.)

DAISY: *(Reflects, then remembers Annie's cry that day.)* . . . Mary, Mother of God?

ANNIE LOCK: I thought I saw her face. *(Pause.)* It could have just been the light.

DAISY: Yes, of course.

ANNIE LOCK: We never can know.

DAISY: No.

ANNIE LOCK: But still. *(Pause.)* I can't seem to forget it. *(Pause.)* So, about your book. We can call it, "Daisy Bates and the History of the Aborigines."

DAISY: *(Pause.)* I will call it, "The Passing of a People" . . . *(Pause.)* It will be a sad book.

ANNIE LOCK: Here's to our sad books, Daisy. *(Annie sits on the edge of stage, beckons to Daisy to sit beside her, opens her bottle of brandy, takes a swig, offers bottle to Daisy who refuses, then relents, takes a modest swig.)* Perhaps when you bring the notebooks, you'll stay for dinner?

DAISY: I no longer eat dinner. *(Pause. It is difficult to say this.)* But I do thank you.

ANNIE LOCK: Another time, then. *(Exits.)*

DAISY: So that's why she ran. *(Muses.)* Ran from the absolute. It's what I have always run towards. Once you live in the center . . . every place else is exile. *(Pause. Returns to tent, crouches by trunk.)* That night I dream I am back in the desert. My red desert. In the heat. In the silence. And the wind comes up. All at once. Like a fury. It tears open the lid of my trunk, seizes my notebooks in its dry hands, rips them apart, and flings them into the air. And I cannot move. I am rooted to the ground like a dead tree. My mouth fills with sand and I watch as the work of my life disappears.

(The trunk opens and a storm of dry leaves are blown around the stage. Each character catches a leaf and it transforms into a notebook page. As they speak to Daisy, they hand her the page.)

RADCLIFFE-JONES: Would you be so kind as to look at these obscene drawings, Mrs. Bates?

GRANDMA HUNT: Hands and heels down, Daisy, head and heart up.

JACK BATES: And what can I offer you, Miss O'Dwyer?

KING BILLY: Kabbarli.

ANNIE LOCK: Sooner than you think your people will be wanting it all back again . . . their history . . . the boomerangs, the corroborrees, the didjeridoos, the totems, and the ceremonies. And the cave paintings. They'll be reading your notebooks, Daisy. And some child in the green hills of wherever will dream of leaving one world and entering another.

RADCLIFFE-JONES: When Daisy died, they gave her quite a funeral. Lots of pomp and ceremony. All sorts of people came . . . scientists and dignitaries and government officials and a man who came all the way from California, said he was her son.

DAISY: *(With surprise and joy.)* William. *(Deep regret.)* I would have so liked to meet him.

KING BILLY: *(To Daisy.)* Come. We must walk many miles into the bush and I will show you the place where the earth prepares the tree. And we will run our hands softly over the branches. See this one has no music in her. *(Pause.)* This one is too young but she will be good in her time. *(Pause.)* But in this one the spirit moves. It has been waiting since the Dreamtime. Waiting to be born. *(Sound of the didjeridoo.)*

DAISY: *(Stands center.)* I see my people walking towards me out of the desert . . . naked and shining. With painted breasts, the old women are dancing. Their granddaughters follow. And we are making such plans!

END OF PLAY

The Last Schwartz

By Deborah Zoe Laufer

To my family, both the one I was born into and the one I married into,
for being so remarkably loving, supportive, and functional.
I'd also like to thank my friends at Juilliard, Florida Stage, Joe Kraemer,
Barry Talkington, and especially David, Alex, and Charlie.

PLAYWRIGHT'S BIOGRAPHY

Deborah Laufer's play, *The Last Schwartz,* received its world premiere at Florida Stage in Manalapan, Florida, in November 2002.

In 2001 she took part in the Cherry Lane Alternative where her play, *Out of Sterno,* was produced. It is now under option for an Off Broadway production. Also in 2001, she completed a playwriting fellowship at the Dramatists Guild, mentored by Arthur Kopit. In 1999 and 2000 she enjoyed a fellowship under Marsha Norman and Chris Durang at the Juilliard School, where she was also a playwright-in-residence and where her play *Fortune* was produced. She is a two-time recipient of the LeCompte du Nuoy grant from the Lincoln Center Foundation and the first winner of the Sklarz-Shapiro Award for playwriting.

Miniatures received a Wedge production at the Hangar Theatre in Ithaca, New York, in July 2002. It won first prize in the Dogwood Competition in Milledgeville, Georgia, and was produced at Polaris North in New York City, and at the Attic Theatre in Buffalo, New York.

Ms. Laufer's plays have received readings and workshops at Juilliard, Playwrights Horizons, Ensemble Studio Theater, 29th Street Rep., New Georges, The Barrow Group, and Rattlestick in Manhattan; The Missoula Colony in Missoula, Montana, the Ojai Playwrights Conference in Ojai, California, and the Chauttauqua Institute in Chauttauqua, New York.

Ms. Laufer is a graduate of SUNY Purchase and Julliard and a member of The Dramatists Guild.

ORIGINAL PRODUCTION

I wrote *The Last Schwartz* during my fellowship at Juilliard in 1999 and am indebted to Marsha Norman and Chris Durang for their brilliant feedback, encouragement, and good humor. During my fellowship at the Dramatists Guild, Arthur Kopit was also extremely helpful in furthering the play's development.

The world premiere of *The Last Schwartz* was produced by Florida Stage in Manalapan, Florida on October 25, 2002. It was directed by Louis Tyrrell with Nancy Barnett, managing director, and James Danforth, production stage manager. The cast was as follows:

Simon . . . . Greg Keller
Norma . . . . Elizabeth Dimon
Herb . . . . Buzz Bovshow

Bonnie . . . . Alicia Roper
Gene . . . . Johnathan F. McClain
Kia . . . . Mayhill Fowler

I am so grateful to everyone at Florida Stage for bringing the play to life with so much talent, generosity, and humor and for reminding me that there's nowhere I'd rather be than in the theater.

In the summer of 2003, *The Last Schwartz* was produced at the Contemporary American Theatre Festival in Shepherdstown, West Virginia.

PLAYWRIGHT'S NOTE

My plays are usually about the things that confuse me. I start with very few answers and a lot of questions, and then I set about creating even more uncertainty for myself

Writing *The Last Schwartz* gave me an opportunity to worry about how hard it is to maintain one's heritage in a society that often devours ethnic and cultural heritages as fads. To what lengths must one go to keep a family history alive, and at what cost? Who must get hurt? Who must pay? Is it ultimately worth the price? As Simon Schwartz says, "Five thousand years is such a short time in the great scheme of things. The dinosaurs were around for hundreds of millions of years, and they're completely gone. What are the Jews next to that?"

I don't know.

The question I get asked most about the play is: "Is that your family???" "Oh, no," I say. "It's a composite of various people and situations I've encountered, drawing from both personal experience and observation." (This is something I heard another playwright say once.) But it was with some anxiety — OK, a lot of anxiety — that I awaited my father's response when I finally gave him the play to read.

"Jesus," he said. "It's like I know these people!"

I was relieved.

The second thing people ask me is, "Why does it have to be a Jewish family?" Well, I guess it doesn't have to be a Jewish family. I mean, I hope it doesn't have to be a Jewish family. I've never lived in a non-Jewish family, but from what I see of my friends' families, they look a little bit like the Schwartz's too.

CHARACTERS

NORMA: Forty-five. The eldest Schwartz. The keeper of the flame. Fervently self-righteous and religious, but hungry for family.

HERB: Forty. The oldest Schwartz brother. Financial wizard.

BONNIE: Thirties. Herb's wife. Generally on the verge of hysteria. Weeps easily. Desperately wants a baby. Has converted to Judaism.

SIMON: Thirty-five. The middle brother. An Astronomer. Going blind. He wears Coke-bottle thick glasses, a very loose-fitting cotton outfit, and white gloves.

GENE: Thirty. The youngest brother. Directs TV commercials. The family's golden boy and a bit of a kiss-up.

KIA: Twenty. A starlet from LA. She lives to have fun. Can turn any interaction into a party.

SETTING

The action takes place in the Schwartz ancestral home in upstate New York.

NOTE ON INTERMISSION

The Last Schwartz was intended to be performed without intermission. However, at Florida Stage we added an act break, which worked very well. As Norma said Kaddish (the prayer for the dead) in the scene after dinner, the lights came down to a blackout, an intermission was taken, and lights came up for Act II as Kaddish resumed.

The Last Schwartz

Act I

Lights come up on the Schwartz ancestral home in upstate New York. Every-
thing in the house has an untouched, old feeling. Antimacassars and doilies
cover every table top, chair, sofa back.

> *Norma is setting a formal dining table upstage. Downstage, in the liv-*
ing room, Herb sits in the ancient easy chair and reads the Wall Street Journal *with his feet propped up on the coffee table, beside the chopped liver. Simon*
is on his knees all the way downstage, staring through a child's telescope pointed
out the window. Bonnie sits on the couch polishing silver and drinking a cock-
tail. She wears a childishly prim dress with a frilly lace collar. She has clearly
been talking for a long time.

BONNIE: And then they roll out these Siamese twins on this huge double-wheel-
   chair-dolly-type thing. And they're joined here, at the top of the head,
   so one of them is facing the ceiling all the time like this . . . *(She demon-*
   strates, though no one is watching.) and one of them is sort of squashed
   under to the side like this.

HERB: *(Not listening.)* Mmmm.

NORMA: *(Calling out.)* Don't fill up on chopped liver everybody.

BONNIE: So they have to take turns who gets to face Oprah which is mostly
   the bottom one . . .

HERB: *(Not listening.)* Huh.

BONNIE: Though there must have been a camera on the ceiling or something
   because when the top one is talking, you do get a pretty good shot of her.

NORMA: *(As she is passing through, collecting some of the silver and bringing back*
   a few spoons.) My goodness Bonnie, are you still talking? Here, you missed
   some spots.

BONNIE: Oh. Sorry . . . I guess I . . .

NORMA: Herb, get your feet off the coffee table, please. Dinner is almost ready.
   As soon as Gene gets here.
   (She exits.)

BONNIE: *(Takes a drink, decides to go on.)* And Oprah asks, like she usually does,
   "What are your dreams and ambitions?", and the one on the bottom, you
   know, like this, says she wants to be a doctor, and the one on the top says
   she wants to be an airplane pilot, and it was just so . . . so amazing and
   inspiring that they had these dreams and ambitions. That it didn't even

occur to them, "Well, gee, maybe my patients won't want my sister lying on my back when I examine them," or "Where is my sister even going to sit in the cockpit?" You know? They were just so young and hopeful.

HERB: Huh . . .

BONNIE: And Oprah says, "If there were a safe operation that could separate you, would you want that? Would you want to be two independent individuals, after a lifetime of, you know, being . . . yoked at the head?" And I'm thinking, "Oprah! Of course they would. Who would want to live that way?"

HERB: *(Not listening.)* Right . . . .

BONNIE: But without even batting an eye they both said no. They *were* one person. They were sisters. There was a connection there deeper than any surgeon could break. And I was so . . . I mean, isn't that what we all want? That connectedness? A meshing of lives and souls and . . . well, in their case various body parts, but, you know . . . Anyway . . . I was wishing so much that I had a sister. Not coming out of the top of my head or anything but . . .

HERB: Right . . .

NORMA: Herb, get your feet off Mama's coffee table. Gene should be getting here any minute now. Could we make the place look nice, everybody? Pick up some of those papers? Bonnie?

(She continues out.)

BONNIE: *(Scrambling to pick up the papers.)* And then this woman in the audience goes to the mike, you know, for audience questions, and asks, "Do you ever want to get married and have children?" Well, I was horrified. I mean, it was outrageous, right? And I'm looking to Oprah to get us out of this. To cover up or change the subject or go to a commercial. But you know what?

HERB: Yeah . . .

BONNIE: They each said they want to get married and have children! The top one actually says, "Three kids." I could feel my jaw drop. And Oprah doesn't say, "What are you, nuts?" or anything like that. She's just sitting there holding one of their hands and looking into their faces, well, the bottom one's face, and nodding and being really serious and sincere. And they cut to the audience and nobody is snickering or laughing. They were all deeply deeply moved.

HERB: *(Responding absently.)* Mmmm.

NORMA: *(Passing through.)* Smells good, doesn't it? Food just smells better in Mama's kitchen. Herb, that's a lazy boy. Use the footrest.

HERB: It's too crowded. It won't open.

NORMA: So move it back.

(She is out.)

BONNIE: And it was just so . . . I mean, really, what are the chances that these girls are even going to find husbands, you know? Look at my cousin Janet. She's pretty and smart and only has one head and she's never found anyone. *(Getting very agitated.)* What are these girls' chances!? And then, if they did get married, could they even have a baby? Would they be good mothers? It was crazy, you know?

HERB: Hmm.

BONNIE: And I didn't want to be mean spirited because it was a very hopeful and positive show, but I couldn't help . . . Well, I couldn't help but to start thinking about myself even though I don't like to harp on that. But I couldn't help but to start thinking about the miscarriages and little Aaron and what we went through even though I'm totally normal.

HERB: Bonnie, you're getting upset. Go get a seltzer, honey.

BONNIE: *(Growing increasingly furious and upset.)* I mean, here I am, totally normal!! And about what a completely great mother . . . how I would have . . . you know, if I could have just had him for a full day even, how much I would have loved him and taken care of him . . .

HERB: Bonnie.

BONNIE: . . . and I would have sung him songs and read to him and just loved him so much. I loved him so much. And I didn't even get a chance. And here are these two FREAKS really, these two freaks who couldn't possibly be good mothers, I mean, they each only had one arm for God's sakes, and here's Oprah, and this whole audience thinking *they're* so special and brave and that THEY should be mothers, and it just made me sick. I just hated those girls so much, I wanted to smack them. Both of them. I just hate them!

HERB: Bonnie . . .

BONNIE: I'm sorry.

HERB: Honey.

BONNIE: I'm sorry. I'm all right.

HERB: Are you all right?

BONNIE: These talk shows.

HERB: You really shouldn't watch these talk shows.

BONNIE: I know.

HERB: Really.

BONNIE: I know. They're terrible.

HERB: They're just terrible.

BONNIE: I know.

NORMA: *(Entering and catching the end of this. Very annoyed with it.)* Oh for . . . *Now* what's going on? Herb!!!

HERB: What??!

NORMA: Get your feet off Mama's table!

HERB: It's an old table. Mama is dead. Leave me alone, I'm trying to read here.

NORMA: That's right, Mama is dead. Show some respect.

HERB: Respect for a table???

NORMA: Respect for your mother. Respect for the other people in this family.

HERB: You're kidding right? Simon, is this upsetting you if I put my feet on the table? Bonnie, do you care if I . . .

NORMA: I care. All right, Herb? I care.

HERB: They left the table to us. So it's my table now.

NORMA: It's not your table. It's all of our table. And I don't want it all marked up.

HERB: It's a crappy table. It's already marked up. How much is it worth? Forty dollars? Fifty dollars?

NORMA: It's not a matter of money. You think everything . . .

BONNIE: Honey, maybe you should just . . .

HERB: You're siding with her now? You're going to side with her over your own husband?

BONNIE: No, I'm just . . .

HERB: *(Getting up and pulling a roll of money out of his pocket.)* Here. Everybody gets a twenty for it — you'll be making a profit, believe me. And then it's my table. And I can sit and be comfortable without everybody riding my back.
(He throws a twenty at Simon, who is still completely unaware that anyone else is in the room. He peels off a twenty and slams it down on the table.)
For Gene when he gets here. Here Norma, here's your twenty.

NORMA: I don't want your money. Everything is not about money, Herb.

HERB: *(Overlapping.)* Take it. Put it in your pocket. What, it's not enough? Here, make it thirty.

NORMA: Everything and everyone can not be bought. Some things are more precious than your money.

HERB: This coffee table???

NORMA: Mama and Papa's memory, us sharing this house . . .

HERB: *(Over her.)* The coffee table??? Sharing the coffee . . .

BONNIE: Honey, maybe you should . . .

HERB: No! Fifty. You all get fifty and this is my table. It's mine now.

NORMA: It is not yours. I do not accept your fifty dollars and I do not accept that this is your . . .

HERB: *(Overlapping.)* It's my table now!!! *(He throws money around the room.)* I'm going to take a knife and carve "Herb" in this table.

NORMA: You are not!

HERB: You want the dining-room table, Norma, it's yours. You take the kitchen table, Simon. Everybody gets a table!!! And this is mine!!
(He puts his foot on the table, as if to climb on it.)

NORMA: *(Overlapping.)* Get off there!!! Get your foot off that table!

BONNIE: Herb, get down. You're going to hurt yourself.
(Norma rushes the table and grabs Herb's foot. Bonnie jumps up and grabs Herb as he is about to fall. The following is all overlapping.)

NORMA: Get down! What is wrong with you? On Papa's Yarzheit you do this?! Get off that table!!!

BONNIE: Herb, careful! Don't step in the chopped liver. Come on now, get down sweetheart.

HERB: Hey, stop it. Let go of my foot. What, are you trying to kill me?

NORMA: You're insane! You have no respect for anyone. You've always been this way.

BONNIE: Honey, please.

HERB: Stop pulling at me! Both of you!
(The struggle escalates. Herb is pulled into a precarious position, when suddenly the three of them freeze. A light comes up on Simon at his telescope.)

SIMON: If only I were going deaf instead of blind. Or if little by little, all my senses melted away as my vision has. No sight. No sound. No taste. No smell. *(Pause.)* No touch. So peaceful. I would become my own capsule. Nothing could get in. Without distractions, with all that quiet, I could solve the mysteries of the universe.
(Lights down on Simon. The action at the coffee table resumes. With much noise and frenzy, all three crumble and are tangled together on the floor.)

NORMA: Get off me! Get off me, you fool!

HERB: Owwww! My leg. I think you've broken my leg. What are you, nuts???

BONNIE: Are you all right, honey?

HERB: No. My leg hurts.

NORMA: Get up. You're not hurt. Just get up. Gene is going to be here soon. Look at this place.

HERB: I'm not sure I can walk.

NORMA: Oh, stop being melodramatic.

HERB: Bonnie, help me to the chair.

BONNIE: Where does it hurt, Herb?

HERB: Everywhere. Just help me out here. Owww. Ohhhh.

(He makes a great show of hobbling back to the chair and putting his wounded foot up on the coffee table. Norma stands for a moment, silently fuming, then decides to drop it. For now. She heads back to the kitchen. Herb returns to his paper, delighted with his victory. Bonnie resumes her polishing. There is a long silence, which Bonnie needs to fill.)

BONNIE: So. Well, I guess Gene will be here soon. *(Pause.)* Herb? *(No answer.)* Herb?

HERB: Hmmm?

BONNIE: I was saying, I guess Gene will be here soon. What do you suppose he's going to do about . . .

HERB: You know, sweetheart, I'd really like to finish the paper. All right?

BONNIE: Oh. Sure. Sorry. *(She takes a gulp of her cocktail. Pause.)* Simon, how was your trip? Do you like Australia? Are the other scientists nice? *(Sigh. She downs the drink and goes to him.)* Simon, do you think you'll be going back?

(She taps him on the shoulder.)

SIMON: Ah!

BONNIE: I was saying, do you think you'll be going back to the aeronautical institute?

SIMON: Oh. N-n-no.

BONNIE: No?

SIMON: No. No, I don't.

BONNIE: Oh.

SIMON: I don't think so. No.

(Pause. He goes back to his telescope.)

BONNIE: Where will you go? Simon?

SIMON: Yes?

BONNIE: Where will you go?

SIMON: I don't know.

BONNIE: No?

SIMON: No.

BONNIE: Oh.

SIMON: I'm going to have to wait.

BONNIE: Wait?

SIMON: Yes.

(He goes back to his telescope.)

BONNIE: What are you waiting for, Simon? *What are you waiting for?*

SIMON: The lunar space station.

BONNIE: Space station?

SIMON: Yes.

BONNIE: On the moon?

SIMON: I don't see any other options.

BONNIE: Oh.

SIMON: For me.

BONNIE: Oh.

SIMON: Of course, it could be some time. Before they build it. And there's a strong movement to start something on Mars first. Strong movement. Very controversial. They're already developing warming pods to release on the Martian surface, to increase the temperature and make it more inhabitable, but I contend that the moon's proximity makes it a more likely venture.

BONNIE: Oh.

SIMON: Yes.

BONNIE: Why are they building a space station on the moon?

SIMON: Why???

BONNIE: Yes.

SIMON: What do you mean?

BONNIE: I . . . Well, I . . .

SIMON: You realize that the earth as we know it is not going to exist much longer. You do realize that, don't you?

BONNIE: No. I didn't realize that.

SIMON: You should do some research.

BONNIE: I should.

SIMON: Yes.

BONNIE: All right.

SIMON: You should be preparing.

BONNIE: All right.

SIMON: There isn't going to be room enough for everyone, you know. You should be preparing.

(Pause. He returns to his telescope.)

BONNIE: How should I be preparing, Simon? *(She crouches uncertainly beside him for a moment.)* What should I do?

(From offstage, we hear voices. It is Gene and Kia arriving. Their conversation is heard offstage.)

GENE: So, this is the front hall.

BONNIE: *(To herself — A breath.)* Oh. It's Gene.

KIA: God, Gene. This place is so fucking old! I don't think I've ever even been in a place that was so old.

GENE: It's only like seventy years.

KIA: SEVENTY years old? God. love it. It even smells old.

GENE: Nah, that's Norma's cooking.

KIA: Oh look, you've got one of these cute little thingies on the door.

GENE: The mezuzah?

KIA: What is it?

GENE: It's for . . . Huh. I don't know actually.

NORMA: Gene!!!

(The sound of them hugging.)

GENE: Hey Nor.

NORMA: Gene, Gene, Gene. Oh, it's good to see you.

KIA: Hi, I'm Kia.

GENE: Kia, this is my big sister, Norma.

NORMA: Gene, I don't think you mentioned you would be bringing a . . . So nice to meet you, Kia. Why don't you go inside and make yourself comfortable. Gene, could I talk to you for a minute?

GENE: Ummm, sure. Kia . . .

KIA: Hey, no sweat. I can make myself at home. See you, sweety pie. *(She enters the living room. She is all legs and boobs and hair. Herb and Bonnie just stare at her.)* Hi, Gene's family! I'm Kia.

HERB: *(Getting up to meet her.)* Well, well, well. Hello, there. I'm Herb.

BONNIE: I'm Bonnie. Herb's wife.

KIA: Hey. Great dress. I love retro.

BONNIE: Thanks.

KIA: *(To Simon.)* Hi there, I'm Kia.

BONNIE: That's Simon. Their youngest brother.

KIA: *(He has not responded.)* Is he deaf?

BONNIE: No.

KIA: Super!

HERB: So, you're here with Gene. That dog!

NORMA: *(Offstage, getting shrill.)* You brought a *date* to Papa's unveiling?

GENE: It's not a date. Kia wanted to come along and . . .

BONNIE: *(Overlapping.)* So, have you known Gene for . . .

HERB: Shhh! Quiet. This should be good.

(They all stand, awkwardly listening while the following is said.)

NORMA: She wanted to come to Papa's unveiling? Why would a perfect stranger . . .

GENE: Well she wanted . . .

NORMA: Is she even an M.O.T.?

GENE: Norma . . .

KIA: *(Whispering.)* What's an M.O.T?

HERB: Member of the Tribe. Shhhh.

BONNIE: She means you're not Jewish.

KIA: Oh!

NORMA: Where is she going to sleep? You didn't think she was going to stay in your room, did you?

GENE: Well . . . yeah.

NORMA: Are you married?

GENE: Norma! Of course we're not . . .

NORMA: Well, if you think you're sleeping together without the covenant of marriage, under Mama and Papa's roof..

GENE: *(Over her.)* Hey, I brought girls here while Mom and Dad were alive . . .

NORMA: Sha!!! Come in the back with me, Gene. I want to talk to you.

GENE: Can't I go in and say hello to everyone? I don't want to leave Kia just . . .

NORMA: Come in back and then you say hello.

(There is a pause while Norma and Gene head for the back room.)

HERB: Damn. So . . . Kia. It's so great to have you here in our little country home-away-from-home.

KIA: Hey, it's great to be here. This place is so old!

BONNIE: You look really familiar. Have you been dating Gene for . . .

KIA: *(Overlapping.)* I do?

BONNIE: Yes, did we meet?

KIA: What if I stand like this?

(She does the Fat No More pose.)

BONNIE: Oh my God! You're . . . You're the Fat No More girl!

KIA: Yeah! Wow. I love this! I love the national recognition. People know me everywhere I go. It's so amazing. Even out here in nowhere. Do you want an autograph? Some people like me to sign their Fat No More box. Would you like that?

BONNIE: I don't use . . . No. Thanks.

KIA: I don't mind. Really.

HERB: I want an autograph. We don't know how famous this little girl is going to get! Here, sign my *Wall Street Journal.*

KIA: Super.

HERB: You are as cute as a button, did you know that? Bonnie, isn't she cute?

BONNIE: Very cute.

KIA: What do I write? I'm sorry, what was your name?

HERB: Herb. Write, "To Herb, who think's I'm a cutey-pie."

(Kia begins to slowly write her message, leaning on the coffee table.)

HERB: Imagine this, the Fat No More girl in our house.

KIA: Is that i-e or e-e or e-y?

BONNIE: Herb, you've never even seen the commercial.

HERB: Well, I'm going to keep my eye out for it now.

KIA: Oh, Gene could probably get you a tape.

BONNIE: Gene could?

KIA: Well, yeah. He directed it, didn't you know that?

BONNIE: Gene directed that? Oh. He didn't tell us . . .

HERB: That dog! That kid brother of mine!

KIA: God, he is so modest. I love that quality, don't you? Yeah. It's such a great story. Here he was, they all were, all the advertising people, they were looking for the perfect Fat No More girl. I mean, it was like a nationwide search, which is so amazing, because I had just come here from LA. So, anyway, they've had the auditions, they've had the call-backs, they're down to two girls who are on what's called "first refusal," which means they should save the day.

BONNIE: Save the day?

KIA: The shooting day. And then, the night before they call one of these girls and tell her she's the Fat No More girl, I meet Gene at this party — he used to go out with the girl whose cousin got me my sublet — so how's THAT for a coincidence. I mean, obviously it was like totally meant to be.

HERB: It was Kismet.

KIA: Yeah. What?

BONNIE: It means . . .

KIA: So, anyway, we just hit it off, and Gene tells me he's directing this commercial, and I had this great blow from this cater-waiter job I just did, and we go back to his place, and the next thing I know, I'm the Fat No More girl!!!

HERB: That is such a great story!!!

KIA: Which is why I totally love NY. I mean, in LA, that would never happen. In LA, they'd tell you how hot you were and all and how they were doing this commercial, and you'd go home with them and everything, and then they'd totally go with the first refusal girl. Do you see what I mean? There's like no honor in LA.

HERB: How awful.

BONNIE: So, how long have you and Gene . . .

KIA: Oh, that was like, three months ago.

BONNIE: Three months . . .

KIA: It's been a gas. And Gene is doing this music video with Trash Compactors, and they need a girl in this cage-type thing that they lower into this pit, and all the executives are like a minute away from it being final that I'm the girl. And THEN, you can imagine.

HERB: Wow.

KIA: Right.

(Gene and Norma enter.)

GENE: Hey everybody! Herb!

(They hug.)

HERB: You dog! *(He hugs him and then tries to wrestle him into a choke hold, but Gene gets his arm behind his back.)* Ow! Ow, ow, ow! I give, I give, you dog, you! *(Thoroughly delighted.)* Rotten kid.

BONNIE: Hey, Gene.

GENE: Bonnie. *(He gives her an awkward hug.)* Simon! How the hell are you? *(Simon is in his trance at the telescope. Gene goes behind him and grabs him, lifting him up.)*

SIMON: *(Very shocked.)* W-w-what!? What?!

BONNIE: *(Overlapping.)* Gene, stop that.

NORMA: *(Overlapping.)* Gene, don't be so rough. Come on now, put him down.

SIMON: Gene! Gene how are you?

(They hug, a painful hug for Simon.)

GENE: Man! Look at you! You look like you should be on some ashram. What's with the pajamas?

SIMON: M-my skin. I can't tolerate that much . . .

GENE: *(Over him.)* And those glasses, man.

NORMA: Come on, everyone. Let's eat, before you completely destroy my brisket, which has been cooking for hours.

GENE: Not *days,* so we could drink it through a straw like Mom's?

NORMA: Now stop that, Mr. Smarty. We should all eat very well tonight, since tomorrow we'll be fasting for Papa's Yarzheit. We should have started at sunset, but with this late one here . . .

(She puts her arms around Gene.)

HERB: Fasting?

NORMA: Well, I'm fasting. I'm hoping you'll all join me but . . .

BONNIE: I'll fast too, Norma. I was planning . . .

NORMA: *(Over her.)* Come, let's eat.

GENE: Hey, did you all meet Kia?

HERB: Oh, yeah. Very nice girl, Gene. Very nice.

KIA: Thank you all for having me. It's so totally cool that you're including me in your whole family ceremony and all. And this house is so great. I love this room.

NORMA: Good. You'll be sleeping out here on the couch. Come on, everyone.
(She herds them to the table.)

NORMA: Herb, you're the oldest male, so you take the head. I'll take the foot. Gene and Simon, here by me. Bonnie. Kia.
(Everyone noisily takes their places as Norma says the prayer over the wine.)

NORMA: Sha. Sha. Baruch atah adonai, elohaynu melech ha'olam, borei pre hagafen. Amen.

Everyone: Amen.
(As she prepares to do the prayer over the bread, a spotlight comes up on Simon.)

SIMON: Walking on the moon must be like walking under water. So buoyant and free. Whenever I'm submerged in a pool I imagine that I'm on the moon. And when I'm alone in my room at night, and it's so quiet that all I can hear is my own breath, I put on my space helmet and practice my moon walk.
(He gets up and begins a very graceful, slow-motion moon walk around the table, like the footage of the first astronauts, and then returns to his place.)
It feels wonderful.
(The spotlight fades on Simon. We hear Norma reciting the prayer over the bread.)

NORMA: Baruch atah adonai, elohaynu melech ha'olam, hamotzi lechem min ha aretz. Amen.

Everyone: Amen.

KIA: Cool.
(The lights start to fade as the cacophony of dinner noise ensues.)

GENE: Pass the bread, somebody,

BONNIE: Could I have some wine, please?

HERB: Hey, where's the horseradish?

NORMA: You're not putting horseradish in my soup. Taste it first.
(And on and on. Slowly, the sound dies down with the light until there is

only a pinpoint of light. There is no sound. The light stays on for a moment, then pops out to blackout.)

Lights up on the dinner table. The meal has been consumed. Simon has already left the table and is back at his downstage telescope. Everyone else sits back exhausted.

HERB: Nobody minds if I undo my pants . . .

GENE: Delicious dinner, Norma. Thanks.

NORMA: I'm glad you enjoyed it. It's nice to have family to cook for. Does anyone want seconds on pie? Thirds?

BONNIE: I'll have some more wine.

KIA: Hey, me too.

NORMA: Simon, sweetheart. Are you sure you wouldn't like some pie?

GENE: He didn't eat any food.

KIA: Yeah, you know, my friend Jody's little brother is autistic, and he never eats like anything either, isn't that weird?
(Pause.)

NORMA: There's nothing wrong with Simon.

KIA: Really?? Wow. It sure seems like . . .

BONNIE: He was never diagnosed. Their parents always refused to have anyone . . .

NORMA: *(To Bonnie.)* Why would they do that? Why would they look for problems?

BONNIE: No, no. I was just saying that . . . that maybe if . . .

NORMA: He's always done beautifully in school. He's brilliant.

BONNIE: No, I know.

NORMA: He's a respected scientist. I don't understand why you always feel a need to look for . . .

HERB: All right. Enough already. I'll take some more pie.

BONNIE: I'll take some wine. Please.

KIA: *(Picking up a pewter cup from the center of the table.)* This is the coolest cup. I totally love it. Where did you get it?

NORMA: Ah, this is wonderful. Tell her, Gene.

GENE: Huh?

NORMA: How Grandma got this cup.

KIA: Tell me!

GENE: How Grandma got the cup . . .

HERB: Oh, boy.

BONNIE: I remember. If you want, I could . . .

GENE: If you could just start it for me . . .

NORMA: Shame on you, Gene!

KIA: Shame on you, Gene!

NORMA: This is our family history. A reminder of where we came from. Of what it is to be a Jew.

KIA: Oh, tell it! I would love to hear what it is to be a Jew.

HERB: Me too!

BONNIE: I'll take some more wine?

NORMA: All right. When our grandparents moved to Lake Huntington they were the first Jewish family. My grandfather opened a small dairy, selling milk and cheese and butter . . .

KIA: I guess that's before people knew about lactose, huh?

HERB: This is a very cute girl you have here, Gene.

BONNIE: Would somebody please pass the wine?

NORMA: No one would shop at my grandparent's store. So one day, my grandfather is not at home, and this group of men comes to the house, carrying guns, looking for trouble. My grandmother sees them coming, she's alone with two small children and she doesn't know what to do. She decides to face them.

GENE: Oh, right. I remember.

KIA: Wait. This *is* about the cup, right?

NORMA: They come into the yard . . .

BONNIE: This is the one, "She's not the Jew — he is." Right?

(There is silence for a moment.)

HERB: Oh, boy.

NORMA: Would you like to tell the story, Bonnie?

BONNIE: No. I just . . .

KIA: *(To Norma.)* Go on, finish it!

NORMA: Well, there's really no reason to tell it now. That was the punch line.

HERB: Oh, boy.

BONNIE: Oh, God, Norma, I'm sorry.

GENE: It's OK, Nor. Tell it anyway. It's no big deal.

NORMA: Well, it hardly seems worthwhile now.

BONNIE: I'm really sorry, Norma.

KIA: Would somebody please finish this story?

BONNIE: *(She begins to get weepy.)* I wasn't thinking. I was just remembering the story and . . . I'm so . . .

HERB: Oh, for Christ's sake, Norma, finish the friggin' story. Who the hell cares what the punch line . . .

NORMA: Don't speak to me in that tone, Herb. Don't use that language in Mama and Papa's house.

GENE: Hey, hey, you guys. Come on. I'm dying to hear the rest of the story. Come on. Tell it, Norma.

NORMA: Well, all right. *(To Kia.)* Try to forget you heard that last part.

KIA: Umm, to tell you the truth, I've forgotten most of it already.

NORMA: All right. So, these men come into the yard, and Grandma goes out to meet them, with Mama and Aunt Yetti clinging to her skirts. And Grandma was feisty. A balabusta. So, she says, "Welcome, gentlemen. You came to see how Jews live? Look around you. I keep a clean house. My children are clean and well fed. I cook, I clean, I pray, I take care of what's mine. This is how Jews live."

KIA: Wow. She said that?

NORMA: Yes.

KIA: How did she know they weren't just coming for milk or something?

HERB: That's wonderful. She's wonderful.

NORMA: *(Giving him a withering look.)* And the men stood there for a long time, embarrassed. They didn't know what to do. And the leader, Joe Poley — Doug Poley's grandfather, Joe finally turns to his friends and says, "All right boys, that's enough, let's go." And sure enough, they all turn around and leave! And as they head off down the road, Joe looks back over his shoulder at Grandma and says, "Hell, she ain't the Jew — he is!"

GENE: Right.

NORMA: And that was that.

KIA: Wait, I don't get it . . .

NORMA: And the next day, Joe comes to the store and gives Grandma this cup — as a kind of peace offering. And he buys some butter. And from then on, our grandparents were in business.

KIA: So, I don't get it. Was she a Jew or not?

GENE: Yeah, Kia. Yeah she was Jewish. The point of the story is . . . Well . . . You know, actually, I'm not sure what the point is.

NORMA: Oh Gene. The point is . . . what the story reminds us of, is the struggle the Jews have always had to prove that we were good enough, that we had a place in the community. It's about how hard it's always been for the Jews and how . . .

HERB: Every story is about how hard it's always been for the Jews. It's our favorite theme. Jew Jew Jew Jew Jew. And who is Jewish and who isn't Jewish and whether that person who isn't Jewish likes the Jews or doesn't. Our father would watch the six o'clock news —

NORMA: Herb! Don't you start in on Papa —

HERB: And for every report there was a play by play about whether it was good for the Jews or bad for the Jews. Every single person who came on — weatherman, reporter, sportscaster, Dad had a running commentary — "That anti-Semite bastard!" "Her, she's a real Jew hater." Or — "That one — always been good to the Jews." And if you achieved greatness, didn't matter who you were — if Dad thought you were great he had some inside info that that you were really a Jew. I was fourteen before I found out that Hank Aaron wasn't Jewish.

KIA: He wasn't, right?

NORMA: Herb, how can you talk disrespectfully about your father? On his Yarzheit.

HERB: It's just true, Norma. Is it disrespectful if it's true?

NORMA: It's disrespectful the way you toss off your culture so glibly. Everyone should have respect for where they come from — it's what separates us from the animals. Where is your family from Kia?

KIA: Ummm . . . California?

NORMA: But where are your parents from? Your parents' parents?

KIA: Yeah, that's a very interesting thing. I kind of got moved around a lot as a kid. So, it's not totally clear who exactly my parents are. But I'm so with you that it's a very cool and interesting thing to know, and one of these days I'm really going to look into it.

NORMA: You have no idea where you're from?

KIA: Well, I mean, I'm generally from around like the Venice Beach area . . .

NORMA: Wait, I don't understand. You don't know who your parents are? How did that happen? Are you an orphan? Were you raised by wolves, or . . .

HERB: Hey, down, Norma. Easy, girl. Kia is our guest here.

KIA: No, that's cool. Well, there was like this group who hung out on the beach and stuff, and you know, sometimes people had babies, and everyone would kind of take care of them or not and stuff. But people shifted around or moved or died a lot, so it wasn't totally clear who was whose, you know? But I think it's great the way you're so into being Jewish and everything. And that thing you said with the bread before was really really cool. I totally loved it.

NORMA: You have no religious background? No faith? What do you believe in?

KIA: Wow. *(She thinks.)* I guess I really believe in having a good time. I really like to have fun.

HERB: That's wonderful. Gene, I think she's wonderful.

GENE: *(Miserable.)* Yeah.

KIA: I guess I'm like totally an American.

HERB: Me too, Kia. I'm an American too.

NORMA: You're an American. Well, Herb, *you* might forget who you are, but believe me, when they come knocking on your door, looking for Jews, *they* won't forget who you are.

HERB: God, you sound like Dad. It's like he walked in the room and pulled up a chair.

NORMA: Thank you. That's the first nice thing you've said to me all day. Now, why don't we clear and have our coffee in the living room. Kia, Bonnie, would you help me? No stacking, please.

HERB: *(Grabbing his paper on the way out.)* I'll be in the library.

NORMA: Gene, why don't you see if you can find some linens for the couch. I think there are some smaller sheets in the downstairs closet.

KIA: Ohhh, I'm so full I could pass out right here on the floor.

NORMA: Whatever you prefer. Bonnie, careful with that pitcher. The handles have been repaired once already.

(Gene disappears after the sheets, Bonnie loads a tray and heads for the kitchen.)

NORMA: Kia, would you rather wash or dry?

KIA: The dishes? There's no dishwasher?

NORMA: Mama didn't believe in machines.

KIA: God, I love that. Wow. I guess I better dry.

NORMA: All right. Take these in and start scraping. I'll be right in.

KIA: Great! *(Exiting, to herself.)* Scraping. Huh . . .

(Norma comes down to Simon. She puts her hand next to the telescope to get his attention.)

NORMA: Simon, Darling. You didn't eat anything. Can I make you something else?

SIMON: No, thank you.

NORMA: You're not hungry, sweetheart?

SIMON: No.

(He returns to the telescope.)

NORMA: Simon. Listen. I've decided that you should come live with me while they're training you. You're not taking very good care of yourself and you'll come live with me, and I'll take very good care of you. All right? Good.

SIMON: No, thank you.

NORMA: It will be no problem, Simon. It will be my pleasure. You can stay in Eric's room.

SIMON: Eric is in Eric's room.

NORMA: No. Eric is with his father.

SIMON: Isn't his father in your room?

NORMA: No.

SIMON: Oh. *(Pause.)* He's not?

NORMA: No.

SIMON: Oh.

NORMA: No, they don't live with me anymore.

SIMON: Oh. *(Pause.)* Why?

NORMA: It's complicated, sweetheart.

SIMON: Oh.

(He turns back to his telescope.)

NORMA: Sometimes . . . sometimes when you do what you know is right, Simon, when you . . . there's a very heavy price to pay. Sometimes it makes it hard for other people to live with you, or for you to live with other people. But the important thing is that you can live with yourself Do you understand what I'm saying? Sweetheart?

(He has not heard her. She puts her hand out to get his attention again.)

NORMA: *(Continued.)* Simon? *(Pause.)* So, you'll come live with me then.

SIMON: No, thank you.

NORMA: It's no trouble, Simon. It's a big empty apartment. It just makes sense.

SIMON: No, thank you.

NORMA: Simon. Sweetheart. Look. *(This is very hard for her.)* I'm all alone, Sweetheart. There's . . . I'm all alone, Simon. You're all alone. We're family. I would take care of you, sweetheart. I would . . . *(She falters.)* Look, we'll talk about this. I think it's best.

SIMON: No. I won't. I won't live with you. No.

(He returns to his telescope. Norma stands for a moment, then goes to the table, takes some plates, and exits into the kitchen. Gene comes out with the sheets. Bonnie returns for more plates and sees him. Sneaks up behind him and puts her arms around him. Gene jumps, startled.)

GENE: Ahhh! Oh, Bonnie, you scared the shit out me.

BONNIE: Sorry.

GENE: OK.

(They stand awkwardly.)

BONNIE: *(Longingly.)* Gene.

GENE: Yeah . . .

BONNIE: Gene. You didn't call.

GENE: Yeah, umm, I've been so unbelievably busy.

BONNIE: I can see that.

GENE: No, no . . . it's just . . .

BONNIE: Why didn't you call? I've missed you so much.

(She goes to put her arms around him. He pulls away in a panic.)

GENE: *(Whispering.)* Bonnie!

(Indicating Simon.)

BONNIE: He doesn't even know we're here.

GENE: Someone could walk in. Please, Bonnie. Herb . . .

BONNIE: Gene. I've been out of my mind. I didn't know what happened. You said you'd call me and then . . .

GENE: Bonnie. It was . . . It was really crazy, you know? I mean, it was a big mistake, don't you think?

BONNIE: No, I don't think.

GENE: But, look, you know, Herb's my brother, and it's just, it was just crazy, you know? It was a crazy night, and a crazy thing to do, and I . . . Can we just . . .

BONNIE: You said you really cared about me. That you'd thought about me, and . . .

GENE: Well, yeah, I mean, you're my sister-in law — of course I care about you.

BONNIE: Is it her? Is it Kia? She said you've been together for three months, is that true?

GENE: Oh, well, Kia. That's just, you know, fun. It's nothing serious. I mean, really . . .

BONNIE: Just fun? Is that what you say about me? Is that what you're telling *her* about me?

GENE: Oh, God no, Bonnie. I would never say that about you. I mean, I haven't told *anybody*, I'm not telling anybody about what happened with us. I mean, we agreed, right?

(She doesn't answer.)

GENE: Right? Right, Bonnie? That was just between us. It's private.

BONNIE: I don't know.

GENE: We talked about this. I would never have done anything if I thought Herb would ever . . .

BONNIE: Are you ashamed?

GENE: Yeah. Of course I'm ashamed. It was a terrible thing to . . . *(He sees her face — she is about to wail.)* Well, no. Not *ashamed*. I don't mean *ashamed*. But, you know. It was . . .

BONNIE: Maybe I *should* tell Herb. Maybe it's best if we get this all out in the open. Maybe we should tell Norma. She'd have some good advice about this.

GENE: What are you doing? Are you threatening me?

BONNIE: No, but if you're so ashamed. Maybe it's best if we . . .

GENE: No, it's definitely not best if they know. *(Absolutely desperate.)* Please. Bonnie. Let's not get crazy here. I'll call you. Please. Let's just let it go for now and I promise I'll call you and we'll talk this out. We'll solve this thing.

BONNIE: Will we get together? Will we meet again?

GENE: I don't know if that's a good idea.

BONNIE: Oh, Gene. Just once more. Just once more meet with me.

GENE: *(In a sweat.)* God, Bonnie.

(She begins to cry in frustration. He looks around frantically.)

GENE: OK. Quiet. Shhh . . . OK, we'll meet again. OK.

(She throws herself in his arms. He pats her back, terrified of someone coming in. Extracts himself.)

GENE: But, but let's just be, you know, sensible this weekend. Let's just get through this weekend, OK?

BONNIE: Just one kiss, Gene.

GENE: Bonnie. Herb could walk in . . . Norma . . .

BONNIE: Kia?

GENE: Please. I'll see you in the city. Please.

(We hear Norma and Kia coming back in for more dishes.)

NORMA: Bonnie? Weren't you helping clear?

GENE: *(Breaking away from this scene.)* I found those sheets, Nor! Just where you said!

NORMA: *(Looking at them oddly.)* Good. Bonnie?

BONNIE: I'll be right there.

NORMA: What are you up to? What were you two talking about?

BONNIE: Nothing . . .

NORMA: Come help clear. And then you can serve the coffee. Don't use the good dishes. Not for the living room.

KIA: Gene, I can't believe there's no dishwasher. This is so wild. We're *washing* the dishes, can you believe it?

GENE: *(Completely adrift.)* That's great.

(Bonnie is staring at Gene.)

NORMA: *(Studying them.)* Come on now, everyone. I, for one am exhausted. We have an early day tomorrow. We need to light the Yarzheit candle and I want to talk about who's going to say something and who's going to lead the prayers — I imagine I will unless you men . . . where's Herb, anyway?

BONNIE: He's in the . . .

NORMA: So let's get coffee over with so we can get some sleep. No more dawdling. Bonnie?

BONNIE: All right.

(She moves to the table and starts clearing.)

NORMA: Come on, Kia. *(Picking up some plates.)* We may as well take some on our way out. Idle hands you know . . . Careful now.

(They exit. Gene and Simon are left alone in the living room. Gene, very shaken, gingerly sits on the couch and tries to regain his bearings. Simon suddenly turns to him.)

SIMON: Hey, Gene.

GENE: Ahh! *(Startled.)* Jeez, Simon. I thought you were . . . Weren't you . . . Have you heard all this?

SIMON: All what?

GENE: Oh. Nothing. *(He gets up and goes to Simon, beside the telescope.)* What are you looking at?

SIMON: Nothing.

GENE: Huh. *(There is a silence between them.)* Nothing? What do you mean?

SIMON: I can't see.

GENE: You can't?

SIMON: No.

GENE: Oh.

SIMON: Everything's going away.

GENE: Huh . . .

(They sit quietly for a moment, staring off. Herb enters, paper in hand.)

HERB: Ah, the men! The men folk, alone at last. Finally we can really talk.

GENE: Herb.

(They all sit, blankly. There is a long silence. Finally Norma and Kia enter, followed by Bonnie with a tray of coffee things.)

NORMA: Everyone clear off the table. We're going to light the Yarzheit candle, decide about tomorrow, drink our coffee, and go to bed. Everyone take your own milk and sugar — faster and easier that way. Bonnie, you pour. *(They all go about doing all that, Norma gets the candle, lights it, and says the prayer. She does it with great feeling, and it's very beautiful.)*

NORMA: Yis'ga'dal v'yis'kadash sh'may ra'bbo, b'olmo dee'vro chir'usay v'yam-
lich malchu'say, b'chayaychon uv'yomay'chon uv'chayay d'chol bais Yisroel, ba'agolo u'viz'man koriv; v'imru Omein.

Y'hay shmay rabbo m'vorach l'olam ul'olmay olmayo.

Yisborach v'yishtabach v'yispoar v'yisromam v'yismasay, v'yishador
v'yis'aleh v'yisalal, shmay d'kudsho, brich hu, l'aylo min kl birchoso
v'sheeroso, tush'bechoso v'nechemoso, da,ameeran b'olmo- vimru Omein.

Y'hay shlomo rabbo min sh'mayo, v'chayim alaynu v'al kol Yisroell;
v'imru Omein.

Oseh sholom bimromov, hu ya'aseh sholom olaynu, v'al kol yisroel;
vimru Omein.

KIA: Excellent! What was that? What did you call it?

BONNIE: Yarzheit.

NORMA: Yarzheit is the one year anniversary of someone's death. We light a
candle the night before, then unveil the headstone at the gravesite.

KIA: Cool!

BONNIE: *(Pointedly.)* We remember the person for his deeds.

NORMA: All right. I assumed I'd be conducting the religious portion of the
ceremony since I'm the only one present who's even stepped foot inside
a temple since Gene was bar-mitzvahed.

BONNIE: Well, I have.

NORMA: Any objections? Fine. It would have been nice if it had been one of
the men, the oldest son, of course, that would have been ideal, but, obviously we're are not living in an ideal world.

BONNIE: I have.

NORMA: What? You have what?

BONNIE: Been inside a temple since . . .

NORMA: Well, I was speaking of the four children, Bonnie. I'm sorry, I though
that was obvious. All right? Now, I would like each of us, each of the children to speak. A memory about Papa, childhood, the family — some sort
of tribute. Of course, it's entirely up to each of you, these are simply sug-
gestions.

KIA: What did he die of? Did you say? Was it cancer or something long and
awful like that?

BONNIE: A crane fell on him.

KIA: Huh?

BONNIE: He was walking up Fifth Avenue and a crane fell over and crushed
him to death.

KIA: Oh, my God. He's one of those crane deaths!?

GENE: Kia . . .

KIA: That's so freaky! I mean, you hear about that stuff happening, but you don't really think it's real people. God! Was it on the news and everything? Was a picture in the paper?

NORMA: Yes. I've hired a gardener to do some plantings and maintain the plot. The rest of the cemetery hasn't been kept up, so I thought we could all contribute to the upkeep of Mama and Papa's plots. Any objections? Good.

HERB: You know, we should really talk about when we're going to put this place on the market.

NORMA: Put what place on the market?

HERB: We've let it just sit around for the past year, pretty much empty while we're paying a buttload of property taxes for nothing. Plus of course, gas and water. Now, it's a bad time with interest rates what they are, but I've done a preliminary work-up of whether our losses due to the market would be greater than our continual tax encumbrance, and of course what we're going to have to pay to get the place in sellable condition, which is only going to increase with time, and I think we should just move on it. I called a broker . . .

NORMA: You what? How could you do that?

HERB: Just to hear what she has to say — to give us some idea of what it's worth, what the market up here —

NORMA: I have no intention of letting this place go to strangers. Absolutely not. It will stay in the family.

HERB: Oh, come on, Norma. None of us comes up here anymore. The town is dead. There's no Chinese food.

NORMA: This is our home.

HERB: It's a two-hour drive to be in the middle of nowhere.

NORMA: It's beautiful here. I love it here.

HERB: Have you come here more than once since the funeral? We haven't. Gene?

GENE: No.

NORMA: Our grandparents came to this country and worked like dogs to build this house. Mama grew up here. Everywhere you look you see traces of their lives, our lives. Papa gave up a career in New York so that he could raise his family in the country, where they would be safe and healthy . . .

HERB: And then he got hit by a crane. So go figure. It's just a house, Norma. And it's kind of falling apart.

NORMA: How can you be so callous? Gene, you don't feel this way, do you?

GENE: Well, no. But . . . You know, we don't really ever come here. It *is* just sitting empty.

NORMA: So, we can change that.

KIA: I think it's an amazingly great house. You should totally hang onto it. I mean, think of the parties you could throw.

HERB: We don't even see each other in the city . . . we're going to drive two hours —

NORMA: I will. I'll come up. Mama and Papa are buried here. Aren't you going to visit their gravesites?

HERB: Norma, Dad didn't visit Mom's grave for ten years. Come on.

NORMA: I did. I came.

GENE: I'm probably going to be moving to LA within the year anyway, Nor.

BONNIE: What?

GENE: Simon's in Australia.

KIA: He's in Australia?

NORMA: This place is our childhood. Our history. Our memories.

HERB: How much property tax are you willing to pay for a memory? Huh? It's going to fall apart. Who's going to take care of it? How can we protect it from thieves, or from vagabonds moving in and taking over?

KIA: Vagabonds!

NORMA: I'm not selling it.

HERB: Do you want to buy us out?

NORMA: Buy you out? Do you hear yourself? Buy you out? I'm your sister, Herb. Have you completely forgotten that?

HERB: No. I haven't forgotten, Norma. But you've got to be reasonable about this. I mean, you don't want to sell — fine. But why should we all pay for it? If you love the house, maybe the house should be yours.

NORMA: I want us to all have it as a family. I want it to be a place we all come to. On Thanksgiving. Rosh Hashana. I want it to be handed down, to our children, our children's children.

HERB: What children? *(There is a silence.)* No, really, what children?

BONNIE: Herb.

HERB: You think Eric's going to want it? Have you even spoken to him in the past three years?

GENE: Come on, Herb. Let's not . . .

HERB: Does he even know Dad died?

NORMA: I wrote to him . . .

HERB: You wrote to him? Your kid? You wrote to him? You see what I'm saying here? You talk about handing the place down, who the hell is it going to?

NORMA: *(Deeply hurt.)* You amaze me Herb. What's happened to us? Mama and Papa, they worked so hard to make this a real home. To make us a family. Why aren't we a real family?

HERB: This is what a real family is, Norma.

NORMA: *(Very upset.)* I don't understand you people. It's like you're strangers. Well, I don't care. I am not selling this place, AND I'm not buying you out. So, Herb, you get together all your lawyers, you go ahead and figure out how you're going to squeeze me out of here. Forcibly. You figure it out. I'm going to bed.

(She exits. There is a silence.)

BONNIE: You're moving to LA, Gene?

GENE: Well, not right away, but . . .

BONNIE: You're going too, Kia?

KIA: Well, when I get work. I mean, eventually I'll be bicoastal, but not now.

BONNIE: When are you moving?

GENE: Not for a long time . . . I just said that, I mean, because of the house. Not for a long time.

HERB: *(To Gene.)* Speaking of . . . the broker is coming on Monday. Obviously I have to be back at work. We can't exactly have Simon show her the place. So, I was kind of hoping . . .

GENE: Ahh. I don't know . . . Norma's really going to be pissed.

HERB: She'll get over it. Her name is Edna something. She'll be here at ten. You just have to show her around and give her a set of keys. Can you do it?

GENE: Gee. I don't . . . Kia, don't you have to be back in the city?

BONNIE: She could go back with Herb! I'll wait here with you, Gene. You know. And then you could drive me home after.

HERB: Sure. No problem.

GENE: I really should be heading back with Kia.

KIA: *(Taking out her datebook.)* Let me look. Huh. I've got a pretty crazy day on Monday.

GENE: *(Trying to head her off at the pass.)* That's OK. I'm taking you back. Don't even look in there. I'm taking you.

KIA: I've got yoga at ten-thirty . . .

GENE: *(Overlapping.)* It's OK, Kia . . .

KIA: . . . which I could definitely miss, but then I've got the abortion scheduled for two, and then an audition for this showcase this girl from my acting class's boyfriend is putting on at four-thirty. So I sort of need to be back by early afternoon.

(There is a shocked silence.)

GENE: *(Jumping in with desperation.)* OK. Well, we'll talk about it and we'll work it out. No need for you to stay too, Bonnie. I could always . . . if it's just keys and all. I can take care of it. God, I'm beat. Shall we call it a night? Kia, you want help making up the bed and stuff?

BONNIE: *(To Kia.)* What did you say?

KIA: Huh?

BONNIE: Did you say you're getting an abortion?

KIA: Um, yeah, but that's not till like two o'clock. So, you know, if Gene can get out by like eleven, that's great, or I'll just get a ride with you guys on Sunday night, right?

GENE: Yeah, great! So, we'll work it all out tomorrow!

BONNIE: You're pregnant?

KIA: Yeah. *(Hitting herself in the head.)* What a dope, right?

BONNIE: Is it . . . is it Gene's?

GENE: Kia. Come on. This is all . . . I can't believe you said anything, Kia.

KIA: Sorry.

GENE: Let's all just call it a night. Let's all just . . .

HERB: Oh, boy.

BONNIE: You're carrying Gene's baby? And you're going to kill it?

HERB: Oh, boy.

GENE: Oh, God. Please please let's not do this. OK? Let's just . . . Kia? Do you need help here, or . . .

(Bonnie runs from the room, weeping.)

KIA: Wow. I'm totally sorry. I've got a really big mouth. Sorry, Gene. I didn't know. Sorry.

GENE: All right. Just don't say anything more. OK?

(There is an uncomfortable silence.)

HERB: *(Awkward.)* OK, then. Well. Guess I'll go find the little woman. *(Pause.)* Good night all.

(He gets up and goes out.)

KIA: Wow. Sorry. I'm a big jerk, huh? I wasn't even thinking . . . I mean, there it was in my datebook and . . .

GENE: Why would you just come out and say that? I mean, don't you have any concept of what's private and what's public?

KIA: God. I guess I don't. Wow. You should have told me not to say anything.

GENE: It didn't even occur to me to tell you that. I thought anyone living and breathing who managed to survive as long as you have would know.

KIA: You're really mad, aren't you?

GENE: No. I just . . . Please, don't say *anything* to Norma. I mean *anything*.

Don't even talk in front of her. Just don't even . . . I mean, if you can help it, just don't even say anything. OK? Around my family, OK?

KIA: Why are you getting like this? This is so not like you.

GENE: No. This is like me. You're . . . you seem so different here. In front of them. You seem so different.

KIA: Hey, I'm totally the same.

GENE: Yeah. I guess you are. Look, let's just get some sleep, OK? Do you want me to help you make up the bed or anything?

KIA: I don't really have to stay out here, do I? I mean, your sister's asleep . . . *(Putting her arms around him.)* Why don't we just sneak into your room and pretend you're in high school again?

GENE: *(Disentangling himself.)* I'm really not up for it, Ki. You'll be comfortable out here. I've slept here myself. It's not bad.

KIA: Oh, man. You're really pissed at me, aren't you? God. I'm such a total jerk.

GENE: No. I'm just really worn out. I need to get to bed. OK?

KIA: OK. *(She gives him a kiss, which he barely returns.)* I'm still going to be the girl in the cage, right?

GENE: The girl in the . . . Yeah. Right.

KIA: Great! Good night, sweetie.

GENE: Night. Night, Simon.

(He exits. Kia goes to her bag and takes out a teeny tiny teddy. She holds it up and is about to undress when she remembers that Simon is there.)

KIA: Simon? I'm going to bed now, if that's OK with you. *(No response.)* I'd kind of like to turn out the light, you know? *(No response. She goes through her bag and finds a joint.)* You mind if I smoke a jay before bed? Cool. *(She lights up and comes beside him.)* You want some? *(No response. She goes over and speaks right into his face, very loudly and distinctly.)* Hey!!!

SIMON: *(Very startled.)* Ahh!

KIA: Whatcha looking at?

SIMON: N-n-nothing.

KIA: Yeah? You been looking at nothing for a long time.

SIMON: Yes.

KIA: How come?

SIMON: I can't see, actually.

KIA: You can't see?

SIMON: No.

KIA: Then, what are you doing?

SIMON: I'm playing back all the star clusters I saw in my childhood.

KIA: Huh.

SIMON: In my head. I can replay years of nights. And, with the information I have now, I can reinterpret what I observed as a child. Reclassify. It's very interesting.

KIA: Can I look?

SIMON: Yes.

KIA: *(Looking through the telescope.)* Wow.

SIMON: What?

KIA: I don't see anything either.

SIMON: You probably need to focus.

KIA: So, what, are you blind?

SIMON: Almost.

KIA: Wow. Tough break, huh?

SIMON: Hmm.

KIA: Are you going to get a dog and all that? Are you going to learn how to read with your hands?

SIMON: I've been sent back to learn Braille. As my work is primarily auditory in nature if I could read I'd still be able to perform my primary functions. But it's become clear that I can't tolerate that much s-s-sensory stimulation.

(He holds up his gloved hands.)

KIA: Wow.

SIMON: And I'm allergic to dogs.

KIA: What are you going to do?

SIMON: There's not very much for me *to* do. Here on Earth.

KIA: What are you? You're like something in Austria they said.

SIMON: Australia.

KIA: Yeah? What?

SIMON: An astronomer.

KIA: An astronomer!!! That is so cool! Can you guess what I am?

SIMON: What are you?

KIA: Come on. I'm easy. And for a professional like you . . .

SIMON: I don't . . .

KIA: Oh, for . . . I'm a Leo!!! Jeez!

SIMON: Ummm.

KIA: Nothing personal, but you could use some more training or more astronomy school or whatever, cause I'm easy easy easy. You know, you've got very sexy lips. *(Holding up the joint.)* You want a drag?

SIMON: Do you mean s-smoke?

KIA: They're all asleep. Let down your hair a little.

SIMON: I don't smoke.

KIA: Never? I'm your first? Oh, my God, this is so great!

SIMON: No, thank you.

KIA: I promise, you'll totally dig it. You'll see star clusters from your childhood like you wouldn't believe.

SIMON: No, thank you.

KIA: You are *so* cute. You really have the sexiest lips. I just want to bite them, you know?

SIMON: I think I better go to bed now.

KIA: Please please please! I'll give you a kiss if you try some.

SIMON: No, thank you.

KIA: I'll give you a kiss anyway.

SIMON: Aren't you Gene's date?

KIA: Oh, he's cool with it. We're totally not into commitment or limiting ourselves or anything.

SIMON: No, thank you.

KIA: Don't you find me attractive?

SIMON: Actually, everyone is very fuzzy right now. At first I just lost my peripheral vision, but little by little a sort of haze has closed in, and now everything is fairly muted.

KIA: This is totally blowing my mind. I'm a knockout!!! I mean, on this coast. I'm gorgeous. In LA I'm not as hot, 'cause there are a lot of girls who've had a lot more work done, but here everybody wants to do me. Do you want to touch me? Maybe you could tell.

SIMON: No thank you. I really don't like a lot of tactile stimulation. S-s-so . . . OK. Good night then. *(He gets up to go. Kia gets in front of him.)* I think you're in my way.

KIA: God, Simon. This is making me so hot! All right, look. Just take one hit and then I'll let you go. OK?

SIMON: No.

KIA: Either one hit or one kiss. Which do you want?

SIMON: Just one puff?

KIA: Yeah. One puff.

SIMON: OK.

KIA: No, no wait. I'm going to change first, OK? Here, you sit down — go back to your telescope and look at your star thingies or whatever, and I'll just duck behind the couch and put on my teddy. *(She goes about doing that.)* God, this is so great. I feel like I'm in junior high again. I love it out here in the country. OK. Let me just get this off, and . . . *(She comes out in her teddy.)* Tada! *(Standing in front of him.)* Can you see this at all?

SIMON: Ummm . . . it's blue, right?

KIA: Wow. OK. Here's your puff. Let me start it, and then you. Here. *(She takes a drag and then puts it up to his mouth.)* Breath it only into your mouth first, and then slowly breath it all the way in and then . . . *(As she speaks, he breaths it in and starts choking and coughing.)* Yeah. The first one's gonna do that.

SIMON: *(Coughing.)* That's . . . I'm dying.

KIA: God. You are like the sexiest man I ever met. Can I just give you one kiss now?

SIMON: You said one or the other. I took a puff — now you have to let me go to bed.

KIA: Jeez! I just want to make you feel good so bad. Could I give you a massage?

SIMON: No, please, don't touch me. I . . .

(He gets up and wobbles.)

KIA: You better relax here for a minute. What if I rub your temples?

SIMON: No . . . please . . .

(She starts to rub his temples. He pushes her hands away, but she goes right back and soothingly does it again.)

KIA: Does this feel good?

SIMON: Just don't . . . do anything else.

KIA: Here, hold on. *(She takes a drag, and then softly blows it into his face.)* Just relax. *(She gets up behind the couch, leans in, and begins rubbing his temples again.)* Can I take off your glasses?

SIMON: No.

(She does. Moves her hands down to his shoulders and begins massaging them.)

SIMON: No! Don't!

KIA: Shhhh.

(As she stands, rubbing Simon, Herb tiptoes into the room. He sees Kia in her Teddy, but can't see Simon. He tiptoes up behind her and quickly puts his hands over her eyes.)

HERB: Guess who! *(Kia shrieks in surprise, as does Simon, who jumps up and crashes into the coffee table.)* Shit! What the hell . . .

KIA: You scared the life out of me!

HERB: What are you doing?

KIA: I was just giving Simon a massage.

HERB: Simon?!

SIMON: Herb. Can I have my glasses, please?

KIA: What were *you* doing?

HERB: I was just . . . I saw the light on. I was coming in to see if you wanted me to turn it off.

KIA: *(She gives him a smooth smile.)* Oh. Thanks. *(She holds up the joint.)* You want a toke?

HERB: Holy crow. Is that marijuana?

KIA: It's really good.

HERB: Christ. If Norma catches you with that shit, you're dead. She'll call the cops on you, honest to God.

KIA: Oh, come on.

HERB: No, I mean it. You better hide that stuff and fast. She turned her own son in.

KIA: What?

HERB: She found it in his sock drawer and she turned him in. Called the cops, had them come take him away. An ambush.

KIA: Wow. That's crazy.

HERB: Lost her husband. Her son. But she wouldn't back down.

KIA: She turned her son in to the cops? How old was he?

HERB: Fifteen. I'm serious. You better hide that, or throw it out the window or swallow it or something. Christ, the room stinks. Open the window. Simon, were you smoking this stuff? I can't believe you.

SIMON: I-I-I . . . Sh-h-h-he, she m-m-made me.

KIA: Oh for . . . You're both so cute, the way you're so scared of your sister. She seemed really sweet and funny to me.

HERB: Well, you've smoked too much of that stuff then. Nothing sweet. Nothing funny about Norma. She's the Gestapo. Simon, you better go off to your room.

SIMON: Th-h-hat's what I w-w-wanted to . . .

(He rushes off, bumping into things along the way.)

HERB: Well. You're a bad bad girl.

KIA: *(Offering the joint.)* Want some?

HERB: No! I'm serious. You should hide that. You never know where Norma's lurking.

KIA: Where's your wife?

HERB: Bonnie?

KIA: Bonnie. She seemed a little uptight. Maybe she could use some.

HERB: Oh, I don't think so.

KIA: You want to sit down?

HERB: No . . . *(Sitting.)* I should really head back in . . . I really just came to check the door, make sure it's locked, you know, that's a very pretty nightgown.

KIA: Thanks.

(She relights her joint.)

HERB: Oh, boy.

KIA: So, where is your wife?

HERB: Oh, she's, you know, getting ready for bed. Putting on her . . .

(She blows smoke into his face. He coughs. She laughs.)

HERB: Putting on her . . . maybe I will take some of that.

KIA: It's really good.

(She holds it to his mouth and he holds her hand steady and takes a hit.)

HERB: *(Holding his breath.)* Sooo . . .

KIA: Sooo . . .

(They both laugh.)

HERB: So what were you doing out here with Simon?

KIA: Trying to help him relax. You've got a very stressed-out family, you know?

HERB: Yes, I know. Could I have some more of that?

KIA: Here you've got this big old house, and all these things — all these really old things, nice things, and money and all, and you're all so uptight. Like, what's the point?

HERB: Right —

KIA: I mean, If this was my house, I'd just come here with all my friends and party out every weekend.

HERB: You're a party girl, aren't you?

KIA: I like to have fun. Do you like to have fun?

HERB: Well, sure. Everyone likes to have fun. But you have to work too, right? You can't have fun if you don't work. Or how do you pay for it?

KIA: Oh, somebody always pays for it. There's usually a way.

HERB: Well, in my experience, you don't really enjoy what you have unless you've worked for it. You have nice things, you go on trips, you own a big house, a fast car, because you've put in the time, the muscle, and then you enjoy it all the more.

KIA: Do you enjoy your things?

HERB: Well, sure.

KIA: Your big house, your fast car, your . . . wife . . .

HERB: Bonnie.

KIA: Bonnie. You enjoy all that?

HERB: Of course you can't enjoy every moment of it. There has to be a down time. Or you can't appreciate the good times.

KIA: Really? I feel like, why not have fun all the time? I mean, life is so short, right?

HERB: Right.

KIA: Why be all serious about it? Why not feel good? I want to feel really really good. Have you ever felt really really good?

(Bonnie walks in in her flannel bathrobe and stands in the back of the room, watching them. She is carrying a fifth of scotch and takes a long swig.)

HERB: Well . . . really *really* good, I don't . . .

KIA: Do you want to feel really really good?

HERB: Well . . . yeah . . .

(She moves in closer.)

KIA: You want to feel really really good with me?

HERB: Well, I'm married . . . *(He moves in on her.)* I'm not supposed to feel really really . . .

BONNIE: Herb? *(He jumps.)* Herb, could you help me out here? I'm having trouble getting my cold cream jar open.

HERB: *(Leaping out of the situation.)* Oh, sure, sure. I was just . . . I was checking on the . . .

BONNIE: Window? Yes, it's very cold in here. Someone left the window open.

HERB: Right. I'll get that . . . that's what I came in here to . . .

BONNIE: Smells a little funny in here.

HERB: I think there may have been a . . . an incense. Kia. Kia was burning some incense.

BONNIE: Ahh. That must be it then.

(They all stand frozen for a moment.)

HERB: Cold cream! Jar.

BONNIE: I was just thinking of getting some more apple pie. Does anyone else want some more pie?

HERB: I could use another slice. Kia?

KIA: Can't be the Fat No More girl on two slices of pie.

HERB: Right. Right. Just us, hon.

BONNIE: Why don't you go get us some pie, Herb?

HERB: Oh! Sure. Sure. *(Nervous to leave them together.)* Okey-doke. I'll be . . . right back then. Right back.

(He goes to the kitchen. Bonnie takes another swig and comes down to Kia.)

BONNIE: So. Kia.

KIA: I'm really sorry if I blew your mind before. You know, about the abortion and all. I didn't realize it was such a big deal with you guys.

BONNIE: You must be freezing. With the window open and you wearing . . . so little.

KIA: No. The cold doesn't affect me. I'm like, totally oblivious.

BONNIE: Yes, I can see that.

KIA: Yeah.

BONNIE: You know, Kia, I've been in my room, I've been lying in my room, drinking this scotch . . .

KIA: Can I have some?

BONNIE: No. So, I've been lying there and I've been thinking about you.

KIA: You've been thinking about me? Cool.

(Herb comes out. He stands and listens, like a deer in the headlights.)

BONNIE: I want to talk with you Kia. I'd like to be your friend.

KIA: You would? Wow. I like totally misread you. I didn't think we connected at all.

BONNIE: No. I feel very connected to you. What is it, Herb?

HERB: Ummm. Pie knife. Can't find the pie knife.

BONNIE: Second drawer on the right.

HERB: Ahh! Rightoe. Great.

(He stands there, not wanting to leave.)

BONNIE: You can't miss it, Herb.

HERB: Right. OK.

(He leaves.)

BONNIE: So, Kia, let's get to know each other.

KIA: OK, super.

BONNIE: Super.

KIA: OK. So, like . . . what do you do?

BONNIE: Me? Well, I'm married to Herb . . .

KIA: But before you were married to Herb. What did you do then?

BONNIE: I was a receptionist. Where Herb works.

KIA: You were like Herb's secretary? Herb was fooling around with his secretary?

BONNIE: It wasn't like that.

KIA: That is so fifties! I love it. Did you stay after hours and come into his office with your little notepad, and tell him you weren't wearing any underwear, and he'd chase you around his desk and you'd squeal, "No, no, no, Mr. —" what's his last name again?

BONNIE: We had a very respectful courtship and as soon as it seemed we were getting serious, I resigned.

KIA: Schwartz! Of course. Duh. Like Gene. No, no, no, Mr. Schwartz! I'm a nice girl. Please stop!

BONNIE: *(Kia has hit the nail on the head.)* It wasn't like that at all.

KIA: So how long have you been married?

BONNIE: Nine years.

KIA: God. Do you have kids?

BONNIE: No. We've . . . we've had some difficulty.

KIA: Yeah? You mean sex? Because I have some methods . . .

BONNIE: No. Kia. No. *(She sighs deeply and takes another swig. Herb rushes in, carrying plates of pie.)*

HERB: Pie!!!

BONNIE: Thanks.

(He begins to sit down.)

BONNIE: Oh, Herb. I'd like some ice cream with that. And a cup of hot chocolate.

HERB: Uhhh.

BONNIE: Please.

HERB: OK. I'll be right back. *(He rushes out again, with the plates.)*

KIA: You know, it's not a great idea to eat all that before bed. It'll go right to your hips.

BONNIE: So, Kia. Tell me about you and Gene.

KIA: Oh, Gene's the best. He's totally changed my whole life. I mean, I guess someone would have discovered me sooner or later, it was bound to happen, but I really wanted it to be while I was in my prime, you know?

BONNIE: Do you love him?

KIA: Gene? Oh sure. He's great.

BONNIE: I just . . . I don't want to see you get hurt, Kia.

KIA: How would I get hurt? I'm not getting you.

BONNIE: I just hope you realize that this isn't a . . . serious relationship for Gene. I don't think he sees any future in it.

KIA: Umm, sorry, but I think you're like totally wrong. He's already told me I'm going to be the girl in the cage. And after that, who knows.

BONNIE: I'm talking about on a personal level, Kia. I just don't want you to get all involved and then find out after some time that . . . that Gene doesn't really care about you.

KIA: How do you know he doesn't care about me?

BONNIE: Well, I don't want to betray a confidence . . .

KIA: Betray a *who?*

BONNIE: Just between us now, Gene told me.

KIA: Gene told you?

BONNIE: Yes.

KIA: Really? Why?

BONNIE: Well, I'm sort of a confident for Gene. We're . . . we're very very close and . . .

KIA: He never mentioned you.

BONNIE: Well, it's a . . . a private thing. I'm sure he doesn't talk about it a lot.

KIA: No, I mean at all. I knew he had brothers but . . .

BONNIE: Gene and I are very close, Kia. We're much closer in age than you and Gene are, and we have a very special . . .

KIA: Yeah? I thought you were like way older than him.

BONNIE: No. Anyway, we talk on a much deeper level than you and he do, and that makes our relationship . . . our feelings for each other . . .

KIA: Oh my God! I get it. You like totally have a thing for Gene! That is so wild!

BONNIE: Be quiet! That's not it at all.

KIA: Oh wow! Did you guys do it? I can't even imagine it. The two of you screwing! That's too weird!

BONNIE: No. We're friends. Keep your voice down.

KIA: Oh, sorry. *(Half whisper.)* So, like Herb doesn't know, right? Wow! You should tell him. Maybe he'd be into it. You could do a brother thing! That would be totally awesome. You know, if you want to make it a foursome or something let me know. I think Herb's really sexy in a fatherly kind of way.

BONNIE: No! No. That's disgusting. I absolutely . . . That's repulsive. No.

KIA: Oh. Well, what were you getting at then? That's not what you were getting at?

BONNIE: No. This is not at all what I wanted to . . . Kia. *(She takes another belt.)* Kia. I want to talk to you.

KIA: Wow. You're getting all uptight again.

BONNIE: Where do you live, Kia?

KIA: What is that, scotch?

BONNIE: How would you like to live in a beautiful apartment on the upper east side with maid service and a doorman, and as time went by, someone to cook for you and make sure everything you wanted was taken care of?

KIA: What do you mean?

BONNIE: I'd like you to live like that, Kia. I'd like to see you taken really good care of.

KIA: Yeah? Who would pay for it?

BONNIE: I would. Well, Herb and I would.

KIA: That's really nice of you.

BONNIE: Yes.

KIA: What would I have to do?

BONNIE: Have the baby.

KIA: What?

BONNIE: I want you to have Gene's baby.

KIA: Wait. Is this a joke?

BONNIE: Look, Kia. Look. It would be seven or eight more months out of your life, and you'd get enough money to live comfortably for years. And then anywhere in the world you want to go, your dream destination — London, Paris, Rome . . .

KIA: Cancun?

BONNIE: Cancun! You could go there. We'd fly you to Cancun. The nicest hotel they've got.

KIA: Yeah? On the beach?

BONNIE: Right on the beach. You live in this beautiful apartment on the upper east side for eight months with everything taken care of. Of course you can't smoke or drink or sleep with anyone or take drugs . . .

KIA: What?!

BONNIE: But for eight months you live like a queen, and then as soon as the baby is born, I'll take that baby, I'll give that baby everything — all the love and attention and everything it needs — you never have to give it another thought, and you're off for an all-expenses-paid vacation to Cancun!

KIA: What about clothes?

(Herb walks in with the plates of pie and ice cream and stands listening.)

BONNIE: You name it. Clothes, food, hotel, spending money.

KIA: A car?

BONNIE: We'd rent you any car you like. Sports car . . . whatever.

KIA: Would you buy me a car?

BONNIE: Well, it's definitely negotiable.

KIA: I'd need my own car.

BONNIE: Fine. You get your own car.

HERB: Hey, what are you gals talking about?

BONNIE: Where's the hot chocolate, Herb?

HERB: The water's heating up. What's all this about cars?

KIA: Your wife wants to give me a car.

HERB: Yeah?

KIA: She wants to give me fancy clothes and a fancy apartment and a maid and a doorman.

HERB: Bonnie? What's going on?

KIA: What do you think, Herb? Do you want to do that too?

HERB: Is this a game? What game is this?

KIA: What about Herb? Do I get Herb too? Do you get Gene and I get Herb?

HERB: Hey you two. What game is this? Can I play?

KIA: I don't know. Can Herb play, Bonnie?

(Just then the tea-kettle whistle blasts.)

BONNIE: Herb, you better get the water.

KIA: You haven't even talked to Herb about all this?

HERB: What's going on?

BONNIE: Herb, get the water.

HERB: No, I want to know . . .

BONNIE: Before it wakes up Norma, Herb. Hurry!

HERB: Oh cripes!

(He rushes out.)

KIA: You and Herb need to talk more.

BONNIE: What do you think? Will you do it?

KIA: I'm the Fat-No-More girl. You think they're going to keep a Fat-No-More Girl with a stomach out to here?

BONNIE: It's only a few months.

KIA: Your body's never the same after you have a baby. My roommate's cousin Jill has a one-year-old and man, you should see her. Why don't you have your own baby?

BONNIE: I can't.

KIA: Why don't you adopt?

BONNIE: I want Gene's baby. I want this baby.

KIA: Wow. This night is totally not going the way I thought.

BONNIE: Kia. Look, Kia, I've always wanted a baby, since I was a little girl. Didn't you always want a baby?

KIA: No. I used to want a horse when I was little, but then I went to the riding stables once with my friend Erica who's really rich, and the place stank. And she had to clean out her horse's stall with a shovel. It was gross.

BONNIE: *(After an exhausted sigh.)* OK. Listen, Kia. All I ever wanted to be was a mother. When I was growing up, my girlfriends had all these ambitions, fantasies, important careers, but all I ever dreamed of was having a baby, my own baby. Someone small to love and take care of.

KIA: Like a dog. Hey, why don't you just get a dog?

BONNIE: No, not like a dog. I want a child . . . I want a family. I want to be a family.

KIA: With Herb? Is he part of it?

BONNIE: Of course he's part of it.

KIA: Yeah? Then why were you screwing Gene? If you don't mind my asking, how does that work?

BONNIE: I do mind your asking. It's none of your business.

KIA: Well, it seems to me if you're going to dress me and feed me and keep me like a pet till I have your kid, it seems like it totally is my business.

BONNIE: *(Getting very upset.)* That's not what I meant. I was just trying to . . . make you see . . . *(Terribly frustrated.)* Achh! I could just . . . I could just strangle you right now! I could put my hands around your little neck and just . . . I could kill you!!!

(Herb enters at this moment with the hot chocolate and overhears this. He is horrified.)

HERB: Bonnie! What's going on here? What are you . . .

BONNIE: Herb, go get me a napkin, please.

HERB: A napkin? What's happening? What are you doing?

BONNIE: *(Completely losing it.)* A napkin, Herb! I need a napkin with my pie! A NAPKIN!

HERB: No, I want to know what you're . . .

BONNIE: *(Coming at him, screaming.)* A napkin! A napkin! Go get me a napkin! Is that so much to ask??? I want a napkin!

HERB: *(Backing out of the room with the hot chocolate.)* All right! I'm going. I'll get you a napkin. All right!

(Pause.)

KIA: Wow. You need to breathe or something.

BONNIE: *(Breaking down.)* Oh, God. What's happened to me? *(A swig. All pretensions gone. A realization.)* You know . . . you know, Kia, I used to be you.

KIA: You used to be me?

BONNIE: I used to be you. I used to be little and blonde and sexy.

KIA: Really?

BONNIE: I know that's hard to believe. Now that I'm old and fat and frumpy.

KIA: You're not frumpy.

BONNIE: I've lost it . . . that thing. What you have. It's gone for me now.

KIA: You know, if you work out, ride a bike, like I said. And the Fat No More thing, it really does work.

BONNIE: When I met Herb, I was you. I was pretty and dumb and I played it to the hilt. Like you. So much like you.

KIA: You know, I'm not just pretty. I'm an actress too.

BONNIE: Yes, I saw the commercial. You know what their father, what Manny said when Herb brought me home to meet the family?

KIA: What?

BONNIE: Well, Herb. She's no genius. She must be really great in bed.

KIA: That's not very nice.

BONNIE: No. No, he wasn't very nice. They weren't very nice. But I wanted it anyway. I wanted a family. I wanted a baby. So I let Manny humiliate me, and I became Jewish, and I quit my job.

KIA: You became Jewish?

BONNIE: I gave up everything that was me. But the baby. A soft, sweet-smelling little baby to love. *(Getting weepy.)* A tiny little baby.

KIA: Hey. Wow. You want to smoke a joint?

BONNIE: Yes, please.

(Kia gets it and lights it and they smoke during the following.)

KIA: Man, so you really wanted a baby, huh?

BONNIE: *(She has to laugh at this.)* Yeah.

KIA: So, why didn't you have one? I don't get it.

BONNIE: Well, we got pregnant right after the wedding. Probably before the wedding, actually.

KIA: Yeah? Great!

BONNIE: And Herb and I were so happy. If you knew us then. We spent six months decorating the baby's room, reading baby books, choosing names. Blissful. Even the family embraced me. Even Manny. Even Norma. I'd visit the baby's room ten times a day, look at those impossibly tiny clothes, and try to imagine that soon there would be a whole new person in my life, a remarkable little person who would fit into those tiny little things. *(Herb returns with the napkins.)*

HERB: Umm, here are the napkins . . .

BONNIE: *(She takes one and blows her nose.)* Thanks, Herb.

HERB: Oh my God, Bonnie, are you smoking?

BONNIE: Yeah, you want some?

KIA: So, what happened?

BONNIE: Well, suddenly it was gone. At seven months. No more.

HERB: Aw jeez.

BONNIE: It had never occurred to us that that could happen. That we could lose our baby. We were in shock for a long time. Cried together. Held each other.

HERB: Honey, why do you want to dredge this up? Come on. And hey, Jesus, you better put that out. Norma . . .

BONNIE: Fuck Norma. But little by little, we recovered. We healed. Together. Till we were brave enough to try again.

HERB: Why do this, Bonnie? Let it rest.

KIA: Hey, let her talk. I'll take a napkin too, please.

(Gene enters.)

GENE: What was that noise? What are you guys doing up? Oh my God. Is that pot?

BONNIE: It was the same thing again and again. But the joy was gone. It was just aching and waiting, swollen ankles, lying in bed month after month trying to keep this one, this next one, this next one alive. Five times. Five times we went through it. Even the doctors begged us to stop. By the time I was pregnant with Aaron . . .

HERB: Bonnie, please, I don't want to hear this.

BONNIE: Then go back to bed, Herb.

KIA: Go back to bed.

BONNIE: By the time I was pregnant with Aaron we had stopped telling people. It was a dark, shameful secret that we were pregnant again. We barely spoke of the baby, barely spoke at all. His family looked at me as if I'd tricked them. Herb's father told him he had no obligation to stay with me. That he had every right to leave.

GENE: Dad said this?

HERB: He didn't say that exactly . . .

BONNIE: And I half expected Herb would leave. Every night when the door opened and he walked in I was so relieved, and just a little disappointed in him that he stayed.

HERB: Jesus, Bonnie.

GENE: Dad said you should leave her, Herb?

HERB: Well . . .

BONNIE: But then, I carried to term. Nine months. We couldn't believe it. We started dreaming again. Hoping. When I was past my due date, we finally let ourselves be really happy. The whole family came to the hospital — even Simon. The baby was kicking me hard all the way to the delivery room. But, then, suddenly, the kicking stopped.

KIA: Oh no.

BONNIE: I told them, I told them in a panic something had changed. They said to relax — everything was fine. But by the time they hooked me up to the fetal monitor, it was clear that something terrible had happened. *(Norma walks in.)*

NORMA: What stinks in here? What are you all doing up? What is that smell?

KIA: Quiet, she's telling a story.

NORMA: Quiet??? You're telling *me* quiet???

KIA: Yeah, chill out. Go ahead, Bonnie.

BONNIE: They turned on the machine, and I lay there in shock. No movement. No heartbeat. Nothing.

KIA: Wow.

NORMA: Oh, you're not reliving all the gory details again . . . This is what you're all up for at one in the morning? What is that — marijuana? Is that marijuana you're smoking???

HERB: Oh, boy.

KIA: It's clove cigarettes, OK? Go on, Bonnie.

NORMA: Well, there's no smoking of any kind in the house. Those are the house rules.

BONNIE: I just started screaming. Not even aware of it. I heard this horrible, hurt animal sound echoing through the hospital, it didn't even seem connected to me. No one could help me, they couldn't help me to stop. So they put me under. And they took Aaron out. It was days before I was conscious enough to really know what had happened. I woke up, a huge empty pouch of a stomach. A huge empty shell. So empty. Even the scream was gone. And Herb was gone too.

HERB: Bonnie, that's not true. You were on so many drugs, you didn't even know what was . . .

BONNIE: *(Over him.)* He couldn't be with me, comfort me any more. I don't blame him. It was too much.

KIA: Man.

NORMA: The whole house stinks. It woke me out of a sound sleep. Put out those cigarettes.

BONNIE: When I got back from the hospital, their father, Manny comes to pay me a visit.

NORMA: All right now, that's enough.

BONNIE: Herb is back at work, they had nurses in all day. And Manny comes into my bedroom.

NORMA: Bonnie, I mean it. Enough is enough.

BONNIE: I'm still barely able to move, I'm all stitched up and swollen . . .

NORMA: What are you trying to do here? What is this? Why do you always feel a need to tear everything down? The man is dead. Have some respect for the dead.

BONNIE: He comes into my bedroom with a checkbook. He sits down and pulls out a pen. "How much?" he says.

GENE: What? Is this true?

NORMA: This is bullshit.

BONNIE: "How much will it take to make you go away?"

HERB: Bonnie, what are you saying?

BONNIE: "This is not for me," he says. "This is not personal."

HERB: Oh, God.

BONNIE: "The Romans, the Pogroms, the Arabs, the Holocaust. We've survived all these attempts at our extermination."

NORMA: Are you drunk? Look at her, she's drunk!

BONNIE: "But I don't know if we'll survive you."

KIA: You??? What?

NORMA: She's drinking. And God knows what she's smoking.

BONNIE: "Our family is the last in a long line. There are no other Schwartzes."

KIA: I know loads of Schwartzes. You should go to Hollywood. There are like tons of Schwartzes there.

BONNIE: "The mix breeding is bad enough, the assimilation, but you can't even give me a grandson. I'll write a check for whatever you like if you'll go away and give Herb another chance at having a real family."

HERB: Oh my God, Bonnie. Why didn't you tell me? How could you let him do that and not tell me?

BONNIE: I was ashamed.

KIA: Why were you ashamed? Did you take the money??? How much was it? Did you take it??

HERB: Why were you ashamed?

NORMA: Yeah. Why were you ashamed? That I'd like to hear.

BONNIE: I stayed. I turned him down. I stayed. (*She begins weeping.*)
(*Herb goes to her and holds her.*)

NORMA: (*Picking up the joint and stubbing it out.*) I don't buy a word of it. Papa wouldn't do that.

KIA: Why did you stay? Why didn't you take the money?

BONNIE: I loved Herb. And . . . and this is the shameful part.

NORMA: Oh for . . .

BONNIE: I still wanted them. I still wanted the family. To love me. To approve. To think I was good enough. I wanted to be part of it.

GENE: Dad did that to you? I can't believe that. I can't believe he would do that.

NORMA: It's nonsense! You were drugged, like Herb said. You couldn't find your own feet, much less understand a conversation. You've always been out to tear this family apart. I don't know what your vendetta is, but . . .

BONNIE: Shut up! Shut up! Stop bullying me already! The old man is dead. Finally. I don't have a baby. I don't even remember who I used to be. What could I possibly have . . . what do I have left that could still threaten you so much?

NORMA: How dare you suggest . . .

BONNIE: And stop pretending you didn't know, Norma. Manny made that very clear.

(Simon enters and stands in the back of the room.)

SIMON: Is it morning?

NORMA: She's a liar! She's always been this way. She's lying.

BONNIE: All this time I've known, and like an idiot I've tried to make you approve of me. I've tried to be a sister to you. Well, no more, Norma. It's over. *(Picking up the joint and lighting it.)* And you can call the cops on me if you want.

NORMA: I just might do that.

SIMON: Why is everyone up? Is it morning? It's so dark.

GENE: My God. I can't believe this. I can't believe it.

NORMA: Gene, it's not like she makes it sound. Papa was a good man. He worked his whole life to keep us safe and healthy. Everything he did was for us. But he knew that to keep the family alive was to keep the faith alive. He knew what it is to be a Jew.

GENE: That's what it is to be a Jew?

KIA: Wait. I thought that story about the cup . . .

NORMA: You know, the Jews have been alive for five thousand years. After five thousand years, is this going to be the generation that ends it all? Or is this going to be the start of the next five thousand years?

SIMON: Oh, definitely not.

(Everyone turns to him, surprised.)

NORMA: Simon. I didn't see you there. Why don't you go back to bed, sweetheart. It's very late.

SIMON: It definitely won't be another five thousand years, Norma. It might not even be five hundred.

NORMA: What won't be?

SIMON: People. No, five thousand years from now, there might be a something on the earth, a new start maybe, there might be some amoebas, or protozoa, or whatever else evolves from what's left of the planet, but there most definitely won't be Jews.

NORMA: Simon, we're discussing something you don't understand, honey.

SIMON: And five thousand years is such a short time in the great scheme of things. The dinosaurs were around for hundreds of millions of years, and they're completely gone. What are the Jews next to that?

KIA: Wow.

NORMA: It's very complicated, sweetheart. Go back to bed, we have an early morning.

SIMON: All right. *(He starts out, but then stops for a moment.)* You know . . . you all should be preparing. I don't know if any of you will be chosen, probably not, none of you knows very much and there's not going to be a lot of room on the way station, but you should at least be preparing for the end.

(He slowly walks out. Everyone sits silent for a long moment.)

KIA: Bonnie?

BONNIE: Yes?

KIA: You're like totally not what I thought and I completely take back all the shitty things I was thinking about you and the fact that I was coming on to Herb and all because I didn't know where you were coming from, you know?

HERB: Oh, boy.

BONNIE: Thanks.

KIA: Yeah. And if there was anyone I'd do this for, it would be you, you know? But, you've got to understand . . . like how you wanted a baby, I want to be the Fat-No-More girl and the girl in the cage. I mean, it sounds really stupid, even my saying it right now, even to me it does, because it's not like on the same level at all, but, it's my dream, you know? I mean, I really need to have a great body right now, you know? I mean, I really can't have this baby.

BONNIE: Yeah, I know.

NORMA: What baby? What?

HERB: Oh, boy.

NORMA: What is she talking about? Is she pregnant? Are you pregnant?

GENE: Kia . . . God.

KIA: Oh, come on . . . you're not still afraid of her, are you? Come on, sweety. I really think you need to like, gain some perspective, you know?

NORMA: Did you impregnate her, Gene?

GENE: Well . . .

NORMA: Eugene Schwartz, is this girl pregnant with your child?

GENE: Listen, Norma . . .

NORMA: Yes?

GENE: Listen . . .

NORMA: Oh, I'm listening.

GENE: *(Pause.)* It's really none of your business.

HERB: Huh.

KIA: Cool.

GENE: Good night, everybody. Kia, it doesn't seem like you could possibly get any sleep out here. You want to come sleep with me?

KIA: Excellent. *(Kia gathers up her stuff and exits with Gene.)*

HERB: Bonnie?

BONNIE: What, Herb?

HERB: Bonnie, do you still want to come sleep with me?

BONNIE: *(A moment.)* Yeah, Herb, I guess I still do.

(He puts his arms around her. They exit. Norma stands in the room for a moment, alone, as the lights fade to black.)

The next morning. Everyone stands before a headstone. Norma is in the middle of Kaddish.

NORMA: Y'hay shlomo rabbo niin sh'mayo, v'chayim alaynu v'al kol Yisroel; v'imru Omein.

ALL: Amen.

NORMA: Oseh sholom bimromov, hu ya'aseh sholom olaynu, v'al kol Yisroel; vimru Omein.

ALL: Amen.

(Each family member puts a stone on the headstone.)

NORMA: Does anyone want to say anything? Any last words to Papa?

(There is silence.)

NORMA: No one prepared anything to say?

(Silence. Lights down.)

Later that afternoon at the house. Everyone is bustling around getting ready to head back to the city. Simon is back at the telescope. He has a space helmet beside him. Norma is putting little colored stickers on furniture and objects.

NORMA: I'm taking the red stickers. You should each choose a color. Just put a sticker on any piece of furniture that you know for sure you want, and we'll decide later who gets what. I know Mama always wanted me to have the breakfront. And the furniture from the master bedroom. Everything else is up for negotiation.

HERB: Yeah. Actually, I think if that woman's showing the house, it probably looks better fully furnished and without little stickers all over everything, so maybe we should all hold off till there's a buyer.

NORMA: You do things in your time, Herb. I'll do things in mine. I just want to warn all of you that if you don't claim something, and I do, when the time comes I'm taking it.

HERB: Yeah. Well, no surprise there. (He grabs a blue sticker and slaps it on the coffee table.) OK. Mine. (He slowly and deliberately steps onto it and stands there for a moment. With satisfaction.) Ah. (He gets down.) You take the rest. (He grabs a suitcase and heads for the door.) You taking Simon back?

NORMA: I think Gene said he was. (Calling out.) Gene! Gene, are you taking Simon?

GENE: (From the other room.) Huh? I'll be right in. We're getting the rest of this packed.

(Bonnie comes through with her suitcase.)

NORMA: Bonnie, I was telling Herb, anything you want to claim, do it now.

BONNIE: It's all yours Norma. Enjoy. (On the way out.) Who's taking Simon back?

NORMA: Gene is. (Bonnie is gone.) You know, I'll go put these on the bedroom set, just so there's no confusion down the road.

(She starts out. Gene enters.)

GENE: Bye, Nor. We're heading out in a minute. You taking Simon?

NORMA: Herb said you were taking him.

GENE: What? We're in the MG. There's barely room for our bags. You're going to have to do it.

NORMA: No, I'm going back to the cemetery for a bit. Tell Herb he's got to do it.

(She heads in and he heads out. Simon sits alone, staring out the telescope. We hear Gene shouting from offstage.)

GENE: Kia, come on. We're going. Herb, you'll have to take Simon, we don't have room. Herb?

(Kia walks through with her backpack. She sees Simon. Comes downstage to him.)

KIA: Hey, Simon. We're heading out now.

NORMA: (Rushing through with her bags.) Whoever is last, make sure you turn the light out. I'm heading for the cemetery and then straight out. Oh, and leave a key under the mat for that realtor.

KIA: *(To Norma.)* Hey, thanks for everything. I had a super time.

NORMA: Unbelievable.

(She leaves.)

KIA: OK. Bye, Simon. It was really cool meeting you.

(She gives him a kiss on the cheek, which startles him.)

SIMON: Ah! Are you leaving?

KIA: We're all leaving now. Are you packed?

SIMON: Yes.

KIA: I think Herb's taking you. Bye.

(We hear a car pulling away.)

SIMON: Bye.

(He goes back to the telescope. Kia takes her backpack and is about to leave. She sees the pewter cup on the dining room table. She looks around. Goes to it. Picks it up. Holds it up to the light. Looks around again. Thinks for a moment. Puts it in her knapsack.)

GENE: *(From offstage.)* Kia, come on already!

KIA: Coming!

(She runs off. We hear another car start up and leave. We hear Herb off-stage.)

HERB: Oh, cripes. The lights are still on. *(He reaches in and turns them off. Simon sits in half darkness.)* Nobody left a key? Oh Jeez . . .

(There is the sound of him putting keys under the mat. The door slams shut. Another car starts up and leaves. Simon sits alone at the telescope for a long moment. He hears the quiet and sits up. Stays listening for a moment. Reaches for his helmet. Puts it on. Slowly, he rises. He stands, taking in the silence. Feels the gravity melting. Arms out, he floats. He slowly begins his graceful moon walk as the lights narrow to a spotlight on him. The spot becomes a smaller and smaller pinpoint. There is just a dot of light and then it pops out to black.)

END OF PLAY

String Fever

By Jacquelyn Reingold

For Maureen (1957–2001)
and for Evan.

PLAYWRIGHT'S BIOGRAPHY

Jacquelyn Reingold's plays, which include *String Fever, Girl Gone, Dear Kenneth Blake, Tunnel of Love, Freeze Tag, Acapulco* and *For-everett,* have been produced in New York at Ensemble Studio Theatre, MCC Theatre, Naked Angels, HB Playwrights Theatre, HERE Arts Center, All Seasons, The Working Theatre; and at theaters across the country. Awards include the EST/Sloan Foundation Commission, Kennedy Center's Fund for New American Plays Roger Stevens Award, New Dramatists' Whitfield Cook and Joe Callaway Awards, two Drama-Logue Awards, MacDowell Colony Fellowships, and the Greenwall Foundation's Oscar Ruebhausen Award, and Ms. Reingold was a finalist for the Susan Smith Blackburn Prize. Her plays have been published by Smith and Kraus, Dramatists Play Service, Samuel French, in *New Dramatists 2000: The Best Plays, Best American Short Plays 1999–2000, 1997–1998, 1996–1997, 1994–1995,* and *Women Playwrights: The Best Plays 1994.* Jacquelyn has written for NBC's *Miss Match* and MTV's *Daria.* She is a member of the HB Playwrights Unit and Ensemble Studio Theatre and is an alumna of New Dramatists. She has written many plays for The 52nd Street Project. Ms. Reingold will receive her MFA in 2004 from the Playwriting Program at Ohio University, headed by Charles Smith.

ORIGINAL PRODUCTION

String Fever was first produced at Ensemble Studio Theatre in New York City; Curt Dempster, artistic director; Susann Brinkley, executive director; Chris Smith, EST/Sloan Project program director; Dylan McCullough, producer; Doron Weber, Alfred P. Sloan Foundation program director. It opened on March 3, 2003. The cast was as follows:

Lily	Cynthia Nixon
Gisli	Evan Handler
Janey	Cecilia deWolf
Artie	Tom Mardirosian
Frank	Jim Fyfe
Matthew	David Thornton

It was directed by Mary B. Robinson. Set by David P. Gordon; lighting by Michael Lincoln; costumes by Michael Krass; sound by Rob Gould; stage manager, Tiffany N. Thetard; assistant stage manager, Elizabeth Nehls; production manager, Timothy L. Gallagher; properties master, Matthew Hodges; assistant to the director, Kevin Lee Newbury.

String Fever was originally commissioned by the Ensemble Studio The-atre/Alfred P. Sloan Foundation Science and Technology Project. *String Fever* was developed at PlayLabs at The Playwrights' Center in Minneapolis.

CHARACTERS

LILY: Just turned forty. A music teacher.

JANEY: Forties. Lily's no-nonsense best friend.

MATTHEW: Forties. Lily's ex-boyfriend. A successful musician. Has problems.

GISLI: Forties. An actor/comedian in Iceland. Bigger than life. Drinks a lotta coffee.

FRANK: Forties. Physicist whose daughter is in Lily's class.

ARTIE: Sixties. Lily's father. A retired salesman. Likes to talk. Talks fast and loud.

DOCTORS A, B: Doctors. Double cast.

PERSON: A person. Double cast.

String Fever

Candlelight on Lily. A group sings.

ALL: *(Sung.)* Happy birthday to you.
 Happy birthday to you.
 Happy fortieth —
LILY: *(Spoken.)* Ohmygod. Forty?
JANEY: Make a wish, Lily.
LILY: I wish I were thirty.
 (She blows out the candles. Lights up. A man is making a videotape.)
GISLI: Hello, how are you? Gisli here. How are you? Hello. OK. Inge and I
 say good morning good afternoon good evening. It's a beautiful day. We
 wish you very well. We are happy to have a new way to have for contin-
 uing good friendship fellowship and for visual communication. We say
 hello on this videotape on this beautiful day and hope you are very good
 very well very good. OK.
 (Another man holds a beach chair.)
MATTHEW: I think it's time we put an end to this.
 (Lily and her friend, Janey, on the phone.)
LILY: I thought he might call.
JANEY: I know. I'm sorry.
LILY: Maybe a present. A card. E-mail.
JANEY: Did you get my present?
LILY: How'd you know I needed a lint shaver?
JANEY: I just knew.
LILY: Maybe I should call him.
JANEY: Oh, sweetie.
LILY: I wish you still lived here.
JANEY: Me, too. Don't fall in love with a Midwesterner. You wouldn't believe
 the way people dress around here. They look awful.
 (A man lies in bed. He moans.)
ARTIE: Bev-er-ly . . . Bev-er-ly . . .
 (Lily and Janey on the phone.)
LILY: So I sent him a card. And some lilies.
JANEY: Lil. You sent *him?* On *your* birthday? You gotta get out more. Are you
 playing? What was your last gig?
LILY: A bank. The opening of a bank.

JANEY: And how's work?

LILY: Oh, that nasty Jennifer had her shower.

JANEY: Ooo, how was it?

LILY: I didn't go.

JANEY: Why not?

LILY: A baby shower? I couldn't.

JANEY: Why don't you call that doctor? You talked about it.

LILY: I wish you hadn't moved. How is it?

JANEY: I just love him so much. It's awful. And now I live in Iowa. Which is truly awful.

(The man with the chair speaks.)

MATTHEW: I think it's time we let this go.

(Videotape.)

GISLI: Gisli here. Hello, how are you? So now it is winter and it is dark all day and all night and as you see I am sending you some video that I hope you will watch. Because you will enjoy it. Here are some clips from my TV show, and I can assure they are very funny, even though they are in Icelandic. And they were made at a topnotch studio, all the trimmings. Topnotch.

(Clips from an Icelandic comedy TV show play.)

GISLI: I know I look different from last time, but my appearance changes rapidly. I like it like that. I am fat, I am blonde, I am dark, I am thin. I have hair. I have none. Inge sometimes doesn't even know who it is she is with. And I am seeing my psychiatrist for twenty years and I haven't had a drink in twelve and a half years. All right then, be well and don't worry, OK? Everything will come together, and if it doesn't, then well, it will come apart and both are good, so be happy.

(Frank, a parent of one of Lily's students, meets with her.)

LILY: So, you're saying that what? It's all connected? It's all — connected?

FRANK: Yes, it's connected.

LILY: String?

FRANK: Strings.

LILY: Not particles.

FRANK: Right. How did we get on to this?

LILY: I don't know. We were talking about your daughter.

FRANK: Yes. Right. Of course.

LILY: She's a good student, talented, musical, a pleasure to have in my class and. What is it you were saying? About your work? About — what was it?

FRANK: I haven't had dinner. Do you want to? I'm last, right, there isn't anyone else — can we get something to eat?
(On the phone to Janey.)

LILY: So, a string can be open like a hair or closed like a loop. And as it travels through time and space, it can either trace a path like a sheet if it's open, or like a tube, if it's closed. I think that's it.

JANEY: What does that have to do with anything?

LILY: I don't know. But I think it does. Somehow. I think it does.
(Lily and Frank at an Italian restaurant.)

LILY: I don't even say I play anymore. 'Cause what I do mostly is teach.

FRANK: Uh huh.

LILY: Which is not bad I mean there are a lot of bad things I might do or less worthy. Well it's obvious, right, those who can't — . You get to a certain age, well I got to a certain age —

ALL: *(Sung.)* Happy birthday to you.

LILY: — No, well, before that. And you have to wonder why and what and Jesus things don't ever turn out like you want, not for anyone I know anyway, right?

ARTIE: *(Moaning.)* Beverly . . . Beverly?

FRANK: Yeah?

LILY: I thought I'd play for the Philharmonic. First violin. I thought I'd be married. I thought I'd have kids.

ALL: *(Sung.)* Happy birthday.

LILY: But well. Fuck shit Christ.

ARTIE: Beverly . . . Where are you? Are you home? Are you here?

FRANK: What?

LILY: I have a place to live, enough to eat, I have friends.

JANEY: Tell me everything that happened today.

ARTIE: Bev? Bev! Please.

LILY: I have nothing to complain about. I have so much. I get to start over. I get to, uh, date. Like now, like here. I'm having a goddamn date. I haven't had a date since, well, ever maybe. But I met you, and look: you're smart, you're good looking, we're eating, we're on a date. So no complaints. I'm healthy. I can be a parent. Like you. Even if it's on my own. Right? Even if it's on my own. And even if I adopt. Even if I never have another date, and have to stop playing the violin 'cause I can't afford it. So I'm not — so I don't make records, and things didn't turn out the way I. Isn't that what being mature is? Acceptance. Gratitude. At a certain point. Everything isn't possible anymore. Isn't that right? It's just that. Maybe a lobotomy. You know? Maybe a goddamn selective lobotomy! That would help.

FRANK: So, did you want to have dinner? Do you eat sushi?

(The restaurant disappears. Frank and Lily are back in her office.)

LILY: You mean now? You want to go out and eat sushi now?

FRANK: That's what I was thinking. If we're done talking about Jessica. She's doing OK, right?

LILY: Yes.

FRANK: Good.

LILY: Oh, I can't tonight. Actually, I can't. *(To Janey.)* So I said I couldn't.

JANEY: Why? Why did you say that?

LILY: I don't know. I don't know him.

JANEY: Well, that's how you could get to know him.

(Chair Man [Matthew] talks to a Person.)

MATTHEW: Hey.

PERSON: How are you?

MATTHEW: I'm all right.

PERSON: Yeah?

MATTHEW: Yes.

PERSON: Good, that's good.

MATTHEW: OK.

PERSON: You doing OK?

MATTHEW: Yeah. Yeah.

PERSON: Good.

MATTHEW: Yeah.

PERSON: Don't forget the chair.

MATTHEW: *I have my chair. I have my chair!*

(Lily goes to a doctor.)

DOCTOR A: OK, so I'll do an exam, and a sonogram, and then on day one you'll call us and on day three you'll call and come in between the hours of seven-thirty and nine and if you started day one after say 4 PM then day one would be the next day, making it day four actually, but for our purposes still day three, we'll check your hormone levels, and then on between days six and ten, using the same 4 PM calculation to start count- ing day one, we'll send you for an HSG, that's a hysterosalpingogram. And we'll take it from there. The nurse will give you some brochures, and then we can get started. And I don't take your insurance, OK?

(Videotape.)

GISLI: Hiya, Lily. How are you? I am today in my Captain Hook outfit for the touring repertory production of *Peter Pan* at the wonderful City Theater, and I'm here to say, the clock is ticking! Don't forget. Even if it's hidden in the belly of a hungry crocodile you still have to watch out! *(He drops his hook.)* Ah! Ha ha. Funny funny. OK. Cuckoo. Tick tock. *(An alarm goes off.)* Ah! Time is running out!

(Lily reads from a brochure.)

LILY: "Hair color, hair texture, eyes, height, weight, blood type, occupation or major." Jeez. "Polish, French, Iranian, J-o-r? Jordanian, Ukrainian, Canadian." OK. "Chiropractor, liberal arts, accounting, Russian studies, human performance? History and animation? Physics." Ooo. "German." Oh well. "Short profiles are available free of charge on our Web site." Oh my. "Pregnancy: Yes indicates that we have received at least one pregnancy report on the donor. No indicates we have not YET received a pregnancy report on the donor. From our experience the donor is on the catalogue for at least six months before we receive a pregnancy report. However this varies according to supply and demand." Oh, God.

(She dials the phone.)

LILY: Hi, Frank? This is Lily, Jessica's teacher?

(Artie lying in bed.)

ARTIE: Beverly. Beverly. If you're here, come here. I need you to come here. Beverly?

(He sees he is covered in blood.)

ARTIE: Bev. Where are you? I think I have a problem here. Ah shit. I gotta big problem. Now what?

(Lily and Frank at a Japanese restaurant.)

LILY: What's that one?

FRANK: Urchin.

LILY: Oh, I've never eaten that.

FRANK: Try it. You'll either love it or hate it.

LILY: Hmm.

FRANK: Go ahead, if you don't like it you can spit it out — and I'll eat the rest.

LILY: *(She takes a bite.)* Oh.

FRANK: Well?

LILY: It's it's very hmm strong, uh, it's interesting, but here.

(She gives the rest of the piece to Frank. He pops it in his mouth.)

FRANK: It's the sex organs of the urchin.

LILY: Oh really well, hmm, I could say something but.

FRANK: Go ahead.

LILY: Well, no, I think it's better left unsaid.

    (Their entrees arrive. His is an entire platter of urchins.)

LILY: Who ordered that?

FRANK: That's what Isidore Rabi, Nobel Prize winner, said after the discovery of the muon particle in the 1930s, "Who ordered that?"

LILY: You're eating a plate of urchin sex organs for dinner?

FRANK: I like them.

    (On the phone with Janey.)

LILY: Well, I mean, you know.

JANEY: What? No.

LILY: Well he'd be at least interested, I mean in bed, I mean look at what he ate.

JANEY: I guess.

LILY: He likes to eat sex organs.

JANEY: Well, what did it taste like?

LILY: Just what you'd think it would taste like, and I didn't want to swallow. But I felt I had to, so I did.

JANEY: And the conversation?

LILY: Strings or something. As a theory.

JANEY: What kind of a theory is that?

FRANK: You really want to hear this? *(Janey and Lily nod.)* There are two theories that are the foundation for modern physics: general relativity, thanks to Einstein, which is a framework for the largest scale: galaxies, stars and what not, and then there's quantum mechanics, which is for the smallest: atoms, molecules, subatomic particles. They're both effective and accurate. *But,* they conflict with each other, so, for decades physicists worked on one, not the other. Which was fine, except occasionally you need to look at both. And when you do, see, things don't make sense. No sense. At all. But you can't throw one out, because they both work. Proven. So, it's a quandary.

LILY: *(To Janey.)* It's based on the idea, I think, that instead of particles being the smallest bits of matter, there are tiny strings, filaments, strands, and —

FRANK: It has the potential, the strings, mathematically, and actually, to bring it all together. What physicists have been looking for. And it was discovered, really, by accident, and now some, like myself, think it could be the theory of everything.

LILY: Theory of everything? That sounds well. Like a lot.

FRANK: Yes. A lot and a little, all together. The big and the small, the utterly incongruous, disparate, incompatible —

LILY: *(To Janey.)* You should have heard him.

JANEY: Hmm.

LILY: *(To Frank.)* And this, these strings, they —

FRANK: Would be a bridge. Encompass quantum mechanics and general relativity, the big divide — you see these strings, depending on the vibrations, they create the different particles —

LILY: And that's what you do. You think about that? You work on that?

FRANK: Yes that's what I do. And I teach.

LILY: Well.

FRANK: Well. You?

LILY: I teach. As you know. And I play the violin.

FRANK: Then you understand about strings.

LILY: Oh. Yes. Yes. I do. *(On the phone to Janey.)* I liked it.

JANEY: What?

LILY: That he thought like that.

FRANK: String theory, for it to work, requires that there be ten dimensions.

LILY: Ten dimensions?

JANEY: Ten dimensions? Where are they?

FRANK: Possibly folded up. Too small to see.

JANEY: And the strings? Can you see those? *(Lily and Frank shake their heads no.)* Kind of hard to believe.

FRANK: See, with so many particles: quarks, neutrinos, muons, bosons, it doesn't seem simple or fundamental. But a string, if everything comes from the same strings, that's simple.

LILY: He's the first man I've liked. First one I liked.

JANEY: True.

LILY: If I could just take out that part of my brain that thinks about Matthew.

JANEY: That would be good.

LILY: I wake up with Matthew, I go to bed with Matthew. I hear him, I see him. I see him. In the mirror. I hear him. In dreams. I talk to him every day, we fight, we argue, we make love, we split up, we get back together, he's right, I'm wrong, I'm wrong, he's right, over and over. Long conversations. Very involved. It just so happens that it isn't really happening.

JANEY: Sounds like he talks more in your head than he did in real life.

LILY: Part of the landscape. Missing Matthew.

JANEY: Sounds like it is the landscape.

LILY: I hope he's OK. You think he's OK?

JANEY: Why don't you call him?

LILY: Bad idea. That last time we talked he said he had to carry around a chair, a lawn chair, a beach chair.

JANEY: Why?

LILY: I don't know. So he could sit? I don't know. I guess when a guy walks around holding a chair, it's time to let it go. At least until he puts it down. And then I heard his mother moved in with him for a while. Can you believe that? He replaced me with his mother.

JANEY: Yeah, Matthew was perfect.

LILY: OK, so I haven't chosen well. So. Maybe I'll be alone. Are those the big questions? Those can't be the big questions.

JANEY: You like this guy, this stringy guy?

LILY: Any man that likes to eat the sex organs of a sea urchin is OK by me.

FRANK: We deal with simple questions that are actually extremely difficult.

JANEY: What's his name?

LILY: Frank.

FRANK: It's elusive. And requires looking smaller and smaller.

JANEY: Has he called?

LILY: No.

FRANK: If we can find what the universe is made of, then we can find how it came to be.

LILY: I hope he does.

FRANK: When it works, when it comes together, you get that feeling of of looking at a piece of art, or a beautiful landscape, it's wonderful, when it comes together and you know it's right.

LILY: Right.

FRANK: Right.

JANEY: What's his number? *I'll* get him to call.

(*Lily and Matthew at a café table. Fantasy.*)

LILY: I just wanted to see you.

MATTHEW: Uh-huh.

LILY: To tell you what I feel.

MATTHEW: Yeah?

LILY: How angry I am.

MATTHEW: Ah.

LILY: That was no way to treat someone.

MATTHEW: Uh huh.

LILY: OK then. Anything you want to say?

MATTHEW: No.

LILY: OK then, that's it.

MATTHEW: Oh.

(*She gets up to leave. Their shoelaces are tied together and she falls. He gets up, the café chair is stuck to him. Lily alone. To the audience.*)

LILY: I was, uh, thinking about the "where things work out dimension." The "I'm always young but smart dimension." The "He still loves me and is really suffering without me dimension." The I can eat whatever I want dimension, the I'm not getting any older dimension. Except of course they're tiny and curled up, and can't be seen by human eyes, isn't that right?

(Artie is in a hospital bed. Matthew sits next to him.)

ARTIE: Well, I had some problems.

MATTHEW: Really?

ARTIE: Yeah, I, uh, put a knife in my chest.

MATTHEW: Ow.

ARTIE: Several times.

MATTHEW: Wow.

ARTIE: I wanted to die.

MATTHEW: Yeah.

ARTIE: But, hey, I couldn't even do that right.

MATTHEW: Right.

ARTIE: I mean, what kind of life is this, I have to shit in a bag, you know.

MATTHEW: Yeah.

ARTIE: I can't go out, I can't go twenty minutes without having to empty it. Of shit. Of my shit. Or gas. You wouldn't believe. It's constantly filling up with gas and shit.

MATTHEW: Hmm.

ARTIE: So I stuck a knife in my chest, right here. In my heart.

MATTHEW: Yeah.

ARTIE: Beverly came home and found me, bleeding all over. She had to buy a new mattress. Scrub the carpet. Everything.

MATTHEW: Jeez.

ARTIE: Called 911. The ambulance came. The police came. Pretty quickly. Read her her rights. 'Cause who knows, right, she could have done it. That happens. God knows that happens. So they read her her rights. Miranda, like on TV, like bloody *Law and Order*. Then they helicopter me here. But Beverly took the car, no helicopter for Beverly. And I went into surgery.

MATTHEW: Yeah.

ARTIE: And this doctor, this Indian lady doctor, she fixed me up, right here, county hospital, she fixed up what all the fancy surgeons at all the top notch medical centers, couldn't figure out. I mean my insides had been put together with Gore-Tex but they were springing leaks and no one could fix it. But now: No more bag.

MATTHEW: Wow.

ARTIE: That's something, huh? *(Matthew nods.)* I had to try to kill myself to get my shit fixed.

MATTHEW: Yeah.

ARTIE: I've had, what, twenty surgeries in the last five years? You name it, I've had it. And then they told me not to eat for six months, I mean that was the one pleasure I had left. They thought it would plug up the holes, but it didn't. You wouldn't believe what my chest looks like. A road map. Of of Los Angeles. With some of it made outta pig skin. I got pigskin. And I got no nipples. Swear to God. One day I coughed and my entire guts spilled out, that's when they put in the Gore-Tex. And then they had me on so many drugs I thought it was 1963. Throw in a breathing tube and some electroshock therapy, thirty-seven antidepressants, and you'll get just a little part of this picture. Not to mention they cut some other parts inside of me that I'd rather not talk about. But certain things are not working right if you know what I mean. And there was no reason to do that, it was a mistake! Hell, you think doctors know what they're doing, that they're experts, that medicine's a science — till you spend as much time in hospitals as I have. Then you realize it's an art. That's right. And just think of all the bad art that's out there. All the terrible terrible art. Most of those doctors are as stupid as the rest of us. But at least I can sit on the goddamn toilet now. Or I will be able to — soon. I mean I got so many problems inside of me it could not last, you know, the connection, but for now it should be all right. Cause of that Indian lady doctor. An artist. Van Gogh. Rembrandt. Picasso.

MATTHEW: That's great.

ARTIE: And you know why I didn't die?

MATTHEW: No.

ARTIE: I stabbed myself in the chest quite a few times. With a knife — this big. A chef's knife. And I didn't die. You wanna know why?

MATTHEW: Why?

ARTIE: The only reason is 'cause I've had so much surgery that my heart is wrapped in scar tissue. How do you like that?

MATTHEW: Wow.

ARTIE: I don't have to shit and fart in a bag cause I got a heart wrapped in scars.

MATTHEW: Wow.

ARTIE: How's that for art? How's that for some goddamn poetry?

MATTHEW: That's something.

ARTIE: I can't wait to get home and go out to dinner.

MATTHEW: Yeah?

ARTIE: And I'm dying for a cigarette. You?

MATTHEW: Oh. I just needed to come in for a few days.

ARTIE: What do you mean?

MATTHEW: I was having some problems with my — I got sick and I thought I was OK at home, but, uh, I wasn't so I came in, and they're keeping me here for a few days.

ARTIE: Hmm. Tests?

MATTHEW: Some. How'd the family take it?

ARTIE: Well, Beverly of course was upset.

MATTHEW: Uh-huh.

ARTIE: I think mostly 'cause I didn't die.

MATTHEW: Hmm. And?

ARTIE: I don't blame her, but. And everyone else was, well, hell, I don't know.

MATTHEW: Lily?

ARTIE: Beverly says not to talk to you about her, if you call or anything, not to talk. That you broke Lily's heart. So for the record, I'm not talking about it. But yeah, she was upset, and, uh, Matthew, she misses you, she hasn't been the same. Believe me I know my daughter. What happened anyway?

(Videotape.)

GISLI: Inge and I say come to Iceland, we will serve you chocolates, beer, and special buried putrid shark meat, a piece for you is included, why, Mick Jagger was here, and he had a very good time, and one of his biggest fans, a man up in the north, was washing dishes, looking out his kitchen window, and saw Mick pass by on a bicycle — and he fainted. Also, we have a very lively cultural life and there is no pollution, did you know that, almost none. As for me I am working on my depression, nothing too bad, but we are happy.

(Lily arrives at Janey's with a suitcase. They hug.)

JANEY: It's so good to see you!

LILY: I know. It's been too long.

JANEY: Thanks for coming.

LILY: It's OK. You can cry. I'll just be here.

JANEY: I made some trout paté, do you want any?

LILY: Yeah.

JANEY: And I got a turkey. And I'll make a pie.

LILY: Great.

JANEY: I locked the cats in the bedroom.

LILY: Thanks. Where's Jeff?

JANEY: Probably at the bar.

LILY: In the middle of the day?

JANEY: He does that. Who knew?

LILY: Oh.

JANEY: And he hasn't been working, so we're behind on the rent.

LILY: Really.

JANEY: I'm so glad you're here.

LILY: Me, too. So, we'll talk. OK?

JANEY: I'm afraid.

LILY: I know.

JANEY: That I'm gonna die.

LILY: I know.

(Gisli and Matthew are soaking in the steamy mineral water at the Blue La-goon in Reykjavik.)

GISLI: Ah.

MATTHEW: Mmm.

GISLI: A surprise to see you here.

MATTHEW: Yes.

GISLI: You know this is how we heat our drinking and bathing water: with this water, the underwater hot spring thermonuclear volcanic type water, and it's perfectly clean of course, but too many minerals for using, so we — what — we soak in it, very good for the skin, wonderful for tourism. We create this place, the Blue Lagoon, for soaking. Many people come, unfortunately some have terrible skin diseases. Look at that girl. Horrible.

MATTHEW: Oh yes. She looks, yes.

GISLI: So.

MATTHEW: So.

GISLI: Why are you here?

MATTHEW: I needed to get away.

GISLI: Yes.

MATTHEW: And Iceland is, well, away.

GISLI: Yes. You took what — Icelandic Air?

MATTHEW: I did.

GISLI: Was it late?

MATTHEW: It was.

GISLI: Always, it's always late. In Iceland, we, uh don't pay too much atten-tion to time, you know, promptness.

MATTHEW: Me neither.

GISLI: Good. Are you sweating?

MATTHEW: Yes.

GISLI: Good. Oh, look at that one, what is that, something awful, eczema or psoriasis, awful. You want a drink?

MATTHEW: No.

GISLI: I know a restaurant, you should try it, they serve this wonderful, uh, cod cheeks, very good, a little too rubbery but good. And maybe you can while you're here come see me in a play I am performing in, uh, *Sunshine Boys,* Neil Simon you must know it.

MATTHEW: Yes.

GISLI: Very funny. Not as funny as the *Odd Couple,* but, funny. OK. Your turn.

MATTHEW: What?

GISLI: To talk, your turn. It's not a monologue. You do talk, don't you? I mean you don't just expect me to say everything, do you? That would be tiresome, no one could live like that, well I suppose some could I mean some who talk all the time, or perhaps they'd turn into someone who talked all the time, like I am right now. And if anyone could I could, but the point is you called me, you came all the way to Reykjavik to sit and soak in the Blue Lagoon where the water is hot and the air is clean even though it's dark out all day, so talk.

MATTHEW: My sister, she told me about this place.

GISLI: Yes.

MATTHEW: She died.

GISLI: Oh. Sorry to hear that. What happened?

MATTHEW: She died.

GISLI: Well.

MATTHEW: It changes things.

GISLI: Yes.

MATTHEW: Priorities.

GISLI: Right.

MATTHEW: I needed to get away. I.

GISLI: Yes?

MATTHEW: I.

GISLI: What?

MATTHEW: I

GISLI: What?

MATTHEW: Miss her, you know. Miss her.

GISLI: Your sister. You miss your sister.

MATTHEW: Yes.

GISLI: That's what you wanted to say, you came to say? From the United States? You could have called, my sister died and I miss her. She's not here, you won't find her here. I mean we can go eat cod cheeks, but you won't find your sister.

MATTHEW: Lily, too.

GISLI: Ah.

MATTHEW: I know the two of you —

GISLI: Are friends. Yes. Good friends. From years ago. So?

MATTHEW: I needed to get away.

GISLI: You said that.

MATTHEW: There's no pollution in Iceland.

GISLI: Well there's some from the cars, but other than that, no.

MATTHEW: What should I do?

GISLI: To call her might help. When did you last call her?

MATTHEW: I haven't.

GISLI: You could.

MATTHEW: Yeah.

GISLI: Or write.

MATTHEW: Yeah.

GISLI: Or leave her the fuck alone.

MATTHEW: Yeah.

GISLI: Yeah.

MATTHEW: I'm trying. I've had some problems. For some time.

GISLI: Yeah, I know. The chair, the goddamn carry around all the time chair. What was the point of that?

MATTHEW: They thought it would help. It felt pretty good, really. I got attached to it.

GISLI: Is that some kind of a joke?

MATTHEW: Oh.

GISLI: What did you do with it? Where is it?

MATTHEW: It's smaller now, but it's still with me. *(He points to his head.)*

GISLI: Unbelievable.

MATTHEW: I think about her all the time.

GISLI: Who? Your sister?

MATTHEW: No. Lily. Why is that?

(Lily alone.)

LILY: If you look close enough, if you look close enough, it seems things don't make sense. They just don't. It's all very jittery that's the word they use,

physicists: jittery. Things make no sense, none whatsoever. And it seems
these strings somehow in some way I don't understand they make it make
sense or at least potentially they make it make potential sense. I like that.
*(The back of the auditorium at Lily's school. Sound of students playing music.
Frank approaches.)*

FRANK: Hi.

LILY: Hi.

FRANK: How are you?

LILY: Fine.

FRANK: I hear you put this together.

LILY: It was something I could do, for my friend Janey. Kind of a video card
from the kids. She loved teaching here.

FRANK: But?

LILY: Oh, she fell in love, moved away, got sick. It was something I could do.

FRANK: It's wonderful. Jess played beautifully.

LILY: She's talented.

FRANK: You think?

LILY: It would be good if she practiced more, but she's a natural.

FRANK: Well, I'll, uh, encourage her. To practice.

LILY: That would be good.

FRANK: She likes you a lot. Talks about you.

LILY: Well, I like her.

FRANK: It's very thoughtful of you to do this . . . for your friend. *(She nods.)*
I'm sorry I haven't called.

LILY: You don't have to say that.

FRANK: I know. I just it's been busy.

LILY: Really, it's fine.

FRANK: I've been traveling. Conferences. Just got back from Austin, Texas.

LILY: Oh, Janey and I went there, ten years ago. We had a wild time. We met
these men and. We had fun. It was . . . Well.

FRANK: Sounds better than listening to lectures on multidimensional spaces.

LILY: Calabi Yau spaces.

FRANK: Uh. Yes.

LILY: I read an article.

FRANK: Really? Well. *(He writes on a piece of paper.)* You might want to read
these. *(Gives it to her. Touches her. A beat.)* I should go. We're having dinner and . . . Nice to see you. I. You look great.
(He drops his hand. Walks away. Video.)

GISLI: You ask how I am and I am OK everything is good. I am very dedicated to my AA program and now have a trainer at the gym 'cause since I stopped smoking, you remember I smoked, well, since I stopped I am getting very fat like a balloon like the Macy's parade balloon and if not careful will get so big it will be out of control and I too will kill innocent ladies by knocking into lampposts. So I have a trainer and I am writing and directing a new commercial for Icelandic company that sells dried fish to Portuese people. And I have enclosed a sample for you. Also enclosed is another little present packed in dry ice. And I hope it brings for you much good fortune for good future. The sad news is I have made some bad behavior with controlling other impulses and very stupid with a young girl, but it turned into my having to move out because Inge has not yet forgiven me but our relationship is very good and she has gone to Florence to learn Italian and to find herself. And I think she will find herself there, because I suspect her self has been in Florence all along. Uh, I had a little visit from Matthew, and I am sorry to say if you do not know already, but his sister passed away. OK. Be well.

(Artie's voice from offstage.)

ARTIE: Hey Beverly. It works. I took a shit. It works!

(He enters.)

ARTIE: Hey Bev. Bev? It works. Holy crap. It works. Bev? Jesus where the hell is she? Bev?

(He looks around. No one's home. He eats a giant candy bar. Lily alone.)

LILY: In quantum mechanics, uh, things — particles can actually move through a wall. And I read that, it's a scientific fact that, if you bang your head enough times against a wall, eventually it will go through. The problem being you'd have to do it so many times that you'd be long dead by the time it would work.

(Artie and Lily.)

ARTIE: Wait wait wait — you're gonna do what?? How about a father a husband a —

LILY: Well, I don't have that and I'm getting old.

ARTIE: You look great, you're gorgeous.

LILY: That's not what I mean.

ARTIE: What about Matthew?

LILY: We broke up, he asked me to move out.

ARTIE: He couldn't help it.

LILY: What do you mean?

ARTIE: We talked. In the hospital. He was there. It was a coincidence.

LILY: What?

ARTIE: Look, it's none of my business, OK. And you're a beautiful girl, I know that, you can have all sorts of men, I know. Bev thinks otherwise, she thinks at your age you're lucky to find an idiot or a deformed idiot at your age, but that's not what I think. I think you're a fabulous gorgeous fabulous girl. So I'm just saying —

LILY: Dad.

ARTIE: A person can make a mistake and then it can take them some time to figure it out.

LILY: He left me.

ARTIE: Out of courtesy!

LILY: I don't think so.

ARTIE: Yes!

LILY: If it were that, he'd have given me the choice. He didn't.

ARTIE: You can't expect someone in his shape to act right. He tried to spare you. I understand this.

LILY: Well either way. I haven't heard from him. It adds up the same.

ARTIE: He'll come back.

LILY: Look I'm forty, heading towards forty-one. I have been waiting, I've waited over a year. And every day, Dad, every day I want to pick up the phone, but I don't, 'cause what good is it? If I could relive it I would, but I can't. So it doesn't help. Hearing this doesn't help. And if one more person tells me to be grateful, that everything happens for a reason, I will probably kill them, and then they'll be dead, and how grateful will we all be? So. I can do it on my own. Lots of women. Do it on their own.

ARTIE: Beverly wants a divorce.

LILY: What?

ARTIE: She wants a divorce.

LILY: What do you mean?

ARTIE: She's had it. She's gonna talk to a lawyer.

LILY: At this point?

ARTIE: She figures she doesn't have too many good years left and she doesn't want them with me. I don't blame her.

LILY: I can't believe it.

ARTIE: Irreconcilable differences. It's over fifteen years. Soon it'll be twenty! You'd think she would have noticed before. She says she wasn't looking. She was busy. I was working, she was painting, I was eating, she was golfing, we were doing different things. Now I'm home. I guess she doesn't like being in the same room with me. I'm nuts about her. Just because *I* feel that way doesn't mean she does. I think it should mean that. My crazy brain tells me it does. But it doesn't.

LILY: I'll talk to her.

ARTIE: Maybe she won't go through with it. I love her. And something tells me you still love him. And we can't help that, can we? We love someone, we love someone.

LILY: Yeah, but we can make choices.

ARTIE: What if he gets better, huh? What if he figures it out? What if he's smarter, more resourceful than me and it only takes a year.

LILY: It's been a year.

ARTIE: Eighteen months.

LILY: I'm forty.

ARTIE: You said.

LILY: It's an important age.

ARTIE: I'm only trying to say —

LILY: I know what you're trying to say. But I haven't even heard from him. She wants a divorce? *(He nods.)* You think she'll do it?

ARTIE: I don't know. I hope not. I don't know. It never stops, huh?

(Lily is lying on an exam table, her legs in stirrups, an unseen doctor doing an exam/test. Fantasy.)

LILY: Dear Matthew, I heard about Dina. I just wanted to express my condolences. I wanted to say I was sorry. I don't know what to say. I'm sorry. Thinking about you, Lily. P.S. I miss you. I wish we could talk.

(Matthew appears.)

MATTHEW: Hey. What's going on?

LILY: Oh, I'm having this test done.

MATTHEW: What is it?

LILY: Well this doctor shoots some dye up my uterus then they take pictures and see if there are any blockages that could get in the way of, you know, fertility.

MATTHEW: Oh.

LILY: I'm sorry about Dina.

MATTHEW: Yeah? I have a new girlfriend. She's twenty-five.

LILY: Oh.

MATTHEW: I'm not really here 'cause I killed myself.

LILY: Oh.

MATTHEW: I've realized I'm gay.

LILY: Oh.

MATTHEW: I'm addicted to pornography, prostitutes, pantyhose.

LILY: Oh.

MATTHEW: I'd like for you to come home.

LILY: Oh?

MATTHEW: I'm completely fine, I just don't want to be with you anymore.

LILY: Oh.

MATTHEW: I've become even more successful since we've been apart.

LILY: Oh.

MATTHEW: My mother moved in with me.

LILY: Oh.

MATTHEW: She sleeps on what was your side of the bed. She doesn't mind my snoring.

LILY: Why'd you leave me like that? You called me from that place and asked me to move.

MATTHEW: I had to.

LILY: I was willing to stick it out.

MATTHEW: I know.

LILY: Are you still with the chair?

MATTHEW: I've moved on.

LILY: Other women?

MATTHEW: Other furniture. That's why I'm here.

LILY: Oh?

MATTHEW: The gurney, it's mine.

LILY: Ow.

MATTHEW: What?

LILY: Nothing it's just — ow.

MATTHEW: You OK?

LILY: They told me it could hurt. Cramping. Ow. Would you mind touching me?

MATTHEW: Sure.

LILY: Or kiss me — just on the forehead.

MATTHEW: Sure.

LILY: That would be nice.

MATTHEW: Sure.

    (He approaches her.)

LILY: I'll give you back the gurney soon as I'm off.

MATTHEW: Sure. Lily.

LILY: Matthew.

MATTHEW: Lil —

LILY: Matt —

    (They almost kiss.)

DOCTOR B: Lily, we're done.

(Matt disappears as the Doctor or his voice appears.)

LILY: Oh. Oh. Oh.

(Lily alone.)

LILY: There's this thing called mirror symmetry and say, you can't figure a certain thing out, you have a problem and it's too complicated; if you look at its symmetrical partner, its mirror, you can get the answer in an instant. You just have to know where to look.

(Lily visits Janey.)

JANEY: I can't even get to the corner.

LILY: You're doing great. You just got out of the hospital and we're walking, that's great.

JANEY: You're right.

LILY: You know it's not bad here, it's pretty.

JANEY: I hate it. It's fucking Iowa, who lives in fucking Iowa?

LILY: I guess you do. How's it going?

JANEY: Well, great sex is great, but when you don't feel well, it's irrelevant. Thanks for coming.

LILY: Not every day your best friend gets part of her body cut off.

JANEY: I was glad to see it go. Take my breast. Please. How are you? Tell me everything. How's shoelace man?

LILY: He hasn't called. No strings attached. But I'm reading this book he suggested. Who knew, the universe is nothing like we think it is. What we think is the whole universe, is just the tiny fraction we can see.

JANEY: I'm fine with the fraction.

LILY: I saw Matt's name in the paper. He's playing on a CD: new composers, best new musicians. I guess he's doing OK.

JANEY: Just 'cause he's working doesn't mean he's doing OK.

LILY: So. All my tests were good. So. I kinda can start anytime.

JANEY: Ohmygod! That's great. I'm so excited.

LILY: I still don't know how I'll manage, at all, but . . .

JANEY: I'll help.

LILY: Yeah?

JANEY: Yes!

LILY: Good. 'Cause I'll need help.

JANEY: We have to plan.

LILY: Yes.

JANEY: Sometime, when I'm better, maybe I can come and stay with you for a while. Can I?

LILY: Uh. Sure.

(Artie and Matthew at a fancy restaurant.)

ARTIE: It's wonderful to eat, isn't it? What is this? Some kind of fish?

MATTHEW: Cod cheeks.

ARTIE: What the hell is that?

MATTHEW: *(Indicates under his chin.)* This part.

ARTIE: *(He tries it.)* It's good, a little rubbery but good. Try eating after not eating for six months, try that sometime. Take all those people who take that Prozac, feed 'em through a tube, tell 'em they may never eat again, and six months later tell em they can eat. *That's* good therapy.

MATTHEW: It's good to see you, Artie.

ARTIE: It's good to see you. I'm delighted you called. How are you? Since the tests? Did they find anything? What were they looking for anyway?

MATTHEW: I'm — uh — thinking of doing some traveling. Across the country. Visit my sister's kid. Out in California.

ARTIE: Sorry about her. It's a terrible thing . . .

MATTHEW: How's Lily?

ARTIE: Fine.

MATTHEW: Maybe you could tell her I said hi.

ARTIE: Why don't you tell her? She's forty, you know. It's a wonderful age. I met Bev when she was forty. I don't understand these men that like little girls. Who wants to fuck a child? A woman, a mature woman, that's a blessing. You don't walk out on that. And if you do, you turn around and you say you're sorry. Why'd you leave her anyway?

MATTHEW: I had some problems.

ARTIE: I know from problems. How are you now?

MATTHEW: On the road to recovery.

ARTIE: What kind of road is it? I mean is it, uh, main street in a small town, or is it I-95 that has to go across the whole goddamn country?

MATTHEW: I'm not sure.

ARTIE: I thought you made a nice couple. Both musicians. Beverly thought you were too quiet, but she thinks I'm too loud. I did some lousy things to her. But you, you're still young.

MATTHEW: Not that young.

ARTIE: Compared to me you are. I got one foot in and one foot out. Anyway, all I'm saying is don't make my mistakes. As an almost father in law. That's what I have to offer.

MATTHEW: You have more than that, Artie. I would have been proud to be your son.

ARTIE: Thank you. What happened? Tell me, I want to understand. Come on.

You can't shock me, I've had seven thousand volts sent through this head. Come on . . .

MATTHEW: I'm thinking it was my left wrist.

ARTIE: Your wrist?

MATTHEW: A few years ago. I had surgery. On my left wrist. But it got worse. And I didn't think I'd be able to play. I had this disorder which can happen from bullets or or surgery or from nothing. I'm not blaming anyone. Because it's me. But. Now my wrist is fine. My wrist is good. Both of them. They're good. And I can play the piano. I'm playing. But the rest of me.

ARTIE: Well that makes sense, when they cut my colon, they might as well have cut my brain, like I had a direct link: colostomy — insanity, goddamn mystery huh?

MATTHEW: Yeah.

ARTIE: All you can do is look at us with awe, that is if you're feeling well enough, if you're not catatonic like I was, *then* all you can see is your own shit bag. For me it was when I lost my colon, for someone else it could be losing anything, a phone number, a set of keys, a library card, a wrist.

(*Matt starts to cry. He hides his face. And cries. Artie puts his arm around him.*)

ARTIE: I know how you feel, believe me. It's gonna be OK. Hey, look at me. I wanted to die, and now I'm so happy I'm alive, I could, I don't know what but . . . You're a good kid.

MATTHEW: I wake up in the morning, and I don't know what to do.

ARTIE: Well, eat breakfast and take a dump. That's always a good start. Why don't you call her?

MATTHEW: I can't.

ARTIE: Don't wait too long.

(*Late. Lily is home. Phone rings. Frank is on the street.*)

FRANK: Lily, it's Frank.

LILY: Oh, hi.

FRANK: I'm on the corner.

LILY: Oh.

FRANK: Can I see you? Can I come up?

LILY: It's late.

FRANK: I know. I've been walking, I've been eating peanuts for two hours and walking, can I come up? Just for a minute?

(*Later. Lily and Frank in bed.*)

LILY: That was longer than a minute.

FRANK: Yeah.

LILY: Was that what you wanted, was that it?

FRANK: Hmm?

LILY: It's fine if that was it, I mean it was more than fine, but I'd like to know. I'd like you to tell me as opposed to waiting for you to call and to find out. I mean I haven't had sex in a long time, so I'm not complaining, it was great, but I'd like to know.

FRANK: *(Frank picks up the phone.)* Hello, Lily, I hope it's not too soon, but I'd like to see you again, of course I don't know if you'd like to see me again, but I would like to see you and while we're still in bed I thought I'd call, 'cause I happen to like you. 'Cause I don't just sleep with anyone. I wanted you.

(To Janey on the phone.)

LILY: And he bakes his own bread!

JANEY: You're kidding.

LILY: No, sourdough!

JANEY: Oh, my.

LILY: And you should see his apartment. It's very nice. Perfect, really. So many books. All alphabetical.

JANEY: Really?

LILY: And he cooks. Things like bouillabaisse. Sea bass in parchment paper. Pear tarts. Pears are his favorite fruit. He has a pear poster. And he's very affectionate with Charlie, his cat. And he likes films from I don't know, 1960s Czechoslovakia.

JANEY: Ew. And the sex?

LILY: Good.

JANEY: OK.

LILY: A little nonspecific, but good.

JANEY: It'll get better. And his daughter?

LILY: They trade off. They didn't get married. Engaged, but then he pulled out.

JANEY: Maybe he should have pulled out a little sooner.

LILY: He has an incredible mind.

JANEY: That's good. After Matthew.

LILY: Matthew was smart.

JANEY: Smart is one thing, having a mind is another.

LILY: He seems very sane. And grown up. And uses words that I have to look up in the dictionary. Not to mention the physics, of course, which I can't at all understand but it sounds like magic like some kind of other language. Flop transitions, deviations from inevitability, superpartners, resonance patterns, heterotic theory, warping time dilation, quantum tunneling, spacetime foam, ATB: after the big bang. Everywhere I look now I see strings. Even where you can't see them, there they are way way way below the surface. We're all made up of these strings.

JANEY: That's good.

LILY: I'm putting the donor sperm on hold.

JANEY: Really.

(Back to Frank.)

LILY: God, I like to touch you. The back of your neck.

FRANK: The back of my neck likes to be touched.

LILY: The back of your back, the front of your back.

FRANK: Mmm.

LILY: The back of your front, the front of your front.

FRANK: I like it that you like it.

LILY: I like it that you seem to want me.

FRANK: I do.

LILY: *(To Janey.)* He seems to want me.

FRANK: I do.

LILY: *(To Frank.)* I want you. I'm impatient. When I see you.

FRANK: Me, too.

LILY: I don't want to go slow.

FRANK: No. Let's go fast.

LILY: Who has time for slow?

(Gisli in Florence. Video.)

GISLI: Ciao, Lily. I am in Firenze looking for Inge look for herself. So far we have both failed. I can't seem to find her and she leaves me notes from place to place that she has not yet found herself. I am hoping perhaps she will next look in Venice for I have always loved that city and have always had good luck with lost objects there, I once lost a camera in the train station and it was quite a miracle to find it, and besides it is a beautiful romantic place and maybe if she cannot find herself she can at least find me. My Italian is not so good and they all think I am some kind of awful German tourist, little do they know I am just a Viking in search of his wife. Oh and I have not read physics book you recommend, but I am happy you have, and now can teach me ins and outs of the secrets of the universe that I want to know but don't want to suffer for. Time is way too short, eh Lily? How is your search going? Are you good? I hope you are seeing again the man with the strings and it all ties up nicely.

Gunar! Gunar! Over here. *(He yells at his son in Icelandic.)* Uh-oh the bambino is running for some gelato, gotta go, ciao bella!

(Lily and Frank in a restaurant.)

LILY: Was it too much? It was too much.

FRANK: No, it was wonderful.

LILY: What was your favorite part?

FRANK: The museum was great. That exhibit.

LILY: Did you know, when did you know?

FRANK: I figured from where you said we should meet we were going to that museum.

LILY: And the rest?

FRANK: No idea.

LILY: Really?

FRANK: Really.

LILY: You were surprised.

FRANK: Yes.

LILY: What was your favorite?

FRANK: The, uh, massage at the Y.

LILY: Oh I'm glad. It was nice?

FRANK: It was great. And the rumba dance lesson.

LILY: That was fun, wasn't it? The way the teacher called you babe and me baby? *(With Spanish accent.)* "OK, baby, you stand like this, while you babe, go like this."

FRANK: Yeah.

LILY: You were good.

FRANK: So were you.

LILY: Well.

FRANK: But I have to say the 3D movie was quite impressive. I'd do that again.

LILY: Oh. Good.

FRANK: And this meal is lovely. I always wanted to eat here.

LILY: So happy birthday. I wanted it to be special. I'm happy you were born. I hope it wasn't too much.

FRANK: It was fine. Fun.

LILY: Oh.

FRANK: It took a lot of planning. Thank you, Lily.

LILY: And it's not over. You can come over. If you'd like. *(To Janey.)* I think it was too much.

(Matthew drops in on Janey.)

MATTHEW: You have what my sister had.

JANEY: That's comforting.

MATTHEW: I didn't mean it that way.

JANEY: I know what I have, Matthew. A lot of women have what I have. It's popular at the moment. They gave it a ribbon. They gave it a 3K walk, a 5K run. They named a month after it. Kind of hard to get away from.

MATTHEW: I'm sorry.

JANEY: OK. What are you doing here?

MATTHEW: Travelling.

JANEY: Through Iowa?

MATTHEW: On my way to California.

JANEY: Look, you could be my brother. OK? And I don't talk to my brother 'cause he's crazy and I choose not to have him in my life. I feel for you I really do, but I choose not to have him in my life. And he's my brother. And you, you're my sweet wonderful Lily's ex who caused her more pain than a sunburn in July, and you can't get to her through me, I won't even tell her that I saw you, and I know you want me to, so if you don't mind, get to the point.

MATTHEW: I was passing through. I thought I'd say hi. Maybe there isn't really any point except. I always liked you. I'm on my way across the country. I wanted to stop by. We were friends, weren't we? And, of course, you're Lily's friend. Of course. How is she?

JANEY: She's doing quite well. Finally.

MATTHEW: Good, that's good.

JANEY: So I hope you're gonna stay away.

(Lily, Artie, and Frank at a restaurant.)

FRANK: Nice to meet you, Artie.

ARTIE: Frank, what's your last name? Plank?

FRANK: Well it's Plahnck. *(Rhymes with honk.)*

LILY: Dr. Plahnck.

ARTIE: So your first name is Frahnk? *(Rhymes with honk.)*

FRANK: No, Frank.

ARTIE: So it's Frank Plahnck.

FRANK: Yes.

ARTIE: As opposed to Frahnk Plahnck or Frahnk Plank or —

LILY: Dad —

ARTIE: Plahnck, isn't that the name of a famous physicist?

FRANK: Yes. Not related.

ARTIE: Anyway, I hear you're a, uh, physicist.

FRANK: I am.

ARTIE: String theory.

FRANK: Yes.

ARTIE: Well I'm a particle man myself.

FRANK: Really.

LILY: Since when did you study physics?

ARTIE: Since don't underestimate your father.

LILY: But —

ARTIE: Feels like a particle makes sense, something you can hold onto, a string feels uh a little wishy washy a little subject to wind or knots or loops. A particle makes sense.

FRANK: You're not alone.

ARTIE: On the contrary.

LILY: She'll come back, Dad. I know she will.

ARTIE: I'm separated, at my age, my wife decided to take a break, a personal retreat, she calls it. Something she read about in one of her groups, she goes to these book groups, four of them, all women, why do you think they don't let men into these groups, as if we don't read? I read. But what they read are these books about a tent or a red tent or whatever Oprah reads, and I like Oprah, I do, but is she married? No.

LILY: Dad.

ARTIE: OK, let's have a drink. I would really like a drink.

LILY: It's a little early in the day.

ARTIE: How bout a Manhattan? Or a stoli with a twist? I finally can eat and drink and hell it gives me pleasure. I'm sure Lily's told you of my troubles.

FRANK: Some.

ARTIE: Well it's all in the past. Medical miracle. I think they're writing me up in the *New England Journal of Alter Cockers*. He should be dead but now he's alive.

FRANK: I'm glad your health is better. Congratulations.

ARTIE: Sorry to give you a hard time, it's just my way. Maybe I took the wrong pills this morning. I got one of those brains where the chemistry is a delicate balance, you know?

FRANK: I understand.

ARTIE: But let me be honest. I liked Matt, just to be frank about it, Frank. Not that I don't like you, 'cause I don't know if I like you, but if there's anything I am, it's loyal, and I'm sure you'd want me to be the same way if it were you.

FRANK: Yes I would. Thank you.

ARTIE: So what are your intentions with my Lily?

FRANK: Uh. To uh. Get to know each other.

LILY: All right, how old am I?

ARTIE: You're my daughter, that's how old you are. When did you meet?

FRANK: Some months ago.

ARTIE: So you don't know her yet?

LILY: OK, let's not do this. This is for you to meet. That's all.

FRANK: This is for Lily. Artie, aren't we doing this for Lily?

ARTIE: Isn't that the truth. Who said you weren't smart?

LILY: No one. No one would ever say that about Frank.

ARTIE: How 'bout a Rob Roy, would you like a Rob Roy? I can't remember when I last had a Rob Roy.

FRANK: Sure.

ARTIE: Lily, he's right, it doesn't matter what I think. OK?

LILY: Well yeah, he's right, but it matters, it does matter.

ARTIE: Strings huh? You really think it's strings?

FRANK: I really think it's strings.

ARTIE: What do you think, Lil?

LILY: I think I'll have a Rob Roy.

ARTIE: *(To waiter.)* Rob Roys! Three of em!

LILY: I think it's strings, too. I think it is. I think I love that it's strings. That it's a symphony, that it's incomprehensible, that it makes sense and it makes no sense, that every time you think you have an answer you end up with another question, that we're made up of filaments that vibrate in hidden dimensions that no matter how hard you look you can't see, that it matters, that the tiniest vibrations matter, and that that people think about these things, that Frank does, and that even though I can't for the life of me understand even a fraction of it, I can understand something that I didn't use to. That meeting Frank has changed the way I see things. And that I want you to get along. 'Cause I love you, Dad, and I want it to work. And I really like him. I liked him instantly. OK? And I want you to see that. 'Cause it matters. What's happening here, matters.

ARTIE: *(Impressed.)* Well.

FRANK: *(Impressed.)* Well.

LILY: Well.

(Gisli, maybe wearing a cowboy hat.)

GISLI: I am sending this from the great west of your country, included here for you is a small piece of sagebrush, yes I I had a bit of a problem along the way and fell off the wagon, well what can I say but I have checked myself into this place for a uh holistic recuperation rehabilitation tune-up dry-out nut-job, and, hell, we don't do it like this in Iceland though I'm awfully grateful for our socialistic government that is paying. Here they help you stay dry and shake out loose marbles and tame all crazy impulses. You do this horse-whispering thing and confront fears and as you know I have quite a few so when it was my turn to get on the horse I told them to go fuck themselves I'm not getting on any goddamned horse in order to lose my fears, how do I know what kind of fears that horse has after carrying around loonies, drunks, anorexic pill poppers, and heroin shooters for years, if I were that horse I'd roll over and crush the next patient that came near me, at which they took me aside and suggested I carry around a chair. Can you believe that, Lily? I have ended up in the place where they give out the chairs! And I took one! And Jesus Christ hell on wheels it's not bad, why it's better than that, it's pretty damn good, so for twenty-eight days I will learn the ups and outs in and outs of chair bonding. OK, sweetie, I'm four days dry and my knuckles are wrapped around the arms of a chair.

(Matthew walks by.)

GISLI: Oh, for Christ's sake.

MATTHEW: Gisli.

GISLI: Yes yes it's me all the way from Reykjavik special command performance, they flew me in to dry out and have an insane conversation with you. What the hell are you doing here?

MATTHEW: I needed some consolidation, you?

GISLI: Too much vodka, too little law abiding. On my way to California.

MATTHEW: Me too.

GISLI: Will coincidences never cease.

MATTHEW: They gave you a chair.

GISLI: Better than a horse.

MATTHEW: Neigh.

GISLI: Huh?

MATTHEW: A joke.

GISLI: You must be feeling better, you're making the jokes and I'm stuck to the chair.

MATTHEW: You'll get over it.

GISLI: Don't comfort me, I fucked up.

MATTHEW: Well you're in a good place.

GISLI: No, I'm not, you asshole. I'm in an awful place. I'm in buttfuck Arizona with your goddamned chair.

MATTHEW: Mine was yellow.

GISLI: Fuckyouyellow.

MATTHEW: Should I get someone?

GISLI: Fuck you get someone.

MATTHEW: You're not violent are you?

GISLI: Ah!

MATTHEW: Should I stay with you?

GISLI: Grrr.

MATTHEW: First time I was here I didn't want to do the horse.

GISLI: Rrr . . .

MATTHEW: But it's not bad.

GISLI: Ewww.

MATTHEW: As good as a chair.

GISLI: Uuuuuu.

MATTHEW: 'Cause you know the chair just kind of sits there, and a horse —

GISLI: Rrrah!

(Lily alone.)

LILY: We went to a museum and we saw pieces of this woman's life, fifty or sixty years of pictures of her lovers her friends family herself, we walked around from decade to decade and suddenly the guard said it was time to leave, two hours had flown by, and I looked over at him and I didn't want to go, I thought, I want to stay here, in someone else's story, I want it to be our story, and I thought, I could. I could stay here. Looking at him. For a long time. I'd like to live that. Paint this picture. I could feel it happen, that melting that longing that thing. I could feel it moving towards him heading towards him my picture of him. Frahnk Plahnck, Frank Plank. Frank Plahnck.

(Lily and Frank in bed.)

LILY: That was great . . . Mmm, how are you?

FRANK: Fine, thank you, how are you?

LILY: So, I guess we'll wait and see. 'Cause — I could be pregnant.

FRANK: Oh?

LILY: Well, I could. I mean the timing and . . .

FRANK: Oh.

LILY: I wouldn't mind.

FRANK: Really?

LILY: Really. I'd like it. I mean. I wouldn't ask anything of you. Well I'd probably ask something but. We wouldn't have to, you know, I mean if it didn't work if it doesn't work out. I mean we're both adults.

FRANK: That's true.

LILY: I'd hope it would be as smart as you.

FRANK: You're pretty smart, Lily.

LILY: Not like you. I'm still reading those books, they're impossible. I mean I like them. It's different.

FRANK: Yeah?

LILY: Like you.

FRANK: How am I different?

LILY: You're sane.

FRANK: Ah.

LILY: And nice. Polite. On time.

FRANK: Doesn't say much about your other friends.

LILY: No, you're very polite. And I'd be happy to have a baby that was part of you. But, if we're gonna keep doing that, I'd like for it to be a decision. Was it? A decision?

FRANK: Well. I just. Didn't want to stop.

(On the phone with Janey.)

JANEY: So, have you talked about it?

LILY: Sorta.

JANEY: Maybe you should have one of those talks.

LILY: I don't want to rock the boat. Things are fine. You know. Afloat. Why go looking for leaks?

JANEY: It's a relationship, not a *cruise* ship.

LILY: How many talks did you and Billy have before you left him? How many did Matthew and I have before he left me? How many therapists did we all go to? What did we learn? How to express what we didn't like about each other? You find out all the wrong things.

JANEY: OK. But. Why are you home on Friday night while he's at a party without you?

LILY: I don't know. I guess we're going slow.

JANEY: I thought you were going fast.

LILY: Well, now we're going slow.

(Lily and Artie.)

ARTIE: I was a salesman for how many years? If there's one thing I know it's people. And this guy? He is the wrong answer to the right question.

LILY: Oh —

ARTIE: He's wearing a nice suit, but the lining ain't there.

LILY: You're just saying that —

ARTIE: 'Cause a Matt? Maybe. At least he has a heart.

LILY: Matt? Maybe he did. Once. Now —

ARTIE: He has a heart! It may not ever work the way it once did, 'cause that happens, but he has a heart. Even if he cannot say it or live it or even talk ever talk to you. Don't question his heart.

LILY: OK. But if I can choose between that and someone who I can actually be with.

ARTIE: Yes. Of course. Good point. Yes. Being with someone. Yes.

LILY: And I like him.

ARTIE: All right. What do I know? He's very nice. Good looking. Smart. Did you introduce him to Bev?

LILY: No.

ARTIE: We're getting together. I've been wooing her. At my age. She's been, uh, somewhat responsive. We're getting together. I think. Next week. I hope she'll, well, we'll see.

LILY: Good. That's good.

ARTIE: So don't listen to me. I just want you to be happy. You deserve the best. I'm very proud. And if you like him, Goddamnit, I like him. Strings and all.
(They hug. Gisli and Matthew on horses.)

GISLI: Ten minutes? I have to stay on this crazy animal ten minutes?

MATTHEW: You look OK.

GISLI: OK? I am terrified I am horrified I am never on horse before and even if I was it would be Icelandic horse which is much smaller not some kind of giant John Wayne horse. He's huge.

MATTHEW: That's Nelly. It's a she.

GISLI: So I can say whoa Nelly? For that it is almost worth it. Whoa Nelly.

MATTHEW: I'm sorry about Inge.

GISLI: There is nothing wrong with Inge. I am the idiot.

MATTHEW: I know how you feel.

GISLI: She is fine and I am stupid man chasing some young girl, then going back to alcohol after twelve years. Is not stupid is moronic, retarded, is no word in English. And I want a drink so bad if I could take Nelly's horse shit and ferment it I would.

MATTHEW: I know how you feel.

GISLI: I am so happy to be in same club as you. I thought you were idiot and now I see I am bigger idiot, you can at least ride horse.

MATTHEW: Pull the reins to slow down . . . Harder . . . Like this . . .

GISLI: I will make comedy routine of this back home. It will be very funny. Some time in the future.

MATTHEW: I hope you find her.

GISLI: With Inge I am stupid, but without her I am nobody, nothing.

MATTHEW: Where is she?

GISLI: Los Angeles I think. Our daughter lives there and she is with her. So I will take plane to LA and hope she has found herself and it includes a picture of me.

MATTHEW: That's good.

GISLI: What is good about it?

MATTHEW: With the horse, you're doing good.

GISLI: It's very simple, Matt, I slipped I fell I fucked up, and Inge left, so now I get up I go after her and if along the way I fall I get up again until each time it is easier to get up and soon I hope falling is no longer necessary I can just skip the falling and keep the getting up that's all. Without Inge the world is for shit. And I am famous in my country, I am like David Letterman famous, I can have girls a lot of girls and let me tell you Icelandic girls are most beautiful, forget California, in Iceland we walk around with a hard-on we are sick from the gorgeous girls, all day it's very inconvenient, but the point is they are nothing next to my Inge. Who is OK past forty years old, who does not have this perfect body anymore. But she is my other me. But I am stupid human being, so I fuck up all the time, every day my dick wants me to follow it around into beautiful young girls and sometimes I go, like dick dick dick I follow you, dick dick, I agree my wife is getting old, dick dick, I do anything you want, but I know better I am forty-four years old and I know better!!! I know if I pick up a drink I am a drunk. I know if I lose my wife less than half of me is left. These stupid therapists say I am codependent, she is codependent, fuck you nothing wrong with dependent. It means I am lucky I found her. I thank God for that. It also means I am human and I push her away. So now I must try to get her back. So first I stop drinking and then I throw myself at her feet and beg she can forgive and if she says no I beg again, I keep at it till she either tells me to never come to her again or she takes me back stupid idiot I am. And I try my best to remember and not forget that she is everything to me. Every day.

MATTHEW: I see.

GISLI: What what do you see?

MATTHEW: What you're saying.

GISLI: You don't see anything, Matt. You're not even looking. What are you doing here? Sucking up more group therapy? How old are you? Fifteen? Twenty? Past forty, aren't you? Tick tock Matt, the clock waits for no one. It's half over if you're lucky. Stop tugging at your own dick and thinking you're doing something. Who cares what your feelings are? Feeling shmeeling! You can spend the next ten years getting in touch with your feelings and then you'll be past fifty, and you'll still be an idiot. Get over it. Grow up, Matt.

MATTHEW: Fuck you.

GISLI: Thank God. You said something real. Finally. Fuck you, too. Pay me. I'll be your therapist.

MATTHEW: You don't know anything about it.

GISLI: Oh yeah? Lily's father died.

MATTHEW: What?

GISLI: He died. The other day. And what are you doing? Getting consolidation therapy in Arizona for twenty thousand dollars a month? Riding horses while she is dating another guy? Get off the horse, Matthew. Get off the fucking horse. Get on plane.

(Matthew gets off the horse and walks off.)

GISLI: Grow up, Matt! Tempus fugit! Carpe diem. Go Nelly!!

(Lily and Frank at Artie's funeral.)

FRANK: You OK?

LILY: Yes. No. It just upsets me.

FRANK: I understand.

LILY: I know it doesn't matter, but Beverly is playing the grieving widow, and I don't think he would have liked that.

FRANK: OK.

LILY: Actually, he probably would have liked it.

FRANK: OK.

(Matthew enters.)

MATTHEW: Hi.

LILY: Hi.

MATTHEW: Hi.

LILY: Um. Hi. Um. This is Frank.

MATTHEW: Hi, Frank.

LILY: This is Matthew.

FRANK: Hello. Nice to meet you.

MATTHEW: I'm sorry. About Artie. How are you?

LILY: I've been better. How are you?

MATTHEW: OK. Um, Lil.

LILY: Nice of you to come.

MATTHEW: Could we —

(Janey enters.)

JANEY: Matthew.

MATTHEW: Hello.

JANEY: Well. You get around.

MATTHEW: Lil, can we talk?

JANEY: What do you have, a homing device?

LILY: Janey —

JANEY: You sure have a way of making an appearance, don't you?

LILY: It's OK.

MATTHEW: Lily —

FRANK: Let's just stay calm.

LILY: I'm calm.

JANEY: I'm very calm.

MATTHEW: Can we talk?

FRANK: Lily, maybe if I —

MATTHEW: Can we?

FRANK: Lil.

JANEY: Lily.

FRANK: Lil.

MATTHEW: Please.

FRANK: Please.

JANEY: Lil.

LILY: Excuse me.

(Matthew and Lily alone.)

LILY: He was fine, after all those years, finally, then Beverly left him, and he thought they'd get back together, they had this date, he asked her to come back, she said she didn't want to, and next day, I swear, his heart gave out. She says they made up — in the hospital. He's on a respirator, and she says they forgave each other. How? He couldn't even talk. I guess that's one way to win an argument . . .

MATTHEW: I'm so sorry.

LILY: Do you still have that chair?

MATTHEW: No, the chair was for a month.

LILY: Did you move on to other furniture?

MATTHEW: What?

LILY: I had this image. I saw you with other furniture.

MATTHEW: That's funny, but no.

LILY: OK.

MATTHEW: So you thought about me?

LILY: Yes, of course.

MATTHEW: I thought about you.

LILY: Yeah well.

MATTHEW: Well.

LILY: What is it you want? What did you want to say?

MATTHEW: I missed you.

LILY: Well, I missed you.

MATTHEW: He sent me the knife.

LILY: What?

MATTHEW: You know, the knife. He sent it to me. A couple months ago. With a note. We talked in the hospital. We had lunch. Can I read it? *(She nods. He reads the note.)* Matthew, I am sending you this knife as a memento of our conversations, which meant a lot to me, and as a reminder of how screwed up a person can get and how much of a miracle it is that he can get better. With love, your friend, Artie . . . *(Beat. To Lily.)* I can get better, Lily. I am — getting better.

(Lily alone.)

LILY: Electrons have something called spin, which is something like but not really like what we think of as spin. For instance, an electron has to rotate through 360 degrees twice in order to get back to where it started. At least it's only twice.

(Lily and Matthew.)

LILY: So what you just show up? You say you're getting better and you show up?

MATTHEW: I can go, OK? I can just go.

LILY: I don't hear from you for what, over a year? I write you letters, I send you cards, I mail you presents and what, what happened, you broke up with your girlfriend? Did she leave you? Or what? You found a pill, a drug to what, to make you want me again? Or what you had your head put back together and now you're fine? You want to allow me to come home? Is that it? After kicking me out of my house, my garden, my office, and what my father died, and you thought you'd come to the rescue? Or you heard I was seeing someone else and you had to make sure I was still available, I was still holding on. You came to give enough encouragement so I'd still be there — in case? Is that it?

MATTHEW: My head was in pieces, it was like like another dimension, like you're walking along and you end up through a wormhole, one of those wormholes and you're in another dimension.

LILY: Why did you say that?

MATTHEW: What?

LILY: About wormholes and dimensions, why did you say that?

MATTHEW: 'Cause that's what it was like.

LILY: Are you reading about physics? Are you reading about physics?

MATTHEW: I have.

LILY: Why are you reading about physics?

MATTHEW: Why wouldn't I?

LILY: Because I am, that's why.

MATTHEW: Well OK, so we both are.

LILY: No, I am.

MATTHEW: Lily.

LILY: I'm the one reading about physics.

MATTHEW: You said.

LILY: Not you, me. The one that's reading about physics is me. M. E.

MATTHEW: Right.

LILY: Fuck you, you're reading physics. Stop it. Physics is mine.

MATTHEW: Uh-huh.

LILY: You hear me?

MATTHEW: Well it's not the kind of thing you can possess.

LILY: Shut up, shut up. You keep your crazy fucking head out of my physics.
    (He walks away. Lily alone.)

LILY: The thing is — with the string theory, I've read more and it isn't that simple. I thought strings, that's simple that's the whole idea, to make it simple, but it turns out it isn't. For one, there are those ten dimensions, and OK let's say they're there, let's say at the big bang the ones we see were the only ones that expanded, OK that's weird, that's almost inconceivable, that means these tiny dimensions that never expanded, that no one can see, OK. But *then,* it turns out, there are five *different* string theories, that's right, not one, but five, which puts a big dent in the idea of simple. Then, a physicist named Witten comes along and says, they're related these five, and he thinks up something called M theory, which kind of encompasses all five but not really, and this M theory requires yet another dimension, so now we're talking eleven. And it also means not just strings! I thought the whole point was strings, but M theory includes branes. As in membranes, as in multidimensional blobs kind of. Like little jello Frisbees. As in string theory isn't even about strings. And no one even knows what the M stands for. Except for this Witten. And he's not telling. So. That's not so simple so elegant so theory of everything to me.
    (Frank and Lily on her couch.)

LILY: Hey.

FRANK: Hey.

LILY: So.

FRANK: So. Well, I think you're wonderful. You're smart, sweet, sexy. We have a great time together. I like talking to you.

LILY: Uh-huh.

FRANK: So I don't at all know why, I can't really explain it but. The thing is.

LILY: Yeah?

JANEY: Where were you?

LILY: On the couch.

FRANK: I don't know how to say this. I mean, I'm sure you've noticed how I've been holding back, the whole time. I'm just very. Ambivalent.

LILY: *(To Janey.)* Ambivalent? I thought he liked me. He called every night. We were having unprotected sex. OK, he never introduced me to his friends, and he always kissed hello on the cheek.

JANEY: You never told me that.

LILY: Well.

FRANK: I just. I just want to stay home and be with my cat.

JANEY: What?

LILY: That's what he said.

JANEY: His cat?

FRANK: I just want to stay home and be with my cat.

JANEY: Oh, my God!

FRANK: I guess I should just go. *(He starts to go.)*

LILY: Your cat? You want to be with your cat? Then why did you go out with me? And call me every night. And kiss me. And fuck me. Regularly. Without a condom. For a very smart man you are amazingly stupid.

FRANK: What if? . . . *(He goes.)*

LILY: I always was jealous of the way he touched that cat. And he had nicknames: Booboo and Choochoo.

JANEY: We're talking deep-seated problems.

LILY: He'd let it get in bed with us, I swear. I'm sneezing, we're having sex, the cat gets in bed, and Frank doesn't do a thing.

JANEY: Oh, that's bad.

LILY: Yeah. I think I'll call him Catman.

JANEY: I think we should write a poem about him. Catman Do.

(They make up a poem.)

Catman DO want to stay home with his cat.

LILY: Catman DO wanna feline love pat.

JANEY: Catman DO like to pet his choochoo.

LILY: Catman DO like to screw his pussy, Booboo.

JANEY: Catman DO take his little kitty cock.

LILY: Catman DO put it in the litter box!!

JANEY: Catman DO —

LILY: Catman DON'T —

JANEY: — Get to be with my lovely Lily . . . *(They're laughing, then Janey is quiet.)*

LILY: Janey?

JANEY: It's in my liver.

LILY: What?

JANEY: Two small lesions.

LILY: Oh shit. Why didn't you say?

JANEY: It's gonna be fine. Lots of new drugs to try.

LILY: Yeah?

JANEY: It's his loss.

LILY: Oh God, I'm sorry.

JANEY: Me, too.

LILY: So —

JANEY: And I talked to this psychic who said I was gonna be fine.

LILY: But.

JANEY: I'm gonna be fine.

> *(Lily and Matthew, on the porch to his house, eating from plates balanced on their laps.)*

MATTHEW: I haven't barbecued since you left.

LILY: *(Straight out to the audience/the rage in her head.)* LEFT!? Left? Who left? I didn't left, you lefted, you left, I only left 'cause you left. *(She talks to him, calm.)* Yeah?

> *(They eat.)*

MATTHEW: Just didn't feel like it.

LILY: *(Out/in her head.)* I can't believe I am here. On this chair. With this fork, this plate, those flowers, his daylilies my forget-me-nots his smell, my fear, his heat, you are right next to me and I could reach over and touch. I want to lock the door, I want to go inside with you and lock all the doors. *(To him.)* Good food.

MATTHEW: Good.

LILY: It's good you kept your career going.

MATTHEW: I did my best.

LILY: Good. You still in therapy?

MATTHEW: Yup.

LILY: How's it going?

MATTHEW: It's going.

LILY: *(Out/in her head.)* I have tried to move on, it's not like I haven't tried, I have. It's a mystery. I mean, it's bottomless. Makes no sense. I want to touch you so bad my hands are shaking, and I can't eat, I'm starving and, well, out of my mind, really, which makes me think there's not that much difference, you know, between us, I keep mine hidden, well so do you, but not a day goes by, Matt, that I don't crave you, that I don't have to have you that I wouldn't stick you up my nose or in my arm, if I could only crush you into a powder, melt you in a spoon, or drink you from a cup. You are in brightly lit close-up and there's nothing else and no matter how you've changed or how you really look, I see the answer, I see this house, I see what I saw when we first met, even if you're frowning I see that smile those eyes that promise that said being close to you would make it better. I keep thinking you're still him, not someone else, not one of those people you feel sorry for. And I can't put the two together. *(To him.)* So, I want to know why I'm here. I want to know what's going on. Let's talk.

(Lights change, they are instantly in Matthew's house. At the kitchen table.)

MATTHEW: I go to the drugstore for my medication, and the pharmacist is chatting and chatting with someone, so I raise my voice, he yells at me, I storm out and accidentally on purpose slam the door and it cracks — the glass, I call to apologize, but next day the police come and give me a summons. At the hearing the DA recommends they put me away forever — because, he says, it's my third strike, he says, I'm a two-time felon, and my lawyer who I found in the yellow pages, looks at me with this why didn't you tell me what else haven't you told me kind of look, and there is so much I wouldn't know where to begin. Should I tell him how there hasn't been a me for two years? But I'm in court for slamming a door so I say nothing, besides, in a way he's right. I have struck out. I know I asked you to leave, I did, but Lily Lil where I was heading I didn't want to bring you. And the judge looks at his papers and says, "Are you Matthew Houseman, born in 1955?" And I say no, I was born in fifty-nine. They realize it's another Matthew Houseman. And the lawyer sighs. The judge smiles. It's a mistake. All I have to do is pay a fine. And I walk out free — to go home, to get back to my life. Which makes no sense whatsoever without you.

LILY: You got a new table.

MATTHEW: Yes.

LILY: But you didn't get a new light fixture.

MATTHEW: No.

LILY: Cause the light was broken, but the table was fine.

MATTHEW: I'm sorry, Lil. I don't know how to say it. But I am. Sorry.

LILY: Last time I was here: 578 days ago, I packed my stuff, Janey drove up, we walked to her car, and I kept turning and looking back at the house. She asked me what I was doing, and I told her I thought it might be the last time I'd see my home.

MATTHEW: I wasn't thinking too clearly back then.

LILY: You sounded clear.

MATTHEW: I was in the loony bin, Lil. Definition of not being clear.

LILY: One day you were this other person, you were, I don't know, one of those people you feel bad for, you say oh isn't it awful, what happened to them, and usually you get used to it, but when it's someone you love, who makes things make sense, who you hold onto, when that person disintegrates, what's left? Invisible strings? Theories? Concepts? That don't hold up? I know it's my little life, I know it's a blink a flash a breath, but doesn't it matter, I mean how well we love, isn't that it? Shouldn't that matter? All I wanted was to wake up with you. What happened?

MATTHEW: I don't know how to explain it. I don't have the words to explain it. I am learning how to live again, Lil.

LILY: I didn't hear from you. Almost two years. You didn't respond.

MATTHEW: What could I say?

LILY: Anything. Hello. How are you. Thank you. I'm sorry.

MATTHEW: Hello. How are you? Thank you. I'm sorry . . .

LILY: You really should get a new light.

MATTHEW: This whole house is about you. How much I wanted to be with you. How much I *want* to be with you.

LILY: When we met I thought he looks like sunshine, I had never met a man who looked like sunshine.

MATTHEW: Well, this is me now.

LILY: I spent how many years waiting for you? Even while we were together. I waited. I won't do that again. Ever.

MATTHEW: OK.

LILY: You wanted to have a family. You said. I thought we were going to do that. That's what you said. We were going to do that. I wanted to do that.

MATTHEW: Me too.

LILY: You didn't want to touch me.

MATTHEW: I do now.

LILY: What?

MATTHEW: Want to touch you. I do now.

(*They kiss. Gisli soaking in the steamy water at the Blue Lagoon, outside Reykjavik.*)

GISLI: With Inge and I apart, I stay busy translating plays like Michael Frayn and Alan Ayckbourn, but also rock mono-musical *Hedwig and the Angry Inch.* Which is fucking hard you would not believe to put into Icelandic. It is traumatic, transsexual kind of lyrics, and not up my alley, literally speaking, if you get my drift and yet I am digging it big time. I usually prefer Cole Porter but this is making me want almost to put on makeup and sing rock 'n' roll but thank God for Reykjavik audiences I will control this impulse . . .

(*Lily, pregnant, enters and puts her feet in the water.*)

GISLI: If I only had small frame to play that Hedwig and was twenty years younger. I would never do it, but maybe I would. I suggest you to get Icelandic fiction book *Independent People* which is most impressive novel I have ever read.

(*Janey, cropped hair and with a limp, gets in.*)

GISLI: It's about a stubborn sheep farmer who has a terrible awful life. You both will love this book very much. We will buy it, go drink coffee, I will show you backstage at both City and National Theater, little Gunar will recite "To be or not to be" speech he has been practicing, and we will go see performance of *Odd Couple* I directed. Oh, my. Look at that girl.

LILY: Who?

GISLI: That one. I remember she had terrible skin disease. And now. Look.

JANEY: She still has it.

GISLI: Yes. And it's worse. But she has very nice bathing suit, no?

LILY AND JANEY: Yes.

GISLI: So after Icelandic adventure trip, you two will —

LILY: Go home. I asked Janey to move in with me.

GISLI: Oh.

JANEY: I want to be with my Lily. And the baby.

LILY: Yes.

JANEY: Until I can't.

GISLI: I see. So, you know if it's a boy or girl?

LILY: I didn't ask. I want to be surprised.

GISLI: Yes, of course. And, uh, if I may ask, uh, the father?

LILY: Well. Could be Frank.

GISLI: Yes. String fellow who loves cat. You and he are — ?

LILY: Not. We are most definitely not.

GISLI: I see.

LILY: Could be Matthew.

GISLI: Ah. Really?

JANEY: Oy.

GISLI: How is Matt?

LILY: Well. Um. Struggling. Up and down. Finding his way. I hope.

GISLI: And you and he are — ?

LILY: Mmm. Not together. I couldn't. I can't. See him. I can't. We talk — sometimes, but. He's. Not together.

GISLI: Yet he is still part of the landscape, yes?

LILY: Well. Yes. But.

GISLI: Picture is bigger.

LILY: Yes. Picture is bigger. Yes . . . Or it could be you.

GISLI: Oh?

JANEY: It could? How could it be Gisli?

GISLI: Dry ice from Iceland. One of our few successful exports.

JANEY: Really? No. Lily, you didn't tell me.

GISLI: I knew I'd sent it, but I didn't think you'd actually . . .

LILY: Well, I did.

GISLI: Oh.

JANEY: I'm surprised.

GISLI: Me, too. Yes.

JANEY: You had a busy month.

GISLI: You did.

LILY: Yes.

GISLI: So, maybe it will be violin player who can do comedy monologue.

LILY: Maybe. It's hard to say.

GISLI: Ah. It's a mystery.

LILY: Yes . . .

JANEY: Yes . . .

GISLI: Yes . . . I guess we'll see. *(He puts his hands on Lily's belly and sings.)* Happy birthday to you

JANEY AND GISLI: *(Adds her hand.)* Happy birthday to you —

LILY, JANEY, AND GISLI: Happy birthday —

GISLI: — Mystery baby —

LILY: Happy Birthday to you.

END OF PLAY

Waiting

By Lisa Soland

PLAYWRIGHT'S BIOGRAPHY

Lisa Soland graduated from Florida State University with a BFA in acting and received her Equity card working as an apprentice at Burt Reynold's Jupiter Theatre. While there, she had the opportunity to work with playwright William Luce, starring as Zelda Fitzgerald in his world premiere play, *Luce Women*. With Charles Nelson Reilly directing, the experience deepened her love for the theater's creative process in which both the playwright and the director are present during rehearsal, working together for the betterment of the play and its production.

After moving to Los Angeles, Lisa wrote her first play *The Name Game,* which received a yearlong writer's grant and was subsequently published by Samuel French. She starred in the world premiere opposite Richard Hatch from *Battlestar Galactica,* and the comedy ran for two months at the Tamarind Theatre in Hollywood.

She received eight Artistic Director Achievement award nominations for her play, *Happy Birthday, Baby!,* which, due to its critical success, was invited to be a part of both the annual NoHo Theatre festival and the LA County-Wide Arts Open House. Her drama *The ReBirth* was also chosen to participate in the LA County-Wide Arts Open House.

Ms. Soland leads a progressive workshop for actors, writers, and directors called the All Original Playwright Workshop. At the end of each eight-week session, their original material is presented to the public and the AOPW Award is given to one of the workshop's writers whose project is most ready for a public staged reading.

In the world premiere production of her one-act romantic comedy *Cabo San Lucas,* Ms. Soland played the part of Grace, whose attempted suicide is thwarted by two house burglars. *Back Stage West* wrote, "Those tired of playing second fiddle to the showier male roles might take a page from the author of this one act, who wrote a meaty starring role for herself . . . a great role for women, by a woman." Monologues from both *Cabo San Lucas* and *Waiting* are included in Smith and Kraus's anthology, *Best Women's Stage Monolgues of 2003.*

ORIGINAL PRODUCTION

Waiting was developed in the All Original Playwright Workshop and produced by Hilde Garcia and the Florida Project at the Tamarind Theatre in Hollywood, California. It was directed by Chip Chalmers with set design by Pat Osos and art direction by Illan Ben-Yehuda. The lighting designer and stage manager was Joe Cabrera II, with still photography by Steven L. Sears. The cast for the original production was as follows:

Betsy	CB Spencer
Sam	Scott Ford
Clair	Patricia Tallman
Bob	Reed Armstrong
Ann	Linda L. Rand
Norm	Jack Kandel
Lindsay	Julie Shimer
Jim	Drake Simpson
Linda	Cynthia Beckert
Truman	King Stuart
Cindy	Miranda Kent
Steve	Joe McClain

ACKNOWLEDGMENTS AND DEDICATION

I would first like to thank *Waiting*'s director Chip Chalmers, who is not only gifted in understanding human behavior and the natural timing of comedy but has a heart large enough to hold both the ideals of a playwright and the desires of a passionate cast. My sincere gratitude goes out to you all — cast and crew. Thank you for sharing your talent so generously.

Waiting originated from a workshop for actors, directors, and writers called The All Original Playwright Workshop because the group's first eight-week session was made up mostly of actors. Only three writers were responsible for creating all the original material. The first act of *Waiting* was written primarily to keep these talented actors entertained and creatively occupied.

The play went for several months with no second act, until The Florida Project selected it for a staged reading. Out of all the plays I had submitted to them, all fully finished and ready for production, they chose the one that was not — *Waiting* — of course! I had two weeks to come up with a plausible second act to complete the story. I had recently met the man I would eventually marry; so much to my surprise, finishing the play came as easily as writing the first act. I would like to dedicate *Waiting* to him — my husband, Deryk.

PLAYWRIGHT'S NOTE

The great temptation in the first act is for the coupled actors to touch each other, but I would recommend that you only touch each other where it is written in the stage directions or as seldom as it is written. If you go with what you "feel" and touch often, you will find that the audience will hold back their response, and we don't want that! Instead, fight it, actors, and receive the rewards of your restraint.

The twelve characters can be played by six actors, depending on your casting needs, as follows: Betsy can play Cindy, Sam can play Jim, Bob can play Steve (and you can still hire a handicapped actor since Bob never has to rise), Clair can play Lindsay, Ann can play Linda, and Norm can play Truman.

The part of Steve should be played by an actor who has at least partial use of his hands. You can cast a nonhandicapped actor or an actor who is paralyzed from the waist down, as written in the script. Our original Steve was played by an actor who is paralyzed from the chest down, so the script was rewritten to accommodate him:

TRUMAN: Waist down?

STEVE: No, actually — chest. Chest down. We're very lucky. The doctors told me if I'd been looking just slightly off to the right, I might have been a higher quad . . . like Christopher Reeve.

TRUMAN: Ah.

STEVE: I'm very happy to have the partial use of my hands. Very happy. *(Beat, to himself.)* Very happy.
(Linda comes out of men's bathroom with red eyes.)

CHARACTERS

BETSY: Twenty-five to thirty, engaged to Sam.

SAM: Twenty-five to thirty, engaged to Betsy.

CLAIR: Late thirties, married to Bob for about fifteen years.

BOB: Early forties, married to Clair for about fifteen years.

ANN: Early fifties, married to Norm for thirty years.

NORM: Early fifties, married to Ann for thirty years.

LINDSAY: About thirty, extremely pregnant, married to Jim for five years.

JIM: About thirty-five, married to Lindsay for five years.

LINDA: Married to Steve for twelve years.

TRUMAN: Eighty-three years old.

CINDY: Twenty-one, college co-ed.

STEVE: A paraplegic, married to Linda for twelve years.

TIME
The present.

PLACE
Act I: The lecture hall, in the psych building, on a college campus.

Act II: The psych lounge and waiting room, just outside the lecture hall.

Waiting

Act I

Scene One

We are in the lecture hall, in the psych building, on a college campus. There is no fourth wall in Act I, so the actors talk directly to the audience, as if the audience were the students in the psychology class. At rise: It is daytime. There are two stools center stage where Betsy and Sam are now seated. Behind them is a long, velvet curtain which is now pulled closed. Also in front of the curtain stage left, is a podium with a college insignia on the front. To the left of the podium is an overhead projector which sits on a small rolling table. There are two doors stage right. The one upstage has a framed frosted piece of glass hanging on it with the words "Lecture Hall" printed on it, backwards. The first invited couple, Sam and Betsy, address the class about waiting.

BETSY: *(To audience.) We are waiting.*

SAM: *(To audience.)* Yes.

BETSY: *Waiting.*

SAM: Hm Hmmm.

BETSY: They say it's best, so that's what we're doing.

SAM: Yes. That's what we're doing.

BETSY: *(To Sam.)* Yes.

SAM: *(Defensively, to Betsy.)* Yes, I said yes.

BETSY: Oh. OK.

SAM: Actually, you're waiting and I'm just waiting along with you.

BETSY: Yes, I suppose so. *(To Sam.)* Thank you.

SAM: You're welcome.

BETSY: *(To audience.)* He's been good about it.

SAM: *(To audience, correcting Betsy.) Very* good.

SAM: Yes. *(Beat.)* Because men don't generally wait.

BETSY: *(From memory.)* No. No, they don't.

SAM: *(To audience.)* But I am.

BETSY: *(To audience.)* Yes. Yes you are.

   (Beat.)

SAM: *(To Betsy.)* Why, exactly am I waiting?

BETSY: Because that's what we agreed to do. We talked about it and we decided that *that* would be best.

SAM: *(To Betsy, a question.)* We did.

BETSY: Yes.

SAM: To wait.

BETSY: Uh-huh.

SAM: *(To audience, trying to convince himself.)* And that's why we're waiting. 'Cause *we* decided to and now *we're* going to follow through with what *we* decided to do.

BETSY: Yes. Well said. *(To audience.)* We're building trust.

SAM: *(A breath.)* Trust. Right.

BETSY: *(To audience.)* So we're waiting.

SAM: Yes.

BETSY: Quietly waiting.

SAM: *(With a sly smile, to audience, he changes the subject.)* And sometimes not so quietly.

BETSY: *(To Sam.)* Excuse me?

SAM: *(Repeating.)* And sometimes, not so quietly.

BETSY: I'm quiet.

SAM: No, you're not.

BETSY: I am as *quiet* as a *mouse*.

SAM: Uh . . . no.

BETSY: *(Correcting him.)* Yes.

SAM: *(Sam rises and crosses downstage, talking to audience.)* I would like to show you, our class today, how quiet she is being when she's being "quiet."

BETSY: *(To self.)* Oh my God.

SAM: *(He imitates the sounds Betsy makes when having an orgasm.)* Ohhh. Ohhhh. Hmm. Oh. Unmm. Oh, um, oh, um . . . Oh oh oh oh . . . OHHHH-HHHHHHH . . . AHHHHHHHHHH!
(Betsy rolls her eyes.)

SAM: *(Crosses back to his stool and sits. Charmingly.)* Now, here's the quiet part. She then curls up into my side and whispers into my now *deaf* ear, "Thank you," ever so quietly.

BETSY: *(Coyly, with a slight smile.)* Like a mouse, quiet.

SAM: *(Smiling, in love.)* Yes, like a mouse.

BETSY: *(Lovingly.)* And I mean it.

SAM: Hmm?

BETSY: *(Genuine, from the heart.)* I really mean that thank you.

SAM: *(Smiling to her.)* Oh, you're welcome.

BETSY: *(Sigh.)* Lovely. You're lovely.
(They kiss, sweetly.)

SAM: *(Directly out of kiss.)* And *you* are sometimes not *quiet.*

BETSY: *(To audience, changing the subject.)* And sometimes I am.

SAM: *(To audience.)* Sometimes.

BETSY: *(Slightly poignant.)* And sometimes *you* are.

SAM: Are what?

BETSY: Quiet. Quiet, that's all I'm saying.

SAM: What exactly do you mean by "quiet"?

BETSY: *(To audience.)* As my fiancee has so amply "performed" for you something that would have been better to remain private between us . . . *(Betsy stands and crosses downstage to audience.)* . . . I too, will act out for you my personal viewpoint of his "quiet" behavior.

SAM: *(Sam rises and rushes to Betsy.)* Oh, no. That's OK. I know what you mean. *(To audience.)* I know what she means. It's not necessary.

BETSY: *(Quietly.)* Sit down.

SAM: I know what you mean and it's not . . .

BETSY: Sit.

> *(Sam quickly returns to seat and sits.)*
> *(Betsy sweetly imitates for the audience Sam's "quiet behavior" approaching orgasm but uses no sounds and very restricted movements. She then counteracts this imitation with her own response by looking as though she is trying to figure out what is going on with him. At the very end there is an almost inaudible groan.)*

BETSY: Uh.

> *(She mimes looking at Sam wondering if that was it, then crosses to her stool and sits.)*

SAM: What? I didn't hear anything.

BETSY: *(To audience.)* Exactly.

SAM: So.

BETSY: *(Betsy timidly and sweetly, begins to ask for what she wants.)* Well, sometimes I would like you to be . . .

SAM: *(Trying to encourage Betsy.)* Yes?

BETSY: A little . . .

SAM: What?

BETSY: Louder . . .

SAM: *(Trying to understand.)* Louder?

BETSY: So I know . . .

> *(Trying to help him guess beause she can't say it.)*

SAM: *(Suddenly getting it.)* Oh, *WHEN!!!*

BETSY: Yes. Exactly.

SAM: *(Raising an eyebrow, enticed by the idea.)* Really?

BETSY: *(Shyly.)* Yes.

SAM: OK. I can do that. Because I've been trying to . . .

BETSY: *(Finishing Sam's sentence.)* . . . be quiet?

SAM: Yes. Pretty much.

> *(Betsy smiles, then gets shy. Sam laughs quietly. Betsy gets embarrassed and giggles.)*

SAM: *(Aroused.)* You are one, sexy lady.

BETSY: *(Feeling the arousal, Betsy turns to the audience, moving on.)* We're waiting.

SAM: *(To audience.)* Right.

BETSY: *(To audience.)* But as you can see, we're not waiting for . . . *everything.* Just the main thing.

SAM: *(To audience.)* The *main thing.*

> *(The next eight lines come quickly, right on top of each other.)*

BETSY: We've had our tests and everything.

SAM: I've given my blood.

BETSY: And everything came out A-OK.

SAM: A-OK.

BETSY: And now we wait.

SAM: Right.

BETSY: We've gotten really good at this part.

SAM: *(An aside to audience.)* Maybe a little too good.

BETSY: *(Quickly with great insecurity.)* You think we're too good?

SAM: Oh honey, no. Of course not. It's just that . . . you are always on my mind. Night and day, day and night, and it makes the waiting very, very . . .

> *(Trying to think of the word.)*

BETSY: *(Coyly, to him.)* . . . hard?

SAM: Hard. Exactly. *(Beat.)* I was trying to find a better word but it just wasn't . . .

> *(Trying again to think of the word.)*

BETSY: *(Sweetly and sexy.)* . . . coming?

SAM: *(Quickly.)* Could you remind me once more why it is we're waiting?

BETSY: *(Quickly, by rote.)* We're waiting because people say that when you wait till after you're friends, the physical sharing is that much more impactful. That's what we're waiting for.

SAM: For us to be friends?

BETSY: *(To audience.)* Friends. Yes.

SAM: *(Suddenly standing, to Betsy.)* Oh, well, we're friends. Jeez!

BETSY: *(Hopeful.)* We are?

SAM: Yes. Yes! Oh, my God. WE — ARE — FRIENDS!!!

BETSY: *(Rising.)* Oh, goody!

(Sam and Betsy embrace.)

SAM: Very friendly!

BETSY: *(Pulling out of embrace.)* Oh, wait. *(Taking him by the arms, seriously.)* Friends or friendly?

SAM: *(To self, turning away.)* Shit.

BETSY: *(To him.)* 'Cause there's a difference, you know.

SAM: No. No, I didn't.

BETSY: *(To him.)* A big, whopping difference.

(Sam sighs.)

BETSY: *(Innocently trying to explain the difference to Sam.)* Anyone can be "friendly" to someone if that someone happens to have something soft . . . and moist . . . and gentle and loving that they want to be inside of.

SAM: *(Turning quickly to Betsy, he takes her softly by the hips.)* I want you now, Betsy.

BETSY: Oh, Sam.

SAM: Please?

BETSY: Oh, Sam.

SAM: Can we now?

BETSY: Oh, yes. Yes. Oh, my God, yes!

(Betsy and Sam embrace and their passion builds as much as it can in front of a lecture hall full of students.)

SAM: *(Sam suddenly stops them.)* No. No. No. No. No. We're going to wait. We've come this far and although we may not know all the . . . secret benefits to this waiting . . . *(A new thought, he sits.)* In fact, I have no idea why we're waiting whatsoever, but we're going to trust it — our decision. And we're going to stick to what we decided to do. It's a sign of character. *(Beat.)* I think.

BETSY: Character.

SAM: *(Trying to convince himself, he sounds very convincing.)* You bet it is. And we're going to stick to it. Period.

BETSY: Period.

SAM: Yes.

BETSY: *(Nodding in agreement, Betsy sits, trying to recover.)* Right. OK.

SAM: It's my choice too, you know. *(To self.)* What little I have of it.

(The next twelve lines are on top of each other.)

BETSY: *(Changing the subject, Betsy turns out in chair and speaks to audience.)* You know, they say that if you wait until the wedding night . . .

SAM: *(Sam turns out on his chair, the opposite way. Under breath.)* "They." Whoever "they" is.

BETSY: *(Continuing.)* If you wait, and you're patient . . .

SAM: I'm waiting for the vows. That's it!

BETSY: and each gets to know each other's faults . . .

SAM: *(Looking slyly at Betsy.)* Which I am.

BETSY: and you build on that foundation of love and acceptance . . .

SAM: You say, "I do." I say, "I do" . . .

BETSY: They say the experience of making love together . . .

SAM: Then I'm going to usher you off to some dark closet.

BETSY: becomes something holy, because you waited for God.

SAM: Great. The *church closet* will be perfect.

BETSY: *(Suddenly hearing Sam, she's sweetly disappointed.)* Church closet?

SAM: *(Finally, with love.)* Honey, that's going to be the best I can do.

BETSY: Oh, me too, Sammy.

SAM: *(Quickly.)* Don't call me Sammy. *(Beat.)* It drives me crazy when you call me Sammy.

BETSY: *(Now realizing what she's done, Betsy goes in for the kill, whispering sensuously.)* Sammy.

SAM: You — are — a — torturer.

BETSY: You torture too, you know.

SAM: Oh, I do, do I? *(Pause, then sensuously trying to drive Betsy over that edge.)* Elizabeth.

BETSY: *(More so.)* Sammy.

SAM: Elizabeth.

BETSY: Sammy, stop. Stop. Stop!

SAM: *(Laughing deviously.)* Ha, ha, ha, ha, ha, ha, ha.

BETSY: *(Surprised by Sam's deviousness.)* You pig!

SAM: Yes, I know. You should know you're about to marry a pig. *(A beat.)* A *blue* pig.

BETSY: *(Smiling, looking pleased.)* Yes, I'm aware of it.

SAM: And you're pleased, aren't you?

BETSY: That secret I will take to my grave.

SAM: You're pleased you're marrying a blue pig.

BETSY: *(To audience.)* Let's change the subject.

SAM: *(To audience.)* Yeah. Let's talk about sex.

(Blackout.)

Scene Two

At rise: We are still in the lecture hall but as the lights come up, we find that Betsy and Sam have exited and a new couple, Bob and Clair, are sitting on the two stools onstage. They are addressing the same topic — "waiting."

BOB: *(To audience.)* We did not wait.

CLAIR: *(To audience.)* No.

BOB: We did not even come close to waiting.

CLAIR: No.

> *(Pause.)*

BOB: I wanted to but . . . *(He makes a head motion toward Clair, suggesting it was her fault, then whispers to audience.)* . . . she's an animal.

> *(Clair gives a small laugh and shakes her head.)*

BOB: Believe me! An animal! *(Beat.)* Never judge a camel by its hump.

CLAIR: *(To him.)* Are you comparing me to a camel?

BOB: *(To Clair.)* No. No. I just didn't want to use the old adage, "Never judge a book by its cover."

CLAIR: *(Agreeing with him.)* Yes, that has been overused.

BOB: *(To audience.)* So, we did not wait.

CLAIR: *(To audience, motherly.)* Though we recommend it to others.

BOB: Oh, yes. It's good to wait.

CLAIR: We just got lucky.

BOB: *(Sexually.)* I got *very* lucky.

CLAIR: He's enjoying me in my late thirties. You know . . . that thing they say about women . . .

BOB: It's true. *(Leaning in.)* All of it.

CLAIR: But we believe people *should* wait.

BOB: Yes. *(Quick beat.)* But not us.

CLAIR: No.

> *(They finish each other's sentences.)*

BOB: We tried. I tried. For the first three hours . . .

CLAIR: . . . of the first date.

BOB: . . . we tried. I tried. *(Beat. To Clair.)* You weren't trying at all, were you?

CLAIR: No.

BOB: The first three hours we did fine. *(Starting to tell the story.)* I took her to Spagos on Sunset. It was still open then and she wore this . . . black number.

CLAIR: *(Remembering.)* Oh, yeah.

BOB: On the first date. *(To Clair.)* What were you thinking?

(Clair smiles.)

BOB: And she had on these pumps with little black straps. The dress was strapless but the shoes had 'em. *(Beat.)* And this bright red lipstick on her lips. *(Beat.)* I did the best I could.

CLAIR: *(Reassuring him.)* You did fine.

BOB: You ordered spaghetti and meatballs. *(To audience.)* She ordered spaghetti and meatballs. Now most women would not order spaghetti and meatballs on the first date, but she did.

CLAIR: *(Admitting it.)* I did.

BOB: Spaghetti and meatballs.

CLAIR: I like it. It's good.

BOB: I barely made it through the meal!

CLAIR: You did fine.

BOB: *(To her.)* Should I describe to them . . . *(To audience.)* I'm going to tell you how she . . . *(Clears throat.)* She sat there, across from me and slowly ingested one strand at a time. And the meatballs she cut into tiny, tiny little pieces . . .

CLAIR: *(To him.)* That's how I eat.

BOB: *(He takes a deep breath.)* Yes, it is.

CLAIR: *(To audience.)* It's better for the digestion.

BOB: *(To audience.)* That's what she always says. She says that it's good for the digestion.

CLAIR: To eat slowly, yes.

BOB: *(Accusing her.)* Oh, and to take such small bites?

CLAIR: Yes.

BOB: Well, it's good for other things too.

(Clair shakes her head.)

BOB: This is the part that kills me. She orders a Coke. A Coke! I ordered a glass of uh . . . red wine, I think . . .

CLAIR: *(Remembering clearly.)* Yes, you did.

BOB: *(Continuing.)* to relax me, 'cause I was a bit nervous. You know, first date — sweaty palms, trips to the bathroom, straightening the tie . . .

CLAIR: You were nervous? You didn't seem nervous to me.

BOB: *(Factually, to her.)* That's because you were too busy eating! *(Continuing with story, to audience.)* She orders a Coke! *(Beat.)* Beware of women who order Cokes.

CLAIR: I like it. It tastes good.

BOB: I barely got through that meal, I'm telling you!

CLAIR: You did fine.

BOB: And of course the Coke has a straw.

CLAIR: *(To audience.)* He remembered the straw.

BOB: *(To her.)* Of course I remember the straw! *(To audience.)* What man doesn't remember the straw?!

CLAIR: Jeez.

BOB: The first time you finished . . . sipping . . . *(To audience.)* . . . she pulled back away from the glass and there was this . . . *ring of red* left around the curve of the straw and I just couldn't get that out of my head. *(Bob removes his glasses and wipes his forehead.)* I tried to eat my potpie . . . but every time she took a sip, the red line just got thicker and thicker. I thought I was going to lose my mind!

CLAIR: *(Suddenly to audience.)* So, we didn't wait.

BOB: *(Not even close.)* Oh, my God, no.

CLAIR: But people should.

BOB: Yes. If they *can,* they *should.*

CLAIR: We just got lucky.

BOB: I got lucky, 'cause I'm telling you, a lot of my friends who didn't . . .

CLAIR: Wait.

BOB: Yes, wait. *(To audience.)* A lot of our friends . . .

CLAIR: Didn't get so lucky.

BOB: No, they didn't. *Unlucky,* I would say.

CLAIR: It's a crapshoot, if you don't wait.

BOB: And we got lucky.

CLAIR: *(To audience.)* Well, we have a lot in common.

BOB: *(To Clair.)* But we didn't know that then. We didn't know anything about each other!

CLAIR: No.

BOB: Next thing you know, we're totally physically addicted to each other and thought that THAT was love, so we got married. *(To Clair, seriously.)* And then we found out what love *really* was.

CLAIR: Yes. *(Flatly, to audience.)* It was the straw.

BOB: *(In reaction to their laughter.)* You think she's joking, but she's not. We keep them in the house.

CLAIR: *(Explaining the facts to the audience.)* He's dedicated an entire drawer in the kitchen, just for straws.

BOB: Not for the kids.

CLAIR: No, he won't let the kids go near them.

BOB: Nope.

CLAIR: Just me.

    (Beat.)

BOB: That's right. *(He quickly turns to Clair, defensively.)* I see nothing wrong with that.

CLAIR: *(Shrugging, casually.)* It's fine. *(Simply.)* It's just hard to explain to your children why their daddy won't let them have one single straw, but he makes mommy use ten . . . at a time.

BOB: *(Defending.)* Hey, everyone has to give a little in the family household.

CLAIR: Yes, you're right, dear.

BOB: But if asked, we *would* recommend that couples wait.

CLAIR: *(To audience.)* But we didn't.

BOB: *(To audience.)* No.

CLAIR: And now I have to spend the rest of my life drinking all liquids through a plastic straw.

BOB: *(Bob quickly pulls a straw from out of his jacket pocket and presents it to her.)* Thirsty?

    (Clair gasps in surprise. Blackout.)

Scene Three

At rise: Lights come up and we are still in the lecture hall. Bob and Clair have exited and now Ann and Norm are sitting on the two stools center stage. Ann has a purse with her, and Norm is sipping the last drop of coffee he brought with him from the waiting room.

NORM: *(Trying to remember, he sets the cup down and turns to Ann.)* Did . . . did we wait?

    (Ann slowly turns to Norm, and gives a look.)

NORM: What? I'm just asking. *(Beat.)*

    Oh, so now you're not going to talk to me 'cause I didn't remember. *(Silence.)* OK, so don't talk to me. *(Turns away, then turns back to Ann.)* I don't know if you've noticed this or not, but after thirty years, I've gotten very good at allowing you to *not* talk to me at times like this.

ANN: "Allowing"?

NORM: Yes, allowing.

ANN: *(Quickly to audience.)* He maintains the power position even at times of having no control whatsoever.

NORM: *(In a huff, he turns away.)* Huh! *(Pause, turns back.)* So . . . did we?

ANN: *(Turning to Norm.)* I'm going to let you find it out on your own. That is why I'm silent. Not to punish you. I'll talk about anything you want, but not that.

NORM: Not that.

ANN: No, not that.

NORM: *(Robustly.)* Fine weather we're having.

ANN: Yes, it is indeed.

NORM: Ah! Just testing. *(He tests Ann again.)* How 'bout those Dodgers?

ANN: It's football season.

NORM: *(Quickly.)* I'm seeing if you're actually listening to me, 'cause sometimes when you shut off and don't talk, you shut off your ears too.

ANN: I'm talking.

NORM: Yes, yes you are. *(Quick beat to catch Ann off.)* Did we wait?

ANN: But not about that.

NORM: "Find it on my own." Jeez, God. *(He rubs his forehead.)* You know my memory. It's shot to hell.

(Ann is as patient as heaven.)

NORM: How's your car running?

ANN: Fine. Absolutely fine.

NORM: Good. Still talking, but not about that. *(He breathes.)* 1967. 1967. April. Vietnam. I was drafted. *(To Ann.)* Were we married *before* I left, or after?

ANN: *(To self, in disbelief.)* Oh, my God.

NORM: What? I'm trying to remember. Can't you love me for my effort?

ANN: *(Factually, to him.)* Oh, I love you. My love for you is not on trial here. That is unchanging. We're not discussing my love for you.

NORM: *(Relieved.)* Oh, OK. That takes the pressure off. *(Rubs forehead.)* Jeez, God. What the hell's wrong with me? *(Suddenly remembering . . . something.)* You need to change the oil on your car.

ANN: *(Lovingly, with reassurance and a smile.)* Yes, yes, I do. Thank you. Thank you for reminding me.

NORM: *(Proud to be of help, Norm's manliness returns.)* Good. Good. *(Back to the business of remembering.)* 1967. Vietnam. *(Beat.)* If I could smell something . . . taste something that reminded me of that night . . . from that night with you. *(To Ann.)* I'm assuming it was night . . . right?

(Ann says nothing.)

NORM: *(Romantically.)* Because it would have taken all day to ease you gently into it and for me . . . for me, the man, to prepare.

(Ann gives a loving, slight nod.)

NORM: Night! Good! *(Norm returns to the task of remembering. To self.)* If I could just smell something.

(Ann turns away and discretely reaches into purse, taking out an old bottle of perfume.)

NORM: *(To self.)* April sixty-seven. *Did we wait.* A very good question. *(To audience.)* Did you ever notice that the "good questions" are always the ones we can't answer?

(Ann dabs a bit of perfume on the inside of her wrists and then behind her ears. She then puts the perfume bottle back into her purse and turns to Norm.)

NORM: *(Smelling the perfume.)* Ah. Oh, I love that. *(To Ann.)* Thank you. *(The memories begin to flood in.)* Oh God, curtains! Blowing! The full moon. I remember the full moon. *(To Ann.)* Do you remember the full moon?

ANN: The moon was very full, yes. Pregnant, they say.

NORM: Full moon and curtains. White, dotted curtains . . .

ANN: *(Confirming.)* Swiss.

NORM: *(The most treasured memory.)* And you. And you. Oh, my God . . . you. You and your soft skin up against mine. You loved me.

ANN: I love you still.

NORM: You loved me and you melted, naked inside of my spoon.

ANN: Yes, I did.

NORM: And you said yes to me.

ANN: Yes.

NORM: You said yes.

ANN: Yes.

NORM: *(To audience.)* It was the most beautiful sound . . . The most beautiful word I'd ever heard.

(To Ann.) I asked you to be my wife and you said . . .

ANN: Yes.

NORM: Yes, you did. *(Beat.)* I remembered!

ANN: Yes, you did. *(Beat, flatly to audience.)* We did not wait.

NORM: *(To audience.)* Uh, no. No, we didn't. *(Beat.)* And the next day, I left.

ANN: *(Thinking back, to self.)* Yes.

NORM: But I came back.

ANN: Yes, you did.

NORM: And I'm never leaving again.

ANN: *(Matter of fact.)* Because you're too old to be drafted.

NORM: And because I love you.

ANN: *(Smiling, Ann touches Norm's face.)* Yes. There's always that.

NORM: *(To audience, answering the question.)* So we didn't wait. *(To Ann.)* Is that OK . . . that we didn't . . . ?

ANN: *(To him, quickly.)* Yes. *(To self.)* Yes.

NORM: *(Relieved.)* Yes. Thank you.

ANN: You're welcome.

(Ann and Norm softly kiss.)

NORM: *(Norm looks over the audience and then suddenly bursts forth in judgment.)* These young kids today!

ANN: *(Quickly correcting him.)* Uh, uh, uh. Remember we said we would never do that?

NORM: What?

ANN: Remember when we were listening to Joan Baez and The Mamas and the Papas . . .

NORM: . . . and Bob Dylan and The Doors.

ANN: *(Continuing.)* We swore we would never say, "These young kids today," because our parents said it to us, about listening to Joan Baez and The Mamas and the Papas . . .

NORM: *(Finishing Ann's sentence.)* . . . and Dylan and The Doors.

ANN: Yes.

NORM: *(Quickly.)* No. I don't remember that at all.

(Norm smiles deviously and Ann realizes he is pulling her leg. She lets out a sturdy laugh.)

NORM: *(Loving to hear Ann laugh.)* I'm kidding. I do remember. *(Beat, then quickly.)* But come on, this isn't music today. There are no stories being told here. These musicians repeat the same thing over and over again till it gives you a goddamn headache! *(Beat.)* There's nothing important being sung about today, like war and wrongdoing.

ANN: Oh, they still sing about war, but it's closer now. *(Ann gently caresses Norm's forehead.)* The war is a little closer now.

NORM: *(He brushes Ann's hand away.)* The music today is just a bunch of energy bottled up, trying to break loose and make sense of itself.

ANN: But that's what they said about us. What we liked.

NORM: Yeah, OK. Maybe you're right. *(Beat.)* But waiting is different. It's good to wait. *(To Ann, referring to audience.)* I don't think young people today, wait.

ANN: *We* didn't wait. You're casting a stone and *we didn't wait.*

NORM: *(Defensively.)* No, no we didn't. But I got drafted and we thought there was a pretty good chance we might not ever see each other again, so we waited for . . . *(With significance.)* . . . that letter.

ANN: Yes, yes we did. *(To audience.)* But not the vows.

NORM: *(To audience.)* Not the vows. No.

ANN: *(Beat, then to Norm, filled with love.)* I love you.

NORM: Yes, yes you do. I remember that. Every day I remember that. *(Suddenly, filled with concern and emotion.)* Do you think I will always remember that?

ANN: *(Very lovingly.)* I don't know. *(Ann knocks on his forehead, the same place she caressed earlier.)* Knock on metal.

(Blackout.)

Scene Four

At rise: When the lights come up, we find an extremely pregnant woman, Lindsay, sitting on one of the two stools. Norm and Ann have exited in the blackout, and Lindsay is alone.

LINDSAY: I'm waiting too, but not for that . . . obviously.

(She rubs belly.)

I'm waiting for my second contraction . . .

(Looking at watch.)

And for my husband, who I called after my first contraction. He was supposed to be here with me today to talk with you about . . . waiting, but he had something come up at work.

(Beat.)

I guess I'm also waiting for him to realize what's most important in life . . .

(A realization, then she takes a positive view.)

But if he wasn't working so hard, I wouldn't be able to realize what's most important in life. Right?

(She rubs hands over pregnant belly.)

So, I'm just waiting for my second contraction, and for my husband, wondering which one will show up here first.

(Beat.)

It's been ten months, three days and twelve hours since . . . Well, since they say we got pregnant. So I've been waiting a long time for this moment, and we waited a long time then too. For the right moment to . . . make love so we could get pregnant. We were lucky. It happened on our first try. That's what they think, anyway.

(Beat.)

My husband was disappointed that we didn't get to keep trying. He liked the changes that occurred in me, with my . . . lovemaking, now that I had some sort of purpose. I was more robust. That's exactly the word he used too — robust. Oh, well. Our first try. I guess I'm pretty fertile. Jeez, that's confusing how they know exactly when it happens. But they say they know.

(Thinking back.)

We knew. We knew the moment it happened. We were holding each other afterwards, and there was this . . . odd feeling in the air that we . . . weren't alone anymore. That we were now a family. A real family.

(She tears up.)

I guess that's when it happens. When a married couple becomes a family — at that moment. Well, that's when it happened for us. And I waited. We waited — ten months, three days and twelve hours and I AM READY TO GET THIS THING OUT OF MY BODY.

(Beat.)

Once it's out, well, then things'll be much easier.

(Beat.)

On my body, anyway. I've had a lot of swelling and enormous back pain. They say I'm carrying a lot of it on the inside too, which is harder on the organs.

(Beat.)

I feel like a horse, grazing all the time. My stomach's so small, it seems I can only eat and digest a single, green pea at a time. Makes you wonder how you can grow this enormous . . . thing, eating such small, little meals. Well, it's probably because my entire life is spent eating, eating, EATING! Oh! And peeing, peeing, PEEING, because my bladder in there, is really tiny too. Everything's all in there, it just got tinier. And don't think that's fun and games, living through the shrinking of your organ.

(Quick aside.)

I know men go through it every other day, but not us women. So I'm waiting for it to be over and done with.

(Beat.)

We don't know what the sex is. We told the obstetrician at our first ultrasound, just to tell us if it's got all the parts. We don't have to know about that one special part . . . and she said, "Yes. All the parts are there." So . . . just waiting now.

(Glances at watch.)

I wonder where he is.

(Feeling somewhat abandoned, she continues.)

I used to feel alone all the time, you know. Like it was just me in this world, but those feelings went away on that night I told you about, when we knew. And it's not so much the baby who makes me feel like I'm not alone anymore, but that *nature* is with me — the miracle of nature, growing something inside of me. It's amazing and kinda scary. Growing, growing, GROWING till you think you're going to burst right open. If there was a seam in here, a seam across my belly, I bet it would just tear me right open, like a pea outgrowing its pod.

(Glances at watch.)

It's waiting that's hard — the waiting. Patience. That's really hard. But I guess I'm going to have to learn about patience because this spunky, little thing is gonna demand it of me. I thought I'd learned enough about patience being married . . . but I suppose I'll learn more.

(Beat, with energy.)

It'll be nice to have sex again. We tried, about two months ago but there was no position that was anywhere near being comfortable. And my husband is rather l . . .

(She stops herself, surprised by what she was about to say.)

Well, there's just no room down there to be adding anything that's not absolutely necessary, so we've been waiting for that too.

(A bit of sadness, loneliness.)

I miss it, because it used to make us feel so close to each other . . .

(Trying to make a joke.)

But now everything feels so close, it doesn't much matter.

(Beat.)

It's weird walking around in the world all the while knowing that something's growing inside of me that's going to be "walking around in the world" too. Like I'm some kind of . . . walking miracle.

(The hormones begin to kick in again.)

Now that I'm pregnant so much more is clear to me — like that I was a miracle all along, even before I was pregnant. My heart beating on its own is a miracle. It's not like I'm telling it to beat. The grass growing up through the cement in our sidewalk, all on its own, finding its way through this cold, hard world.

(Her eyes well up with tears.)

Miracles happen all the time. It's like life has some sort of higher order that you can't see quite clearly unless you're pregnant . . . or drunk or just really, really quiet.

(Almost whispering.)

And that's the most amazing thing of all. When I'm really, really quiet and I'm lying down and my baby is lying down inside of me, I think about how many aches and pains I went through that day, and how many aches and pains my baby will go through in his life.

(Beat.)

OH! HIS! I said his. I wonder if it's going to be a boy!

(Beat.)

Anyway, how many worries my husband goes through at work, and I know that nature or God or miracles isn't just the time between contractions, like now, the time you're waiting, it's the *contractions* too. It's the *pain* too. It's everything. Miracles are the things that happen while you're waiting for the miracle.

(Her husband, Jim, enters from the hallway, upstage right door.)

LINDSAY: Oh, there he is. *(To audience.)* Here he is.

JIM: *(Crossing directly to Lindsay.)* I'm sorry I'm late. I had a client cancel so I had to . . .

LINDSAY: *(To Jim.)* Say hi to the audience, honey.

JIM: *(Jim looks over the audience with head lowered and then dismisses them with one word.)* Hi. *(To her.)* So how are you? Are you done here?

LINDSAY: *(Happily getting another contraction.)* Oh! Oh! Ahhhh. Lookie here, I got myself a second contraction.

JIM: Really? What can I do? Just tell me.

LINDSAY: *(Suddenly frightened by a possible problem.)* Oh, gosh. That doesn't feel right. Owww.

JIM: *(With concern.)* You OK?

LINDSAY: Uhhm . . . I think so. *(She looks at watch.)* Thirty-five minutes. Not bad. *(To audience.)* See? Yet another little miracle — I got them both at the same time. *(To Jim, noticing he doesn't have her bag.)* Where's my bag? I asked you to bring my bag.

JIM: *(Almost condescending.)* Yes, I know. *(Almost defending.)* It's in the car.

LINDSAY: I'm going to need it *now*, honey.

JIM: *(Not hearing her.)* Can we go? You ready, 'cause I've got to get back to the . . .

LINDSAY: *(Trying to slow Jim down.)* Hold on now, sweetie. You're going to have to slow down now. *(Contraction eases up and ends.)* Ah, there we go.

(She stands.) Yes, I'm ready but I'm going to have to use the ladies room on our way out.

(They begin to exit together.)

LINDSAY: Say good-bye to the audience, sweetie.

JIM: *(Same look over audience and dismissal.)* Good-bye.

LINDSAY: *(To Jim, on their way out.)* Would you get my bag from the car . . .

(Jim quickly exits, leaving Lindsay to walk alone.)

LINDSAY: *(Calling after him.)* . . . and I'll meet you in the waiting room. *(Lindsay crosses back to her stool and takes a deep breath.)* We arrive into this world alone and we leave alone. That's what he helps me to remember. *(She smiles.)* I'm sorry we weren't able to talk with you about whether we waited or not. It's an interesting story. *We didn't,* but it's an interesting story.

(Blackout.)

Act II

Scene One

Lights come up and we are now in the faculty lounge, the waiting room, which is just outside the lecture hall. The fourth wall is now in effect. The two stools, podium, and table with projector from Act I, have been struck. The curtain has been pulled open, revealing four chairs against the back wall. Stage right of the chairs sits an old, freestanding radiator and stage right of the radiator is a faculty mailbox full of mail and memos. There is a coffee table downstage left with a thermos full of coffee, coffee cups, snacks, and straws. Arranged near the coffee table are two more chairs of the same design. A watercooler with small cups stands against the wall; upstage left is a faculty bulletin board hanging beside it. The same two stage right doors remain, but now there are handicap bathroom signs hanging on them — the downstage sign reads "Women" and the upstage sign reads "Men." The door upstage left has a framed, frosted piece of glass hanging on it with the words "Faculty Lounge" printed backwards on it. There is a working red light hanging above the door. At rise: Steve is offstage in the men's bathroom in his wheelchair and Lindsay from Act I is offstage in the women's bathroom. Truman is sitting quietly in the far left chair. Linda is standing, waiting patiently near the women's bathroom door. Cindy, with a backpack full of schoolbooks, enters upstage left.

CINDY: *(Crossing to Linda.)* You waiting?

LINDA: Yes, I am.

CINDY: Oh. OK. *(Cindy steps into line close behind Linda. A long silence as Cindy and Linda wait.)* God, I hate this.

LINDA: *(Trying to be polite.)* Hmmm?

CINDY: This . . . standing here like this, just because there's only one.

LINDA: Yes.

CINDY: I mean, when are they going to figure it out that they should have two women's for every one man's. When?

LINDA: Hmmm. *(Beat.)* They have it that way at baseball stadiums.

CINDY: Baseball stadiums?

LINDA: Yes — twice as many women's as men's.

CINDY: Oh. *(Really trying to think.)* You think a lot of women attend those things?

LINDA: I don't know. *(Beat.)* I don't.

CINDY: Me neither. *(Beat.)* But I should, I guess. At least then I wouldn't have to wait. *(Beat.)* I mean, look at this! *(Referring to line by men's bathroom.)* Here we are the two of us waiting and no man. Jeez, that pisses me off.

LINDA: *(Trying to be polite.)* Hmmm.

CINDY: I mean, why do they put a little girl sign on one and a little boy sign on the other? Are they actually that different inside? Why don't they just hang an androgynous sign on both doors and call it a day.

(Linda shrugs.)

CINDY: I mean, here I am in pain, when there's probably no man in there at all. *(She quickly opens the men's bathroom door. Linda tries to stop Cindy but is too late.)*

STEVE: *(Offstage.)* *(From inside men's bathroom.)* Hey! I'm in here!

CINDY: Ooops. Sorry. *(She closes the door again, then shouts at Steve through closed door.)* Why don't you lock the door?! *(Realizing what she did.)* Oh, my God. I can't believe I did that. *(Speaking confidentially to Linda, woman to woman.)* I saw him. He was sitting in there. Sitting on the . . . Oh, God. Squatting. I've never seen a man squat before. Have you?

LINDA: Yes.

CINDY: Really?

LINDA: Yes. I have. *(Beat.)* Him, actually. He's my husband.

CINDY: Oh, my God. I'm so sorry.

LINDA: *(Kindly.)* That's all right. It was a mistake.

CINDY: I'm usually not this impatient. It's just that I'm getting a urinary tract infection and when I get those it hurts to wait. I mean, really hurts. I'm very sorry.

LINDA: I understand.

CINDY: *(Continuing.)* I also don't think very clearly when I'm in this kind of pain. I mean, it's an icky kind of pain.

LINDA: I'm sorry you have to go through it.

CINDY: Yeah. I shouldn't have waited this long to try to find a bathroom. I shouldn't have waited this long to see a doctor. *(Quickly and loudly.)* God, what is taking this woman so freakin' long. What's up with that? Why can't women just pee and get the hell on with their lives.

(We hear the toilet flush from inside the woman's bathroom.)

CINDY: *(Quickly covering her own mouth with her hand.)* Oh, God, she probably heard me. *(Beat.)* That's another symptom of an approaching urinary tract infection — I have no control over my mouth either. *(Loudly, as if to woman in bathroom.)* Just have to pee, that's all. Just have to pee.

LINDA: You can go before me, if you'd like

CINDY: Oh, can I?!

LINDA: Yes.

(Linda steps out of the way.)

CINDY: *(Stepping forward into Linda's waiting position.)* Oh, thank you. Thank you. That's very kind of you. Thank you from the bottom of my . . .

LINDA: *(Cutting Cindy off.)* Sure.

(Pause. Cindy and Linda go back to waiting, then . . .)

CINDY: The last time I got one of these, I was nearly hospitalized 'cause I waited too long to go to the doctor. I was trying to heal it homeopathically. With cranberry juice. That's what they tell you to do. I drank so much freakin' cranberry juice that I developed sores on the inside of my upper lip from the acid. Who would have known. Too much of a good thing. Never again. 'Course I say never again and here I am. *(Beat.)* It was on Valentine's Day. My friend, Eric, finally took me to campus emergency 'cause I couldn't physically drive, or stand up straight, for that matter. My boyfriend at the time was out with his *mother*, so he said.

LINDA: *(Knowing.)* Valentines Day.

CINDY: Yeah. *(Beat.)* They IV'd me and everything. My white blood count was sky high, and they told me I had a kidney infection and it was bad. *(Thinking back.)* They scolded me. Do you believe it? A twenty-one-year-old woman and they're talking to me as if I'm some kind of kid.

LINDA: Hmmm.

CINDY: They asked me if I was a dance major and I said no. I guess dancers get them because of the tights they gotta wear. I said, "No, just starting another relationship." *(To self.)* Just starting another relationship. *(Beat.)* I get them when I start sleeping with a new partner. I guess my body isn't used to it or something and I get them, but he finally showed up.

LINDA: *(Totally lost.)* I'm sorry, who?

CINDY: My boyfriend. *(Explaining.)* The one at the time.

LINDA: Ohh.

CINDY: *(Continuing, with a pleasant memory.)* And he had this big ol' heart-shaped box of Lady Godiva chocolates and I was starved, so we sat there and ate them together while the nurse came in and out poking me. And he kept telling me all these stupid jokes I had already heard a million times. *(Beat.)* From *him. (Beat.)* I mean, what's up with that?!

LINDA: *(Seeing the sadness in Cindy's story.)* I don't know.

CINDY: It's like they don't even remember they told you them, and it makes me feel like I could be anybody. Just anybody lying there in the emergency room. *(Beat.)* I tried to laugh but I kept thinking, "This isn't funny. Why does he keep trying to make me laugh?"

(Linda nods. Cindy turns back toward the bathroom. There is a pause. They wait.)

CINDY: *(Over the shoulder to Linda.)* Very painful. I get them all the time. It sucks really. I don't know what's up with that. *(Turning to Linda.)* They tell you if you pee just before you have sex, or just after sex, that that will take care of the problem. I guess it's some sort of "healthy preparation," but it doesn't work. It doesn't work. I've tried it. I've tried everything.

LINDA: Did you ever try not having sex?

(Beat.)

CINDY: You're joking, right? *(Beat.)* Do you ever get them?

LINDA: I used to, but not any more.

CINDY: Oh? What did you do?

LINDA: I got married.

CINDY: *(This hits her emotionally, just a bit.)* Right. *(Deciding to ignore this information, Cindy turns back to the bathroom.)* Jeez, God. *(Bangs on bathroom door.)* Could you please come out of there? One of you? Just come the hell out, for God's sake. What the hell are you doing anyway, having a fucking baby or something!

JIM: *(Jim enters stage left carrying his wife Lindsay's bag. He crosses to center stage and hearing Cindy's rude comment, he stops.)* Excuse me.
(Cindy and Linda turn and look at Jim, but have no idea who he is. Jim crosses to bathroom door downstage right, and Cindy and Linda move just enough out of his way.)

JIM: Honey, I've got your bag. Do you want to open the door and I'll . . . *(He knocks.)* Honey, are you . . . *(He tries the doorknob and it's locked. He bangs on the door and there is no sound from within.)* Honey? Come on now. I don't have time for this. Open the door.
(He bangs again and is starting to get nervous.)

LINDA: Is that your wife in there?

JIM: *(Almost coldly.)* Yes. *(Very rudely.)* Could you get out of my way — please?
(Linda and Cindy move away from the door. Linda is startled by Jim's rudeness and a bit put off by it.)

JIM: *(He tries to struggle with the door, anything to open it.)* Goddammit. Open, you fucking door. *(It doesn't budge.)* SHIT! *(Turning around to the others.)* Do any of you have a pin of some sort?

CINDY: A hairpin?

JIM: Yes, great. Get it.
(Cindy pulls a hairpin out of her hair and hands it to Jim.)

JIM: *(Impatiently grabbing it from Cindy.)* OK. Honey, I'm coming. I'm right here and I'm coming. *(On his knees before door, he struggles to open it, using hairpin.)* Oh, to be James Bond!

(The men's bathroom door opens and Linda's husband, Steve, enters in his wheelchair.)

STEVE: *(To Linda.)* Is there a problem?

LINDA: *(Crosses to Steve.)* Yes, his wife is in there and he can't get her out.

JIM: Oh God, I never could do this hairpin thing. Shit. Someone call an ambulance, please.

(He throws Linda his cell phone from his pocket and Linda dials 911.)

STEVE: *(Wheeling over to the bathroom door.)* Here, I can help you with that.

JIM: Great. Go.

(Jim gladly hands Steve the pin. Steve goes to work on opening the door with hairpin.)

CINDY: *(To whomever.)* She's been in there a long time.

LINDA: *(Into phone.)* Yes, operator. We need an ambulance. A woman is locked in the . . .

JIM: *(To Linda, correcting her.)* *Pregnant* woman. Tell them she's pregnant.

LINDA: A pregnant woman.

JIM: We've had problems before, with the pregnancy. *(Wiping his eyes.)* Tell them that.

LINDA: Yes, there's trouble. Please come right away.

STEVE: Got it.

(Releasing the door, Steve backs up, out of the way.)

JIM: *(Rushing into women's bathroom, panicked.)* Honey, oh God. Honey. Come here, sweetie. *(He pulls Lindsay out, onto the stage. She looks lifeless.)* I've got you now. *(To Cindy.)* Could you get some water, please?

CINDY: Sure.

(Exits into the men's bathroom, looking for a glass and water.)

LINDA: We are at . . . uh . . . *(To anyone in the room.)* Where is this? What's the address here?

TRUMAN: *(Plainly and calmly.)* Six, two, five, Oakland Ave . . .

LINDA: Six, two, five, Oakland Ave. . . .

TRUMAN: The psych building . . .

LINDA: *(Into phone.)* The psych building.

TRUMAN: East campus.

LINDA: *(Into phone.)* Yes. Yes, that's right — East campus. How soon can you be here?

JIM: God. Honey? Can you hear me?

LINDA: *(Into phone.)* Great. Thanks.

JIM: *(To others, in defense of himself.)* I was just running to the car to grab her bag and my beeper went off. So I just thought I'd make a quick call . . .

LINDA: *(Into phone.)* Yes, operator, she's unconscious.

JIM: *(Continuing through.)* Oh, God. I was just going to make one, quick call to my office.

LINDA: OK, hold on.

JIM: *(Thinking.)* Or maybe it was two.

LINDA: *(To Jim.)* Can you take her pulse?

JIM: Actually, I'm wrong. It was three. *(With slight awareness of wrongdoing.)* I made three calls.

LINDA: *(Touching Jim to help him focus.)* Take her pulse.

JIM: *(Tries to feel Lindsay's pulse at her wrist.)* I don't feel it. *(He puts his hand on her chest.)* I don't feel anything.

LINDA: *(Into phone, becoming emotional.)* He says he doesn't feel it? He doesn't feel anything.

(After the long search for a glass of water, Cindy has discovered the faculty lounge water dispenser upstage left and fills a cup. She then crosses to Jim and hands it to him.)

CINDY: Here ya' go.

(Jim takes the water and drinks it himself.)

LINDA: *(Into phone, making note of Jim's actions.)* OK. Yes, we'll keep her still. *(She hangs up.)*

What did they think we'd do? Run her around the block?

JIM: I don't feel anything. There's nothing there.

LINDA: They're going to be here in just a few seconds. Supposedly there's an, uh . . . ambulance place right near by.

CINDY: *(To Linda.)* Campus emergency.

JIM: *(Stroking Lindsay's hair, Jim fights becoming emotional, or is it that he can't feel anything?)* She's always talking to me about priorities, you know? What's really important in life.

LINDA: *(Trying to comfort him.)* It's going to be OK.

JIM: She's right, though. She's absolutely right. *(Beat.)* And I hear her when she reminds me and then life starts up again . . . work . . . and I'm right back into, the externals as she calls them. the externals. God, I just want what's best for us. *(Beat.)* I wanted a house, you know. A house.

LINDA: *(She's got Jim figured out.)* A nice house.

JIM: Yes, of course. With a sunroom for her to sit and read. She likes to read. And the cars? Safe, well-made . . . German cars.

LINDA: Beamers.

JIM: *(To Linda.)* Yes! Yes, exactly. Safe. *(Beat.)* For the children. *(Back caring for Lindsay.)* Oh, sweetheart. If you can hear me, please just hang on. Someone's on the way and it's going to be OK. *(To others.)* If you only knew how often she tells me . . .

LINDA: Oh, I can imagine.

(Cindy, still desperately needing to pee, slowly tries to exit into the women's bathroom, unnoticed. Facing the audience, she sidesteps her way there and quietly shuts the door behind her.)

JIM: *(Not listening to Linda.)* . . . and I never, never . . . Oh, God. I just keep forgetting. Over and over and over again. It's like I never learn the lesson. I never learn the goddamn lesson.

CINDY: *(Reentering from women's bathroom.)* It's all wet in there. It's all wet all round the . . .

JIM: My darling. My sweet, sweet darling. You tried, didn't you?

(The sound of an ambulance is heard and drawing near.)

TRUMAN: Ah, the sound of hope.

(Blackout.)

Scene Two

At rise: Lapse of time of about twenty minutes. Jim and Lindsay have exited and Truman continues to sit in the same chair. Steve is in his wheelchair, stage right of the row of chairs. Linda is standing upstage right by the radiator, facing away from the audience, wanting some time alone. Cindy is in the men's bathroom. We hear the toilet flush.

CINDY: *(Entering from men's bathroom, drying hands on paper towel, and putting on her backpack.)* Do you have any idea how hard it is to pour a glass of water when you have to pee as badly as I did. Holly macaroni. *(With hands now dry, she looks left, then right for a trash can, although there is one right behind her. Not finding it, she puts wet paper towel in her pocket.)* Ah, that's so much better. *(She crosses to exit door and looks out.)* Gosh, I sure hope she's OK. *(Pause.)* It kinda makes you not know what to say. *(Looks at watch and turns to the others onstage.)* Well, you guys take care. I'm late for my next class. See ya. *(She exits.)*

STEVE: Dear God.

LINDA: I'm going to . . . use the bathroom here.

(She exits into men's bathroom and closes door behind her.)

TRUMAN: I was here when his wife came in. Nice woman. Lovely.

STEVE: Are you here for the . . . ?

(Motioning to the upstage left door.)

TRUMAN: Yes, the uh . . . *(He motions to the door upstage left.)* Good idea. Don't you think?

STEVE: Yes. Yes, I do.

TRUMAN: They teach us everything in school but what counts.

STEVE: Yes, I know. It's strange, isn't it? The most important things are always kept secret.

TRUMAN: Yes, so it seems. *(Motions to men's bathroom.)* Your wife?

STEVE: Yes. Yes, she is.

TRUMAN: She OK in there?

STEVE: Gee, I sure hope so, after that. *(Quickly calling out to Linda.)* Honey?

LINDA: *(From offstage.)* Yes, sweetheart. *(We hear the toilet flush.)* I'll be right out.

STEVE: *(To Truman, simply.)* She's probably crying because of the trauma. Trauma makes her cry.

TRUMAN: Ah, yes.

STEVE: *(Looking toward bathroom, to self.)* Makes her cry.

TRUMAN: Yes. *(Beat.)* What happened to you?

STEVE: Oh. *(Simply.)* Seven days back home from our honeymoon, I had returned to work. I worked for UPS. Still do, actually. They gave me a desk job.

TRUMAN: *(Already knowing Steve's answer.)* How's that?

STEVE: Ah, well. You know. I like people. Being out. *(Plainly.)* It sucks.

TRUMAN: Yes. *(Beat.)* You were saying?

STEVE: *(Continuing story, simply.)* Yeah. I was, uh . . . The hills, you know. Those sharp curves up in the hills?

TRUMAN: Yes.

STEVE: I was coming around this corner, looked down quickly at my clipboard, and . . . *(He shrugs.)* that was that. I had my seatbelt on, but it, uh . . . didn't seem to matter.

TRUMAN: Waist down?

STEVE: Yes. We're very lucky. Just the waist down. The doctors told me if I'd been looking just slightly off to the right, I might have been a quad . . . like Christopher Reeve.

TRUMAN: Ah.

STEVE: I'm very happy to have the use of my hands. Very happy. *(Beat, to himself.)* Very happy.

(Linda comes out of men's bathroom with red eyes.)

STEVE: Hi, sweetie.

LINDA: Hi.

STEVE: Everything OK?

LINDA: Yes, thank you. *(She sits beside Steve in stage right chair.)* I just . . .

STEVE: *(Knowing.)* Yes. *(He takes Linda's hand and kisses it, then holds it. To Truman.)* We still get to hold hands.

TRUMAN: Yes. It's lovely.

(Linda looks up shyly, sensing they've been talking.)

STEVE: That was always my favorite thing anyway.

(Linda smiles.)

TRUMAN: How lucky are you?

LINDA: *(Whispering to Steve.)* Can I get you anything? I'm going to see if they have a vending machine somewhere.

STEVE: Uh, no. I'm fine. Thanks, honey. You go. *(She doesn't move.)* Go.

(Linda exits with purse.)

STEVE: She has to walk around a lot when she's feeling stuff. She walks. She'll walk up and down the hall. Just walking. It helps her.

TRUMAN: *(Watching Linda exit.)* Lovely.

STEVE: Yeah, she is. A gem. I gotta tell you, a real gem. Shy. She doesn't like meeting new people since the accident. She just got shy. *(To self, trying to understand.)* She didn't used to be that way.

TRUMAN: Things change.

STEVE: *(Smiling, poignantly.)* Yeah, they sure do.

(We hear the sound of laughter from the lecture hall, off left. Steve looks at his watch.)

TRUMAN: They might be a while in there, those two.

(Motions to door.)

STEVE: Oh, that's fine.

TRUMAN: They're a gay couple. *(Leaning forward a bit.)* Gay couple.

STEVE: *(Watching Truman, who represents another age.)* Really.

TRUMAN: Yes. I expect they have a lot to say. I talked with them a bit before they went in. Both real talkers. Interesting stuff, but when *both* people are talkers, you've got yourself a *War and Peace* novel.

STEVE: Are we scheduled to go next or . . . ?

TRUMAN: Yes, you two. Then me.

STEVE: *(Referring to the event.)* I'm glad to be here. Glad to be here. Good idea, isn't it?

TRUMAN: Yes it is.

STEVE: How do we know when to . . . ?

TRUMAN: Go in?

STEVE: Yes.

TRUMAN: That red light goes off there.

(Motions to red light above door.)

STEVE: Oh, it just lights up?

TRUMAN: Yes.

STEVE: Great.

(Silence, Steve and Truman wait.)

STEVE: I guess everyone waited back then, huh?

TRUMAN: Oh, no. *(Beat.)* No. They didn't wait then either. *(Beat.)* Well, more did than didn't, I suppose. But I'll tell ya what — the engagement periods were shorter. Much shorter. *(Beat.)* Gave us a chance in hell! *(Beat.)* There was more faith back then — believing in something even though you couldn't see it. Pure faith. *(Beat.)* Now trust? — that you gotta wait for, but faith . . . Well, we had faith and then the trust comes.

STEVE: Yeah.

TRUMAN: They tried to get me on that Heraldo show, a few years back. You know, that aggressive fellow with the jet-black hair . . .?

STEVE: Yes.

TRUMAN: . . . Who keeps opening things that are empty?

STEVE: *(Nodding, smiling.)* Did you go?

TRUMAN: Hell, no.

STEVE: But you're here.

TRUMAN: This is education. That's a three-ring circus. *(Beat.)* No one listens to anyone anymore, even when they have a good story. There's too much hype and too much money. "Where lies your treasure, there also lies your heart." *(Beat.)* That's what my Anna used to say. I think it's from the Bible. She read the Bible for two hours before starting every day. I'm glad I didn't need her to milk the cows . . . 'cause cows don't wait for nobody. Not even God.

STEVE: You milked cows?

TRUMAN: Hell, yes. Every morning for sixty-three years. Every morning and every night. Dairy farm. No one else could do it, except my sons when they got old enough. Matthew. He finally took over the farm a few years back. I took it over from my father and he took it over from me. He wanted to and I'm glad of that. *(With a twinkle in his eye.)* I would have hated to twist his arm. Father's get such a bad rap for that kind of thing. *(Beat.)* And hell, he was bigger than me. He got bigger than me so fast. *(Looking back.)* It all goes by so fast.

STEVE: How many children did you have?

TRUMAN: We had six, Anna and I — five boys and one girl. Thank God for that. The boys made it easy to run the farm. They were easy to raise, so I was glad there were more of them. *(In thought.)* The girl was hard on me, without Anna.

STEVE: Anna was your wife?

TRUMAN: Yes.

(The door opens and Linda enters.)

STEVE: *(With supportive enthusiasm.)* Hey, there she is.

LINDA: *(Smiling, holding up the remains of her candy bar.)* They had my But-terfinger. Very exciting.

(She takes the last bite.)

STEVE: Excellent. Honey, do you have a moment?

(Motioning for Linda to join him.)

LINDA: *(Throws wrapper in trash can, stage right.)* Yes, I'm sorry. I was just walking . . .

STEVE: *(Knowing.)* That's fine. I would like you to meet my friend . . . uh?

TRUMAN: Truman.

STEVE: Truman, this is my wife Linda and I'm Steve.

(Linda actually shakes Truman's hand.)

TRUMAN: How very nice to meet you both.

(Linda sits left of Steve. There is a short sound of laughter coming from lecture hall, offstage left.)

LINDA: What's taking so long?

STEVE: We're next, honey.

LINDA: Oh, that's good. *(Beat.)* How do we know when to . . . ? *(She motions to go in.)*

STEVE: Go in?

LINDA: Yes.

STEVE: The light.

(Pointing to it.)

LINDA: Oh. *(Beat.)* I wonder how she is. Do you think someone will come back and tell us?

STEVE: I don't know who would.

LINDA: *(Loud, direct, and absolute.)* Certainly not her husband. The self-absorbed *fuck.*

(Silence. Silence.)

TRUMAN: You know . . . I was feeling ambivalent about that man's character, so I'm very glad to have heard your opinion.

(They all laugh, lightly.)

LINDA: I'm sorry. It just upset me.

TRUMAN: And well it should. *(Beat.)* You two make a lovely couple. How long have you been married?

STEVE: *(Knowing.)* Oh, what has it been, honey?

LINDA: Twelve years.

TRUMAN: Isn't that something?

STEVE: Yes.

LINDA: It has been.

STEVE: *(To Linda.)* Can you. . . do you have the pictures of the kids with you, honey?

(Linda reaches for purse and pulls out wallet.)

TRUMAN: *(Surprised.)* Children??!

(Linda shows photos to Truman.)

STEVE: We had decided to just have one, because of the . . . uh . . .

TRUMAN: *(Looking at the photos, delighted.)* My, oh my!

STEVE: But then the twins came.

TRUMAN: *(Surprised.)* Twins?!

STEVE: *(Continuing.)* You see, I can hold 'em, but I can't run them down, so Linda's got her hands full.

TRUMAN: *(Trying to understand.)* And you didn't adopt?

STEVE: Oh no, no. She had 'em.

LINDA: I had 'em, all right.

STEVE: *(Tongue in cheek.)* One at a time, of course. It's easier that way.

TRUMAN: *(Tentatively, mostly to Steve.)* So . . . you can . . . ?

STEVE: *(With enthusiasm.)* Oh, yes. I can.

LINDA: He can!

TRUMAN: But you can't . . . ?

STEVE: No, no I can't.

LINDA: *(Plainly, with sadness.)* He can't *feel* a goddamn thing.

TRUMAN: I see. *(Beat.)* Children. What a blessing.

LINDA: *(Out of the silence, she begins to speak.)* You know, the pain never comes from where you expect it to come from. If it did, then it would be easy. Life would be easy. But it doesn't. It comes from where you don't expect it. It sneaks up behind you when you're not looking and it takes your heart and stretches it in directions you . . . really wouldn't want it to go. *(Steve and Truman don't know what to say. Linda has surprised even Steve.)*

LINDA: You see, you'd expect me to be sad about him, that he can't walk, or do anything for that matter, because this is . . . a life of action. It's an active world. *(Sarcastically.)* Hell, everything worth while requires action.

Right? So you'd think I'd be in pain about that. There's hiking, camping, skiing . . .

STEVE: It's OK, honey.

LINDA: Traveling, sightseeing . . . But I'm not. That doesn't bother me.

STEVE: I know, sweetie.

LINDA: *(To Steve.)* It doesn't bother me, honey. It never has.

STEVE: I know, it's OK.

LINDA: And if I was like most pigs I've seen, like that . . . *(Almost insinuating Cindy's breasts.)* . . . perky co-ed we . . . experienced earlier, I would be upset because my husband couldn't please me sexually, but believe me, that's not it either.

STEVE: *(Tongue in cheek.)* I sure hope not, 'cause I work very hard at that.

LINDA: *(Seriously, to Steve.)* Absolutely not, because you do. You do please me ALL the time.

STEVE: *(Trying to understand.)* OK.

LINDA: It's standing behind you, that bothers me. That's where the pain comes from — behind you. *(To Truman.)* Steve enters a room, and I enter behind him and I watch them. *(To Steve.)* I watch *people* watch *you,* and I can't tell you how that hurts my heart. I just can't tell you. It's the pain where you don't expect it. *(Getting to the core of it.)* They live a sickening shallow existence because they believe what their eyes tell them, and they never trust what they cannot see. They cannot be patient, they cannot be silent and they can not hear the subtle beating of their own hearts. *(Steve and Linda kiss.)*

TRUMAN: *(Watching.)* So, I take it you two waited.

STEVE: *(Bewildered.)* How did you get that from what she just said?

TRUMAN: I'm eighty-three, and I listen. And I too was married. *(Beat.)* Am I right?

STEVE: Oh, yes. We sure did. And we talk about that all the time — how grateful we are that we *did* . . . wait.

LINDA: *(Explaining to Truman.)* Not that we were virgins.

STEVE: No, no. *(Beat.)* Because we weren't. *(Beat, teasing her.)* Well, I was, but not Linda.

LINDA: *(Surprised by Steve.)* Listen to you!

STEVE: *(A laugh, then he continues.)* We'd both just been through so much with other relationships that we thought we'd try something ENTIRELY different. And it worked. 'Cause we never could have survived this . . . *(A breath.)* . . . the *accident* . . . *(Finally able to say the word.)* . . . had we not . . . waited. I know that. I know that now.

LINDA: You're probably right.

STEVE: I know I'm right. We love each other in a way that . . . I can't explain 'cause I honestly just don't see much of it. When I was a kid, I was so confused because I *felt* that what Linda and I share was possible . . . I *felt* it somehow . . . but I just never found it. Never. I couldn't even put my finger on it, what it was I was looking for, but I knew it was there, somewhere. *(Beat.)* I know it sounds . . . silly and all.

TRUMAN: No, I'm with you.

STEVE: I just never gave up on it and I'm glad about that. I finally got to the point where I decided I was going to live the rest of my life alone and I knew I could do it too and that's when we met. *(To Linda.)* Jeez, I'll never forget that.

TRUMAN: Isn't that something.

STEVE: Oh, yeah. And I'm sure my whole family thought I was gay, being an artist and everything.

TRUMAN: Oh, you paint too?

STEVE: Pencil, yes. Mostly nudes of Linda now.

LINDA: *(Quickly.)* Steven!

STEVE: Don't even tell me you're embarrassed by that, at this point!

(Linda smiles.)

STEVE: *(Continues.)* But yes. A great hobby for me. *(Beat.)* What about you, Truman? Your wife? How long has she been . . . ?

TRUMAN: Forty years. Forty years today.

STEVE: Today?!

(Truman nods.)

LINDA: So you remarried.

TRUMAN: Uh, no. No, I did not.

STEVE: You raised those children?!

TRUMAN: Yes, I did and I'm a better man for it.

STEVE: Why? Why in heaven's name didn't you . . .

TRUMAN: *(Plain and simple.)* Listen. It's plain and simple. I have one heart. One. I had one wife. You give it away and that's all you got.

STEVE: But forty years. Didn't you get lonely?

TRUMAN: Yes, after I would put the kids to bed and watch the news and turn out the lights and hit the pillow. Yes, but only then. And even then I had to believe that my Anna was with me. Maybe not physically, *really* there. But I could almost feel her lying beside me, whispering in my ear, coaching me on what to do to get through the next day. Because I didn't have a clue. *(Beat.)* You see, *I'm waiting too*, because before she died, and it was a slow death so we had plenty of time to talk . . . Before she died, the two of us decided we would meet up again. I crawled into bed next to her and laid my hand on her heart and could feel it pushing its way into my hand. She said, "My True Man . . ." That's what she would call me, "My True Man, don't go wasting a perfectly good life, pawing about in the dirt. The children need you. Those ol' cows, *they* need you. So live. And live fully. I'll be here when you're ready to come home." *(Beat.)* And then no more. No more life. It lifted out of her.

STEVE: She sounds amazing.

TRUMAN: *(Nodding.)* Yes. That she was. *(Beat.)* You remind me of her, Linda.

LINDA: Me? No. No, I can't take that credit.

TRUMAN: Oh, yes.

LINDA: *(Humbled.)* Was she as filled up with anger as me?

TRUMAN: *(Loving, compassionate.)* Oh, it's not so much anger, as it is . . . maybe a loss of hope.

LINDA: *(Thinking to herself.)* Hmm. Yeah, I guess I have lost hope. Hope in basic . . .

TRUMAN: Humanity?

LINDA: Yes. *(Beat.)* I just don't know what it takes. I don't know what it takes for a person to make that . . . leap.

STEVE: A leap of growth.

LNDA: Yes — a leap of growth. Or maybe even a crawl. A crawl would do. *(Explaining it better.)* You know — a person who you would least expect to take a chance toward kindness. A leap. It just seems people are so busy buying into . . .

STEVE: The externals.

LINDA: Yes. Like him. *(With anger.)* Like that . . .

STEVE: *(Tongue-in-cheek.)* Careful, honey.

LINDA: *(It pops out.)* That . . . "beamer" of a husband.

TRUMAN: Not that age always brings wisdom, but I've found that it is important to try to keep a tiny place . . . Even if it's a very, tiny, little place left open inside your heart for people to surprise you. For people to leap.

STEVE: *(Simply.)* Sometimes they do, honey.

TRUMAN: *(Simply.)* Yes they do. When they are ready for the leap, they come to you and sometimes they do.

(Cindy enters.)

CINDY: Hey, guys. What's up?

STEVE: Hey!

TRUMAN: *(Robustly, with a twinkle in his eye.)* Well, look what we got here.

CINDY: I skipped my class so I thought I'd just stop back by here and let you guys know that she's going to be OK. Oh, and so's the baby.

(The next two lines are simultaneous.)

STEVE: Excellent!

TRUMAN: Oh, good!

(Linda's speechless.)

CINDY: Her heart was beating all along, he just couldn't feel it. Weird, huh? Him not being able to feel his own wife's heart beat?! I thought that was really odd, myself. *(To Linda.)* Oh, and thanks a lot for being nice to me. I got some Bactrim so I'm cool. I dated an intern last year in the campus emergency and that's where they brought Lindsay. Lindsay's her name. They're doing a C section on her. Pretty gross, but it's all cool. He gave me this . . . *(Holding up the Bactrim.)* Nice guy. I'm already feeling better.

LINDA: *(Rises and crosses to Cindy, with passion.)* You are amazing. You absolutely amaze me and I want to thank you so very much for coming back here to tell us that. *(Beat.)* Can I hug you? Is it OK if I hug you?

CINDY: Oh, sure.

(Linda hugs Cindy.)

CINDY: I also needed to use the bathroom again. I like this one because they have free tampons in there. *(Beat.)* Excuse me. *(She crosses to women's bathroom, then turns back.)* Tampons are so freakin' expensive. *(She exits into women's bathroom.)*

LINDA: Hey, I'd call that a leap.

TRUMAN: That was a leap if I ever saw one.

CINDY: *(Enters from woman's bathroom with hand jammed full of tampons.)* It's still wet in there. What's up with that?

(Exits into men's bathroom.)

STEVE: Absolutely amazing.

(There is a loud sound of applause coming from the lecture hall offstage left, and then the red light, above the door, lights up.)

STEVE: Ooup. There's the light. What do we do? Just go in?

TRUMAN: Just go in.

LINDA: Now?

TRUMAN: *(Factual.)* That's all we got.

LINDA: *(Referring to Cindy in men's bathroom.)* But I want to tell her how much I . . .

TRUMAN: *(Simply.)* You've told her all she can hear.

LINDA: Yes. *(Rising and crossing to Truman.)* Listen, thank you. Thank you so very much. You are such a little angel. *(Linda hugs Truman.)* Anyway, thanks. I really have enjoyed talking with you, so very much.

STEVE: *(Crosses to Truman and shakes his hand.)* Nice to meet you, Truman.

LINDA: Yes, it sure has been.

(They turn to go.)

STEVE: *(Stopping, he turns to Linda.)* Honey, honey. You go first. Let me come in behind you.

(Linda looks at Steve.)

STEVE: Let me come in . . . behind *you.*

(Linda smiles a very warm smile to Steve, then lets Steve exit behind her. We hear a toilet flush and Cindy enters from men's bathroom, drying hands on paper towel and putting on her backpack.)

CINDY: Hey, what's up? Where'd they go?

TRUMAN: It was their turn to go in.

CINDY: Oh, cool.

(With hands now dry, she looks left, then right for a trash can, although there is one right behind her. Not finding it, she puts wet paper towel in her pocket.) So what's up with you?

TRUMAN: I'm here to tell my story about my wife and myself and how we're waiting.

CINDY: Waiting? What do you mean, waiting? Like, what for?

TRUMAN: *(With a twinkle in his eye.)* Do you have a minute?

CINDY: Yeah, sure.

(Truman pats the seat next to him and Cindy crosses to the chair and sits.)

TRUMAN: *(Takes a breath and begins his story.)* My wife and I, we met at a wedding, in a church. Do you believe that?

CINDY: Not really. I've never met anyone there.

TRUMAN: *(With the same twinkle, Truman continues his story.)* We met in a church at a wedding. I was an usher for my friend's wedding and she was a guest and I ushered her down the aisle. *(Lights begin to fade.)* She was so pretty, I have to tell you. She was wearing a calico dress, with ivory lace around the collar. I trembled when I held her arm because she was so darn pretty . . .

(Blackout.)

END OF PLAY

PERMISSIONS

The Psychic Life of Savages © 2003 by Amy Freed. Reprinted by permission of the author. Contact: Peter Franklin, William Morris Agency, 1325 Avenue of the Americas, New York, NY 10019; Tel: (212) 903-1550.

The Dianalogues © 2003 by Laurel Haines. Reprinted by permission of the author. Contact: Susan Schulman, A Literary Agency; 454 West 44th Street, New York, NY 10036.

Daisy in the Dreamtime © 2003 by Lynne Kaufman. Reprinted by permission of the author. Contact: The Susan Gurman Agency, 865 West End Avenue, #15A, New York, NY 10025-8403.

The Last Schwartz © 2003 by Deborah Zoe Laufer. Reprinted by permission of the author. Contact: Lazarus & Harris LLP, 561 Seventh Avenue, 11th Floor, New York, NY 10018.

String Fever © 2003 by Jacquelyn Reingold. Reprinted by permission of The Gersh Agency. Stock and amateur stage performance rights are controlled exclusively by Dramatists Play Service, 440 Park Avenue South, New York, NY 10016. Written permission for professional and nonprofessional performance of the play must obtained in advance from the Dramatists Play Service. For inquiries concerning all other rights, contact: The Gersh Agency, 41 Madison Avenue, 33rd Floor, New York, NY 10010.

Waiting © 2003 by Lisa Soland. Reprinted by permission of the author. Contact: Lisa Soland, P.O. Box 33081, Granada Hills, CA 91394.